Mixed Race Amnesia

Minelle Mahtani

Mixed Race Amnesia
Resisting the Romanticization of Multiraciality

UBCPress · Vancouver · Toronto

© UBC Press 2014

All rights reserved. No part of this publication may be reproduced, stored in a retrieval system, or transmitted, in any form or by any means, without prior written permission of the publisher, or, in Canada, in the case of photocopying or other reprographic copying, a licence from Access Copyright, www.accesscopyright.ca.

21 20 19 18 17 16 15 14 13   5 4 3 2 1

Printed in Canada on FSC-certified ancient-forest-free paper
(100% post-consumer recycled) that is processed chlorine- and acid-free.

Library and Archives Canada Cataloguing in Publication

Mahtani, Minelle, 1971-, author
    Mixed race amnesia : resisting the romanticization of multiraciality / Minelle Mahtani.

Includes bibliographical references and index.
Issued in print and electronic formats.
ISBN 978-0-7748-2772-0 (bound). – ISBN 978-0-7748-2773-7 (pbk.)
ISBN 978-0-7748-2774-4 (pdf). – ISBN 978-0-7748-2775-1 (epub)

    1. Racially mixed people – Canada. 2. Racially mixed people – Canada – Race identity. 3. Racially mixed women – Canada – Interviews. 4. Race – Social aspects – Canada. 5. Canada – Race relations. I. Title.

FC106.R33M34 2014   305.8'0500971   C2014-903653-1
                                                 C2014-903654-X

Canadä

UBC Press gratefully acknowledges the financial support for our publishing program of the Government of Canada (through the Canada Book Fund), the Canada Council for the Arts, and the British Columbia Arts Council.

This book has been published with the help of a grant from the Canadian Federation for the Humanities and Social Sciences, through the Awards to Scholarly Publications Program, using funds provided by the Social Sciences and Humanities Research Council of Canada, and with the help of the University of British Columbia through the K.D. Srivastava Fund.

Printed and bound in Canada
Set in Garamond and Formata by Artegraphica Design Co. Ltd.
Copy editor: Robert Lewis
Proofreader: Jillian Shoichet Gunn

UBC Press
The University of British Columbia
2029 West Mall
Vancouver, BC V6T 1Z2
www.ubcpress.ca

برای فریده ک. افشار
همیشه پر شور، با محبت، مهربان، و الگوی زندگی من

Baray-e Farideh K. Afshar,
Hameesheh por shoor, ba mohabat, mehraban, va olgooye zendegi man

AND

Kishin L. Mahtani
1933-2006
That's Life in the Big City

AND

To Cole and Zhenmei – the future of multiraciality

Contents

Acknowledgments / ix

Introduction: Disentangling Our Curious Affection with Multiraciality / 3

1 Mixed Race Mythologies: Toward an Anticolonial Mixed Race Studies / 29

2 Mixed Race Narcissism? Thoughts on the Interview Experience / 60

3 The Model Multiracial: Propping Up Canadian Multiculturalism through Racial Impotency / 95

4 Beyond the Passing Narrative: Multiracial Whiteness / 140

5 Mongrels, Interpreters, Ambassadors, and Bridges? Mapping Liberal Affinities among Mixed Race Women / 166

6 Mixed Race Scanners: Performing Race / 207

7 Present Tense: The Future of Critical Mixed Race Studies / 243

References / 259

Index / 274

Acknowledgments

Many people were remarkably patient with me as I persevered with the completion of this book. I am grateful to those in the Department of Geography at University College London who befriended me when I was a doctoral student. I thank Tracey Bedford, Ben Malbon, and Simon Pinnegar for their generous friendship and for introducing me to the pleasures and pains of Port. I have been sustained by the laughter of several wise and wonderful girlfriends: Joylyn Chai, Sylvia Fuller, Renisa Mawani, Marichka Melnyk, Brenda Nadjiwan, Risa Schwartz, Ing Wong-Ward, and Mary Lynn Young.

Many colleagues were generous in reading over innumerable early drafts of this manuscript and providing useful commentary. They include Camie Augustus, Abbie Bakan, Lawrence Berg, Paul Bramadat, Andrea Choi, Francis Henry, Habiba Ibrahim, Jayne O. Ifekwunigwe, Jack Jedwab, Danielle Kwan-Lafond, Michelle LaFlamme, Gary Lemons, Katherine McKittrick, Daniel McNeil, Mary-Jo Nadeau, Brenda Nadjiwan, Jillian Paragg, Steve Pile, David Roberts, Scott Salmon, Jennifer Simpson, Miri Song, Paul Spickard, Sarita Srivastava, Leanne Taylor, and Cynthia Wright. I am particularly indebted to Margot Francis, Renisa Mawani, Rainier Spencer, and Juanita Sundberg, each of whom offered critical comments on drafts. Dan Hiebert was a thoughtful mentor while I was completing a postdoctoral fellowship at the University of British Columbia. Finally, I am grateful for the encouragement and mentorship of Sherene Razack, which came just when I needed it most.

I was fortunate to spend a sabbatical in Sydney working on this book. Mary Zournazi kept me laughing. Dee and Mark Swinchat opened their

Balmain, Sydney, home to a complete stranger, offering me a convivial place to write while in Australia. I am indebted to them for their generosity.

I had the most efficient and capable research assistant working with me on this project. To Tamir Arviv, I offer not only my most sincere gratitude but also my ongoing admiration. His intellectual prowess and keen eye were invaluable.

My uncle Shahrukh Afsheen corrected details about my family history. I was inspired by his own book about our family, *Under Five Flags* (2011). I was honoured to work with a talented and insightful editor, Emily Andrew, whose "mind is a palace," to quote Anne Michaels in *Fugitive Pieces* (1996, 176). Most of all, I am grateful to Bruce Baum, who made the process of completing this book so much more joyful. You are my soul mate. And to my son, Cole Asher Baum Mahtani, know that your presence animates every page. I love you both.

The current text has undergone substantial revision since portions appeared in "Mixed Metaphors: Situating Mixed Race Identity," in Jo-Ann Lee and John Lutz, eds., *Situating "Race" and Racisms in Space, Time and Theory* (Montreal: McGill-Queen's University Press, 2005), 77-93; "What's In a Name? Exploring the Employment of 'Mixed Race' as an Identification," *Ethnicities* 2, 4 (2002): 469-90; and "Interrogating the Hyphen-Nation: Canadian Multicultural Policy and 'Mixed Race' Identities," *Social Identities: Journal for the Study of Race, Nation and Culture* 8, 1 (2002): 67-90. The publishers graciously permitted me to adapt these articles for publication here.

Portions of Chapter 2 appeared in an earlier version as "Not the Same Difference: Notes on Mixed-Race Methodologies," in Rosalind Edwards, Suki Ali, Chamon Caballero, and Miri Song, eds., *International Perspectives on Racial and Ethnic Mixedness and Mixing* (London: Routledge, 2012), 156-69. Parts of Chapter 6 appeared as "Tricking the Border Guards: Performing Race," in *Environment and Planning D: Society and Space* 20 (Winter 2002): 425-40.

The lines from the poem "Declaration of the Halfrican Nation" by Wayde Compton (*Performance Bond* [Vancouver: Arsenal Pulp Press, 2004], 15-16) in Chapter 3 are reprinted courtesy of Arsenal Pulp Press.

The lyrics from the poems "Why I Don't Say I'm White" by Alexis Kienlen, "The Land Knows" by Shandra Spears Bombay, and "Conversations of Confrontation" by Natasha Adiyana Morris quoted in Chapters 4 and 7 are kindly permitted by Inanna Publications and Education Inc. (Toronto).

Mixed Race Amnesia

Introduction
Disentangling Our Curious Affection with Multiraciality

> I was beginning to understand what it meant not to be purely black or white. There were the strangers who gawked at me and tried to unlock the mysteries of my lineage, who saw Ethiopia in my forehead, Polynesia in my hair, Nepal in my freckles.
>
> — MACLEAR 2012, 22

This book explores multiraciality in the contemporary postwar context in what has been optimistically imagined as a postcolonial, liberal, and multicultural Canada. It asks, *What work does the "mixed race" label do to support a romanticized notion of race?* I look at the experiences of those who are perceived to be from a plethora of places all over the globe, whose faces are routinely scrutinized for geographic clues, much like Toronto-based novelist Kyo Maclear's mixed race protagonist Marcel in *Stray Love* (2012). Engaging with interviews conducted with twenty-four self-identified women of mixed race in Toronto in the years 1996-98, I examine how they contemplated race by charting their personal stories. I make the case that Canada's romance with multiraciality governs both public perceptions and personal accounts of the mixed race experience in Canada. This curious affection requires some disentangling. I explain how Canadian mixed race identity is a product of colonial formations created and reflected through various cultural representations and facilitated through certain forms of cultural amnesia or strategic forgetting.

In the past ten years, in particular, scholars from a variety of disciplinary homes have drawn from and contributed to what is now commonly referred to as critical mixed race theory (see, for example, Camper 1994; Ifekwunigwe 1999; Christian 2000; Hill 2001; Makalani 2001; Parker and Song 2001; Daniel 2002; Dalmage 2004; Ifekwunigwe 2004; Alcoff 2006; K.M. Williams 2006; DaCosta 2007; Squires 2007; Beltrán and Fojas 2008; Sexton 2008; McNeil 2010; Elam 2011; Spencer 2011; Bettez 2012; Ibrahim 2012; G. Carter 2013; and R. Joseph 2013). Through an analysis of qualitative, open-ended interviews, this book makes an effort to capture the experiences of individuals who see themselves as belonging to more than one racialized group.

Olumide (2002) points out that research on mixed race people has traditionally followed an extremist agenda, rarely defining them on their own terms. She claims that mixed race people have been either pathologized as having no place to call home, envisioned as torn and confused about their racial identity, or celebrated as holding the solution to the world's race problems. This text moves beyond these popular stereotypes of multiraciality by asking not only how they have limited a fuller understanding of the mixed race experience but also how the superficial celebration of multiraciality has worked to further oppress other racialized groups (including black and Indigenous populations). I make the case that we need to look at the cartographies of multiraciality – not at the objectifying "What are you?" question, which seems to distinguish so much of the mixed race experience, but at the "Where are you from?" question, which invites us to go beyond superficial analyses of the experience of the first generation by paying much closer attention to those complex diasporic life histories that inform the process of identifying as mixed race. The emphasis on experiencing multiple diasporic geographic locations, on the *where,* is a redirection from the "What are you?" question. I develop this idea more in Chapter 7, where I introduce and critique the idea of the *present tense* as a way of making sense of the epistemological framework that currently structures so much research in mixed race studies.

Obviously, the category of mixed race is more than a black and white issue. In the Canadian context, it is important to see beyond black and white in order to understand the issue through different kinds of racialized lenses, including Asian Pacific and Indigenous lenses as well as other multidimensional axes of identity. The literature on multiraciality in the academic context has focused mostly on the American experience of mixed race identity, which has been primarily seen as a black-white or Asian-white issue. This book makes the case that we must draw from broader global cartographies to inform a revitalized understanding of racial mixing.

This book has five goals in its attempt to situate the interview findings within a broader interdisciplinary realm. First, it provides a space for those who identify beyond the black-white binary (and the Asian-white binary) that so commonly characterizes definitions of mixed race identity in scholarship emerging from the United States, Canada, and the United Kingdom – those countries that are understood as multicultural liberal democracies in the global North. For most people in these locations, when "mixed race" is uttered, a partially white ancestry tends to be assumed. Why? Given that many women who identified as mixed race in this study did not claim any white heritage, there is clearly more to multiraciality than claiming one is half-white. I reveal the stories of women who did not claim any white heritage yet still identified as mixed race, particularly in Chapter 4, through an interrogation of critical whiteness studies. This book aims to challenge the predominant whiteness that characterizes studies of multiraciality on both the ontological and epistemological scales, paying attention to those who identified as black-white or Asian-white but also to those who did not claim any white descent. At the same time, however, I heed Andrea Smith's (2012) cautionary words about attempts to challenge the black-white binary. I do not want to "add and stir in" other members of communities of colour in this analysis, for such a project would only contribute to a superficial politics of multiculturalism, purporting that "if we just *include* more peoples, then our practice will be less racist" (ibid., 75, emphasis in original). As this book makes clear, such a project would not address crucial questions of settler colonialism or challenge the conditions of the creation of the settler state itself. Instead, I work in this book to remember that "the consequence of not developing a critical apparatus for intersecting all the logics of white supremacy, including settler colonialism, is that it prevents us from imagining an alternative to the racial state" (ibid.).

The field has become skewed toward a focus on people of partially white heritage. It is vital to recognize the role of the legacy of North American transnational slavery practices, where mixing between whites and blacks was punishable by death. In the late nineteenth century, mixed race people were tenaciously marked by the one-drop rule, where you were considered to be black if you had one drop of black blood. This is not to essentialize the wide range of responses that accompanied interracial intimacy; rather, it is to emphasize that anti-miscegenation laws in North America from the colonial era to the mid-1900s played a significant role in who was allowed to identify as white or black and subsequently as belonging to one, both, or neither of these groups. In the public and academic imagination, "mixed race" automatically implied mixing with white because of the logic of white supremacy. However, where do people who identify as mixed race yet do not see themselves as being partly white fit in to this picture, and under what circumstances do they claim this racial identification given the historical legacies of the "mixed race" label? *How might we reimagine the place of nonwhite mixed race subjects?*

Second, this book makes the claim that identifying as mixed race is not patently unique and different in and of itself. Nor does it represent a social or democratic good (see McNeil 2012), despite the ongoing social mania assuming that mixed race people portend an optimistic racial future, representing "fleshy confirmation that racial equality has arrived" (Elam 2011, 9). As Nyong'o (2009, 174-75) reminds us, "the impossibly burdened figure of the biracial child cannot conceivably do the work of utopia that we repeatedly impose upon her." Mixed race people do *not* possess special talents or abilities simply because they call themselves racially mixed. Instead, it asks why this stereotype often emerges in interviews with people who identify as mixed race.

Makalani (2001, 94), in his critique of mixed race identity, tells us that "it is doubtful that ... the [mixed race person] is naturally imbued with objectivity, rationality, and a keener intelligence that would allow him or her to assume the vanguard of ... race relations." We are not the purveyors of a new racial order based primarily on our mixed racial parentage, nor are we the people of the future. What we do share, if anything, is a similar set of racialized experiences that cannot be understood without unravelling the cultural capital that some, but not all, people who identify as mixed race share. In other words, I hope to divest mixed race subjects of their privileged status and reflexively analyze why they are seen as cultural commodities – emblems of a utopic future.

Third, this book emphasizes the crucial importance of remembering that race mixing is *not* new, in spite of relentless journalistic reports from the global North celebrating mixed race futures in modern liberal democracies (see Squires 2007). Mixing has occurred in the global South for generations, including Latin America (see Twine 2000a) and India (see Blunt 2003), yet mixing there is not seen as equally newsworthy. No one is racially pure, of course, but some people experience the privilege of being perceived as mixed more than others. As Elam (2011, 6) reminds us, the question should not be, "Why are there more mixed race people now?" – instead, we ought to ask, "Why do we see more people *as* mixed race now?" (emphasis in original).

Fourth, this book focuses on mapping forms of multiraciality in *Canada*. More precisely, it asks, *What work does Canada do – as a state, as a racial backdrop, as a formative geography – to impact definitions of mixed race in the Canadian context?* American (and to a lesser extent, British) literature dominates the field of critical mixed race studies, and this literature is not always easily transferable to the Canadian context, given our different racial pasts. As a result, I suggest that this incompatibility has led to mixed race in Canada being relatively understudied (although, of course, there are some notable exceptions: see Hill 2001; L. Taylor 2008; Lafond 2009; and McNeil 2010).

DaCosta (2007, 34) writes that multiraciality has "always been linked to the broader system of racial domination that demarcates white from black." I show in this book that multiraciality has been linked to the broader system of racial oppression and domination in Canada, which demarcates Indigenous from non-Indigenous as well. The motif of mixing plays a complicit role in ensuring ongoing white supremacist practices that allow for the systemic racism that structures the lives of both blacks and Indigenous peoples.

I argue that Canadian multiculturalism as a policy, practice, and ideology intertwines complicitly with liberal multiracialism. Mixed race agency offers a means through which liberal multiculturalism is enacted, in turn supporting an ongoing colonial project. For some Canadian mixed race women in this study, identifying as mixed allowed for a racial impotency, a concept I elaborate upon in Chapter 3, providing a space for some of them to be seen as racially unique without necessarily adopting an antiracist stance that would have bound them to a progressive politics. Some experienced the privilege of a particular form of exoticized difference, without recognizing or acknowledging the freight and legacy of historical racisms. Being perceived as racially ambiguous was opportune for some of these women, providing a way to opt out of race politics and instead access the white privilege that so often accompanies the experience of multiraciality – not only for those who see themselves as black-white or Asian-white but also particularly for those who do not claim partially white descent. I delve into this in more detail in Chapter 4, where I interrogate the ways that some mixed race women spoke about accessing white privilege.

Fifth, this book asks, *What is "critical" about critical mixed race studies?* It is important to distinguish here among three overlapping but separate arenas – first, studies that broadly consider mixed race identity; second, the newly emerging field that is called critical mixed race studies or critical mixed race theory; and finally, critical race theory – for these three things are definitely not the same. If we are committed to a politically progressive, truly critical mixed race studies, it would serve us well to consider how we might more carefully map out complex diasporic family histories in relation to imperial colonial legacies and critical race theory. More than thirty years ago, a rigorous school of thought emerged that has since explored the nexus of race, racism, and power, placing civil rights, ethnic studies discourses, and the law within a broader perspective under the rubric of critical race theory (Delgado and Stefancic 2001). Critical race theory interrogates the very foundations of the liberal order, including a careful examination of legal theory and reasoning, opening up a window to ignored and alternative realities of the experiences of people of colour and emphasizing the personal dimensions of the racial political project. Focusing on intersectionality, anti-essentialism, and tensions between assimilation and nationalism, critical race theory has shifted the contours of the study of race. However, it remains an open question how studies on multiraciality have been informed by critical race theory more broadly, and vice-versa. I make the suggestion throughout this book that a critical mixed race studies is possible only through a prolonged exchange both with critical race theory and with anticolonialism and anti-imperialism debates, which do, of course, inform critical race theory as well. But these intersections have not always been made plainly clear, and white privilege continues to shape studies of multi-raciality more broadly (Sexton 2008; Elam 2011; Spencer 2011). *How do colonial formations inform mixed race social geographies in Canada, and how then do contemporary mixed race geographies re-inform colonial formations?* I emphasize that our analytical vocabulary for describing the experience of multiraciality is not yet up to the task of telling a more complex story about whiteness, race, diasporic mobility, and grids of racial intelligibility in a white-settler society within what is understood as a multicultural liberal democracy. This book tries to expand that vocabulary. Before exploring these themes in more detail, I ask what fuelled my own desire to study multiraciality.

Intimate Social Geographies

> We were supposed to be the next generation, all newfangled and melting-potted, but instead we were like Russian nesting dolls. When you opened our parents' bodies you found a replica of their struggle, no matter how hard we tried to transcend it.
>
> — SENNA 2011, 180

We often write about what intimately touches us. I chose to write about mixed race because of the ways that it has influenced my own life. In sharing the following story about myself, I admit to some anxiety because I think this approach can teeter into a form of narcissism, an issue I explore in further depth in Chapter 2. Moreover, I make the case in this book that we must be wary of the political limitations of citing the lived, personal experience of individual mixed race people and using that as the sole basis for our theoretical discussions (see also Makalani 2001; and Ibrahim 2012). The field has developed, however, in part because scholars who identify as mixed race have provided the impetus. Personal experience has been a crucial component of critical mixed race studies, and although I explore how this approach has prevented a more robust analysis of race, I share my own story both to make transparent my initial desire to pursue this topic in a scholarly context and to emphasize how particular colonial histories have shaped my experience and interest in pursuing multiraciality as an academic investigation.

I see myself as mixed race. It wasn't always that way. I was born in Canada, but both of my parents were racialized immigrants to this country. My mother, Farideh Afshar, is Iranian and Muslim; my father, Kishin Mahtani, was from India and identified as Hindu. However, my mother spent some of her early childhood in India, and she speaks not only English and Farsi but also Urdu and a smattering of Bengali. I have spent a great deal of my life being asked to define myself because I am perceived as racially ambiguous – my racial background is hard to pin down, apparently. I have joked ironically for years that I have been called every single racial slur in the book, yet it is rare that someone actually gets it right.

I was in Hawaii several years ago and was strolling alone along the boardwalk, the dappled waters shimmering as the sun began its slow descent into the ocean. Suddenly, a woman ran up to me and tugged my t-shirt excitedly. "Excuse me," she stammered. "I know this must seem pretty forward, but do you mind me asking where you're from?" Before I could respond, she exclaimed, "No, no, let me guess! Moroccan, right? No, no, Algerian!" I experience variations on this episode about once a week, wherever I go, and despite that frequency, I still don't know how to respond to a question about my heritage without launching into a whole history of explanation. Am I Indian? Iranian? or Indian Iranian Canadian? Although I feel as Canadian as "snow and ice" most days (Philip 1992, 17), I am often not considered Canadian even though I was born in Canada, raised there, and returned there to live and teach. I never really know how to answer when people ask me the ambiguous question "Where are you from?" because I know they are not inquiring about my place of birth or my childhood geographies – they are asking me this question because they want to racially categorize me.

This story might resonate for some mixed race people because it is not uncommon for many of us to be continually queried about our racial identity. As I hinted at earlier, the question "What are you?" is one with which we are intimately acquainted, and conversations about how we answer this question are almost like a rite of initiation into what I ironically refer to as the "Mixed Race Anonymous" confessional club ("my name is X, and I'm mixed race"). This book attempts to unravel the complexities of the identification of mixed race beyond its use as a catchall phrase for people who experience a constant barrage of questions about their racial identity just because they look racially ambiguous. Certain people are seen as mixed race, whereas others are not. How that is determined depends on a variety of factors, including the currency of whiteness, an issue I discuss in more depth in Chapter 4.

Part of my personal as well as professional project has been not only to try to understand my own racialized experience but also to consider how we might more productively locate a study of multiraciality within a broader, colonial and imperialist global context that takes into account the diasporic colonial experiences of our families and their personal histories. Their complex transnational movements across countries and oceans require that we pay attention to the experiences of those whom Walcott (2008) deems double migrants – those who left so-called Commonwealth countries for Britain but ended up in Canada because of perceived improved opportunities and a vague sense that racism was milder there. As Walcott points out, despite many immigrants of colour desiring to emigrate from former (and continuing) British colonies, Canada's policy of requiring British citizenship was written to explicitly exclude those who were nonwhite.

My parents were among those nonwhite immigrants who, by virtue of British passports, managed to travel from their respective places of birth to London and then finally North America, people whom the novelist Jhumpa Lahiri (1999, 197) refers to as moving to the third, and final, continent. Whereas my mother initially entered London with an Iranian passport, my father was from the Commonwealth and was automatically issued a British passport. My mother eventually came to Canada as a British national, having been granted this status because she was married to my father. They both rescinded their British citizenship once they came to Canada. They wanted their entire family to share the same citizenship, and for them, that was to be Canadian.

My father was originally from Hyderabad Sind, which was part of India but is now in Pakistan. Coming from a family with seven brothers and sisters, he worked painstakingly hard to scrounge together enough savings after graduating from St. Xavier's College in Mumbai in order to travel to London to study at St. Martin's College of Art and Design. His ultimate goal was to pursue a career in advertising. His mother was illiterate, yet she made sure all of her children obtained an undergraduate degree. In contrast, my mother had a more circuitous path to London, where she eventually met my father.

Unlike my father, whose upbringing was impoverished, my mother came from an upper-middle-class family in Iran, where her father was a well-respected engineer. He studied in England on a scholarship from the Iranian Oil Company, pursuing a graduate degree in engineering at Loughborough University.

My mother's paternal grandmother adored her. When my mother was barely a toddler, her grandmother was about to leave on an extended vacation to India and Burma (Myanmar) and pleaded with her son and daughter-in-law to allow my mother to accompany her. After much hesitation, they acquiesced to my grandmother's wishes, so my mother set sail for the shores of Kolkata, India. It still makes me wince to think about how hard it must have been for her to be away from her parents at such a tender age.

The plan was to return to Iran to reunite the family fairly quickly. However, weeks turned into months, and months turned into years. It became clear that fate had another plan for my mother. It was 1944 and the Second World War was ravaging the world. Travel across national borders soon became treacherous. There was no way my mother could return to her parents in Iran, nor could her parents leave Iran to reunite the family. After the war ended, my mother's parents rushed to Kolkata, and they ended up settling there for many years.

My mother's happiest childhood memories revolve around her early years in Kolkata. Her face becomes wistful as she recalls the intoxicating beauty of the blossoming bougainvillea that covered the elaborate front gate and the walls of her home on Park Street. She traipsed through New Market, giggling with her girlfriends, proudly sporting her school uniform. Almost ten years ago, I was invited to give a talk in India, and I persuaded my mother to travel with me to Kolkata. We visited her old haunts, and she showed off her old family home, tears welling up in her eyes, as she shared stories with me.

When her family returned to Iran years later, my maternal grandfather continued to work as an engineer in the Anglo-Iranian Oil Company (yes, that was its name). My mother pursued her dream to become a paediatrician and started her medical degree in earnest in Lahore, Pakistan. She was about to embark upon her final year of medical school at the University of Brighton in England when her passport was stolen in Istanbul during the long road trip to the United Kingdom with her father. As a result, her studies were abruptly halted because she was stranded in Turkey, missing the first few months of classes without any chance of re-enrolment.

When she finally made it to England, she found herself in London without funding or any sense of what her next move would be. Ultimately, she would never complete her medical degree because of lack of financing. She eventually decided to take a course on the Montessori method of teaching, and she now runs her own successful Montessori school in Markham, Ontario, which is celebrating its thirtieth year of operation as I finish this book.

My mother met my dad at a party in London, England. Given her time in India, it was not surprising that they had some things in common despite their differences. They fell in love and eventually married, much to the chagrin of my mother's father. However, my grandfather was unable to pay much attention to his daughter's burgeoning new romance, as he was too busy grieving the loss of his wife, who had tragically died in a house fire. My grandmother apparently fell asleep on the sofa one afternoon, and her cigarette slipped from her fingers. If my mother's mother had been alive, I suspect news of my mother's marriage would have been met with outrage. My mother always told me that her mother would have, in her words, "skinned me alive" if she had known her daughter would marry a Hindu. Such is the premium that is placed on whiteness, and such is the legacy of hatred between Hindus and Muslims that continues to haunt our family.

My parents experienced both virulent and subtle forms of racism in London during the first few years of their marriage. Although they expressed a certain nostalgic fondness for Britain, no doubt influenced by their shared experience of the Commonwealth spectre in India, they would often speak in hushed tones to their Indian friends at the pub about their desire to abandon the colonial way of life. One evening, their best friends – coincidentally, another mixed Indian Iranian couple – excitedly told them they were going to try to immigrate to Canada. My parents knew nothing about the country, and their interest was piqued. They concocted a plan where all four would move to North America and start a new life together.

My mother started the long process of sending out resumes to Montessori schools in Toronto with the hope of finding work, and my dad applied for advertising jobs, praying he would get some lead. In 1968 they moved to Canada but without their friends who had made the suggestion in the first place. They had changed their minds at the last minute and decided to stay in London. They now have a daughter, who is also Indian and Iranian and about the same age as me, but she has grown up in Britain. She was raised among her extended Iranian family and speaks fluent Farsi, whereas I can barely mumble a few phrases, and when I do, they are marred by an awful accent. When we see each other, we chuckle about how different both our lives might have been if her parents had made the trip across the Atlantic with mine.

Over the years, my parents have carefully parcelled out which stories to share with me about their first few years in Toronto. I'm sure this was done to protect me from hearing about the racism they faced. They told me that when they first arrived, if they ever saw anyone who was Indian on the public transit, they would immediately smile, wave, and initiate a conversation because such a sighting was rare at the time. It was a way to make friends in a strange country where family was scarce. Now, as my mother likes to remind me, South Asians make up the majority of the population on the bus. If they did that today, they'd be so busy shaking hands and exchanging pleasantries that they'd never get off at their stop.

Not unlike other immigrants, they developed a network of South Asian friends whose homes we would visit on the weekends, friends we all referred to as uncles and aunties. We would pile into the car for the long trip out to Mississauga, moving from one person's house to another's, the fragrance of biryani in the air, the sound of jubilant laughter among the men, the clink of ice cubes in scotch glasses, the lilting Indian accents of the women, including my own Iranian mother's. The weekends were safe havens for my parents, a chance for them to engage with others who had fled the country of their birth. During the weeks, however, my parents participated in a wholly white world.

My parents tried to cocoon my brother and me from hearing how difficult those early years must have been for them. It was only recently on a trip to Australia that I learned from a friend exactly why my father abandoned advertising as a career and ended up employed as a civil servant in the Ministry of Education for the rest of his working days. I knew he had a passion for advertising and I had always wondered why he abandoned his beloved choice of profession. I found out why when I was on sabbatical hiking with two friends and fellow academics, Mary Zournazi and Paul Sheehan, through the Blue Mountains of Sydney. As we reached the crest of one of the mountains, the view of the Pacific Ocean stretched out in front of us. I lay on the grass, marvelling at the scene, and drank in the warmth of a beautiful Australian summer day. Paul had visited Toronto in 2000 and had stayed with my dad, taking him out for a drink (or three) in exchange for a place to sleep. It was at that moment in the Blue Mountains that Paul chose to tell me a story that my dad had shared with him over scotch. This was particularly poignant for me because my father had died of a sudden heart attack a few years earlier, and I missed him intensely. I longed to hear more stories about him.

Paul explained that my dad had confessed to him that he had experienced racism in the advertising world in Toronto back in the late 1960s. Apparently, his boss confided in him one day that it was unlikely that he would ever be promoted because of the shade of his skin. "I'm sorry Kish," he apologized. "You're simply too *Oriental* for us to make you an advertising director." I remember a chill going through me that day, even though the sun was beating down on us so brightly.

My brother and I struggled to make sense of the ostracism we both felt from my mother's side of the family. Many of our relatives were immigrating, as this was the late 1970s and trouble was brewing in Tehran. It is hard to describe the feeling of alienation we felt from our extended family of

Iranian cousins and aunts and uncles. I felt haunted by a shadow of disdain whenever we visited their homes. This may have been because of our darker skin and because we were seen not just as half-Indian but also as half-Hindu, an emphasis that was understandable given the violent, bloodied histories between Muslims and Hindus, but as children, those histories were unknown to us. My dad certainly never felt accepted by my mother's Iranian side of the family. My brother and I acutely sensed this rejection and began to avoid family gatherings with my mom out of loyalty to our father, perhaps intuitively trying to provide him with some emotional support. We'd cozy up with him on the couch under a tattered, raspberry-coloured wool blanket and watch hours of tennis championships on television. But it wasn't just with my mother's family that we experienced isolation.

My mother and I would visit India every other year, as she felt very much at home in Mumbai and particularly Kolkata, given her experience growing up there, and missed India terribly. But she had no family there of her own, and we stayed with my dad's sisters whenever we went to Mumbai. Without my father present, however, his sisters belittled my mother, and I felt they laughed at her behind her back, even while she made unsuccessful and feeble attempts to be warm and generous with them. I could not make sense of these encounters, and it wasn't until I was older that I began to recognize that this ill treatment was due not only to my mother's fair skin but also to the class differential between her and these women.

My parents chose to raise us in the town of Thornhill, Ontario, a newish suburb just north of Toronto, which, at the time, was predominantly Jewish. My high school was populated with the kids of Jewish immigrants from places like Poland, South Africa, and Romania. Their parents, like my own, wanted to establish an upper-middle-class life for their kids. Most of my friends were Jewish (my family was one of the only non-Jewish families on our street), and they warmly welcomed my brother and me into their homes. As a result of countless lunches and dinners with them, I learned about aspects of Judaism in a casual setting. I began to yearn to go to Hebrew School and felt jealous when all of my friends were busy on Wednesday afternoons reciting and memorizing the Torah at synagogue. I dreamed about having my own Bat Mitzvah and inviting all of my friends to celebrate the day with me. I was invited to *Seders* by my friends and loved the sacred nature of the ceremonial practices of the Friday-night Shabbat dinner. I would beg my mom to buy me *gefilte* fish from the supermarket, and I would eat it furtively with a fork out of the glass jar by myself at home. My mother and I would still say our prayers together as the sun set every night, both of us hitting the mat and reciting Arabic verse, yet I longed to learn more about Jewish culture, to become part of that larger community of my teenaged friends, and to go to synagogue.

My own immersion in some aspects of Jewish culture shaped my own pronouncements and beliefs about multiraciality too. Mixed race scholarship has not yet unravelled the complexities of mixed religion and mixed race, which are definitely not the same even though they inform each other.

I tell these stories with trepidation. But I feel it is important to do so in order to indicate some of the complexities of my own complicit relationship to multiracialism, which is not only informed and influenced by my own colonialist and imperialist histories but is of course further embedded through complicated and unearthed religious histories that remain hidden to me. These personal family stories inform our experiences of multiraciality – but they go well beyond my parents' generation, extending back to my grandparents' generation and earlier. Studies of multiracialism have not been very strong on exploring the context-specific histories of the production of mixed race knowledges. They seem generally timeless and poorly historicized. I am curious about how my parents' wildly different and complicated voyages from colonial and imperialist lands influence and define my own understanding of multiraciality. *What is the shadow cast by imperial historical formations that inform intimate contemporary social geographies of mixed race?*

I have already said that mixing between racialized groups is not novel, despite the plethora of news media accounts that seem to herald the dawning of a new mixed race or postracial era. We are, of course, all mixed in some form or another, but certain combinations and computations of mixed race hold different value, with mixes of white descent firmly on top. For mixed race to be seen as an exciting and progressive racial category, a strategic forgetting has to take place – a forgetting of our parents' past and of our grandparents' past. Rowe (2008, xi) explains that this kind of forgetting

> comes from knowing more about what you are trying to become than who you are leaving behind. Its power is that it comes with a wage that compels you to devalue what's lost because you believe that you need to belong to a certain kind of future ... The privilege of belonging to this future comes at the price of betrayal to that past.

Critical mixed race theory has provided a space for a certain sort of forgetting of complex diasporic histories through a focus on a particular kind of temporality. It allows for an unwriting of history, proffering a form of historical amnesia, particularly for those mixed race people who have experienced internalized racism. It can be seductive to see oneself as part of that bright, raceless new future and simply identify as multiracial. In my case, it was much easier for me to identify as mixed race than as Indian or Iranian. This identification befuddled people. At times, but not always, it provided safety from a barrage of diverse racial slurs, like "Chink," "Paki," or "terrorist." Through the proud declaration that I was mixed race, I would sometimes sidestep more direct questioning. But by doing so, I was participating in a form of racial epistemological violence that is enacted when we wilfully and not so wilfully discard the complex trajectories of our families' histories – stories that inform and influence who all of us are. *How can the "mixed race" label be used to avoid confronting either ourselves or the ongoing racialization of our bodies?* Ahmed (2012, 2) tells us that "forgetting has its uses." I see mixed race identity as creating a space for some multiracial women to enact a particular kind of strategic forgetting of complex colonial histories.

This study is informed by a variety of interdisciplinary sources, but it is also firmly ensconced within the field of social and cultural geography. There are particular reasons why I have chosen to explore mixed race identity within this discipline. Those of us who teach social and cultural geography often face puzzled looks when we announce what we do at dinner parties, where we are often greeted by the now-familiar refrain, "But that doesn't sound like geography as I remember it. For me, geography is about maps, soil erosion, and peninsulas." But, of course, geography is much more than just these things. Human geography offers a way for us to map and decipher the ways that we live out our lives in a complex, multilayered world – one that calls for a drastic revisioning of previous models of identity affiliation. Geographers in some ways are ideally situated to capture and chart the fluid and shifting nature of the forces shaping our daily lives. The idea that all social relations are spatial, occurring within particular physical contexts, is pretty much taken for granted among geographers (Kobayashi and Peake 1994; McKittrick 2006; McKittrick and Woods 2007). Thus racism as a process and procedure works to map particular spatial patterns through which both spatial and racial domination are actively entrenched and maintained. Some critical geographers are committed to grasping the longstanding and lingering effects of these dominant spatial formations by identifying the ways that racism continues to infiltrate spaces and to shape our experiences in those spaces.

It sounds trite to say that race and geography have long been intertwined, but it is worthwhile repeating. The interplay of environment and geography was one of the first and most persistent theories advanced to explain racial difference. Although large North American cities have become increasingly racially diverse, supposed physiological differences that mark racial difference continue to speak to geographical origins, despite the distance from these places: "Where you are from, where your parents are from, where your ancestors are from" (Kawash 1997, 9). Kawash (ibid.) notes a telling detail that exemplifies her point: "the semantic shift from 'black' to 'African-American,' [which] evidence[s] a certain substitutability between the language of race and the language of geography." As Goldberg (1995, 185) notes, "Just as spatial distinctions like 'West' and 'East' are racialized in their conception and application, so racial categories have been variously spatialized more or less since their inception into continental divides, national localities, and geographic regions." In other words, geography has acted as a complicit agent in racial discourses: "The delimitations of racial difference have been understood to correspond to a global map" (Kawash 1997, 9). Through the particular illogic of cartography, separate human populations and attendant racial groups are fixed in particular geographic spaces. Kawash (ibid., 10) reminds us that "the history of positive racial science has been Modern Geography applied to human diversity; the races are the natural, physical formations that make up the social world." She insists that "race, like the places geography takes as its object, is reduced to physical objects and forms, and naturalized back to a first nature so as to become susceptible to prevailing scientific explanation in the form of orderly, reproducible description." She suggests that if we see it this way, "the human division of races is of the same order as the continental division of a mountain range or the expanse of [an] ocean ... simply a natural fact out there in the world, to be described in the most neutral and objective terms possible" (ibid.).

Any critical human geographer worth her salt will tell you that human geography is concerned with challenging this assumption. Our focus is on repudiating this tautology. This book pays particular attention to the personal and political geographies that some mixed race women create in relation to others' perceptions about their racialized bodies. Not only is there a historical specificity to perceptions of racial mixedness, but there is a definitive geographical specificity as well. Those geographical specificities have wildly varying political co-ordinates, as I make clear in Chapter 3.

At the same time, however, I do not cite specific locations in the city, like street corners or names of places, where mixed race women contest and play with systemic racial formations. I am far less interested in asking mixed race women about the specific material spots where they feel at home or in place because I think that geographies are unstable and shifting yet at the same time can be unyielding as well. I draw here from McKittrick (2006), who encourages us not only to conceptualize geography as a location in time and space, firmly rooted in the ground and in the soil, but also to consider what philosophical work social and cultural geography can do to inform critical understandings of race through the creation of new epistemological and ontological spaces. I choose to look at the spatial acts employed by some mixed race women and to ask whether these spatial acts *contest and challenge existing racial and colonial ontological and epistemological formations.* Here, I see spatial acts as "identified through expressions, resistances, and naturalizations" (ibid., xix). For me, the real power in drawing from social and cultural geography both as a discipline and as an analytical tool is that it can help us to understand the ways that race operates through these spatial acts. As Sexton (2008, 29) points out, race can also work as a medium, or connecting tissue: "Race is a production of meaning or a form of value and hence operates as communication, as an element of exchange." Racial communication takes place in a physical and geographical place and, in turn, alters space. *How does space constrict, refuse, conform to, allow, or create opportunities for different kinds of racial reconfigurements?* I investigate how different geographies on a variety of scales shaped the actual intensity and experience of race for the women in this study. The book tries to show that mixed race people have been made intelligible in ways that reinforce both racialized and gendered categories, their bodies routinely disciplined through ongoing processes of regulation to keep them securely *in place.*

As I have hinted here, I was driven to explore mixed race identity in an academic context because my own experience of racial identity throughout my life seemed to be radically different from that in the literature I had encountered. I have participated in countless conversations with other mixed race people over the years, and inevitably, we have remarked upon the paucity of literature available on how we negotiate and challenge interpretations of our racialized identities, especially in Canada (but see Camper 1994; Hill

2001; and DeRango-Adem and Thompson 2010). Although we are witnessing a proliferation of new texts that explore the experiences of mixed race identity in the United States and the United Kingdom (Camper 1994; Ifekwunigwe 1999; Olumide 2002; Kwan and Speirs 2004; DaCosta 2007; Sexton 2008; McNeil 2010; Elam 2011; Spencer 2011; Bettez 2012; Ibrahim 2012; R. Joseph 2013), few studies have explained how individuals of mixed race identity negotiate their racial identities under various circumstances, over time, and at different times in their lives. This gap in the literature led me to consider a wide array of questions: How do we challenge static stereotypes of our identities as mixed race women? Why is there an assumption that there is a quintessential mixed race look? Why is it that some mixed race women are considered exotic beauties and seamless cultural navigators, ambassadors of the new global economy? Are there ways of understanding our identities beyond vacant euphoric celebrations of our mixed ancestry, where our bodies are seen as portending a colour-blind future?

I contend that the seeming invisibility of some insidious racist and sexist discourses in the Canadian context works to undermine a more careful understanding of the mixed race experience. As I make clear in this book, there are other ways to understand the mixed race experience outside of the prevailing paradigm of the mixed race individual as either confused and torn or able to solve the world's race problems by emblematically ushering in a postracial future (as though such a future could exist). The experience of mixed race is also not the same from place to place, of course. One cannot consider interviewing mixed race people without asking more about the ground upon which they live out their lives (see King-O'Riain et al. 2014) – for example, as Anglo-Indians (those of mixed Indian and British descent in India) or as Korean Americans (children born to women in Korea during the Korean War, some fathered by white servicemen and some by African American servicemen), not to mention as individuals born of the various forms of racial mixing in South America (see Twine 2000b).

I pursued this study of mixed race identity because so much of the literature on multiraciality has emerged from an American- and British-based context, with the modalities of race in both countries subsequently influencing epistemological turns in mixed race studies. I ask how we might understand the experience of mixed race identity in Canada – a modern, white-settler society imagined as a liberal, multicultural democracy. I am not alone in articulating the value of looking at the experience of those who identify as mixed race through a study of those located in a particular arena; indeed, Maria Root (1990), one of the key scholars contributing to mixed race theory, has proposed that among the factors and criteria affecting the experience of mixed race identity, environment must play a significant role. Keeping this in mind, I decided to limit my focus to Canada, particularly Toronto.

I conducted research in Canada's largest urban centre not just because it has the nation's largest foreign-born population but also because it was a city with which I was intimately familiar and where I had retained close personal and professional ties. The number of interracial relationships in Toronto is increasing, and interracial unions increased 35 percent between 1991 and 2001 (Mahoney and Alphonso 2005). Although we have no precise figures confirming the number of people who identify as mixed race in Canada, the Ethnic Diversity Survey conducted in 2001 shows that out of the 29,639,035 respondents, 11,331,490 indicated belonging to multiple *ethnicities,* but the census did not ask about *racial* origin (Statistics Canada 2003). I deliberately chose to carry out research in a city with a diverse ethnic population since it has been suggested that mixed race people growing up in places with more documented incidents of racism are less likely to have the freedom to choose their racial identity, a point I touch upon later in the book (Root 1990).

Most of these interviews were conducted in the mid- to late 1990s. This particular period and its corresponding politics, policies, and projects influenced and informed the gathering of interview material. Obviously, the contours of race have shifted since that time. Significant shifts to neoliberal forms of government and policies in Canada occurred during the 1990s. The government of Prime Minister Jean Chrétien, which rose to power in the 1993 election, reduced the federal contributions to national and provincial social and welfare programs. In 1995, just before interviews began, Ontario's Progressive Conservative government (under Premier Mike Harris) was elected. The Harris Cabinet was explicitly and uncompromisingly neoliberal and "perhaps the most interventionist government this province/city has ever seen" (Keil 2002, 588). The Ontario Conservatives devalued many services to municipalities and initiated numerous restrictive laws that affected the everyday life of the general population in Ontario, especially Toronto. These shifts to neoliberalism at the various levels of government led to an increase in spatialized socio-economic polarization and inequities, including inequities in the distribution of resources and in access to opportunities, with racialized minorities and immigrants mostly affected. As I make clear in Chapter 3, this context shaped the responses I received in interviews.

Race 101

> To study race ... is to enter into a world of paradox.
>
> — OMI AND WINANT 1994, XI

> To say "race" seems to imply that "race" is real ... but "race" has been the history of an untruth ... the truth of racism as a lie: that is what we need to unpack before we successfully put behind us the ugly and brutal regime of race.
>
> — RADHAKRISHNAN 1996, 81

Somerset Maugham in *The Razor's Edge* (1944) warns the reader that he can very well skip a particular section of the chapter without losing the thread of the story; indeed, I would be surprised if the reader did not already understand many of the concepts I discuss here. But, like Maugham (ibid., 218), I concur that "except for this conversation, I should not perhaps have found it worthwhile to write this book," and I feel it is important to include this section, especially for those new to the study of race.

One of the most crucial issues in the field of critical mixed race studies, particularly in different national contexts, is who identifies as mixed race. What does this identification really mean? Of course, what actually constitutes race is a crucial question. But how one defines mixed race is also valuable to consider. Can you identify as mixed race if you are Indian and Iranian, like myself? Or are you mixed only if you identify as black-white or Asian-white – mixes that have governed both popular and intellectual understandings of the multiracial experience?

More than a decade ago, April Moreno and I wrote an article that asked whether we, as self-identified Indian Iranian and Mexican Chinese women, respectively, could consider ourselves to be mixed race subjects (Mahtani and Moreno 2001). What was our place in the discourse about multiraciality, and how did the existing epistemological framings in critical mixed race studies reveal a disturbing tendency to rebiologize race by focusing on who was and who wasn't allowed to be part of the mixed race movement? It is impossible not to consider these questions without a contemplation of the ontology of race and racism.

Dei (2007, 55) rightly points out that the "intellectual gymnastics" surrounding race have taken on a variety of forms, and in the past ten years, we have witnessed an explosion of work about the ontology of race and racism (see, for example, Saldanha 2006; and Sexton 2008). Although most scholars recognize the dangers in defining race, I think it is important before considering these questions to remind the reader of the arbitrary connection between anatomical features and political meaning, where certain physical differences (like skin colour and hair type) have been used to indicate crucial power differentials between individuals. This becomes particularly potent for people who identify as mixed race, as their very bodies can become a minefield of racial marking.

In most social-science literature, race has predominantly come to be viewed as a social construction based on an arbitrary affiliation of phenotypical characteristics with social and cultural inferiority and superiority, an issue I return to in Chapter 1. However, I must admit that I still encounter bewildered looks and blank stares when I state unequivocally to others, "Race is a social construction." Despite this reality, race remains systemic and a powerful mode of division. Although race always works with other identity markers like gender, ethnicity, class, and further forms of social stratification, race remains deceptively difficult to discuss. Barzun (1938, 94) provides a particularly productive and revealing definition of race-thinking: "a tangle of quarrels, a confusion of assertions, a knot of facts and fictions that revolt the intellect and daunt the courage of the most persistent. In its mazes, race-thinking is its own best refutation. If sense and logic can lead to truth, not a single system of race-classification can be true." Despite Barzun's claim that not a single system of race classification can be true, myths about race remain tenacious. Race remains ubiquitous, and there is a murky acceptance in popular discourse that the world is divided into specific races – which comprise easily identifiable and always stable categories. To understand the debates discussed in this book, it is crucial to remember that race is but a regulatory fiction, an imaginary construction with its origins in biological myths. As the critical mixed race scholar Jayne O. Ifekwunigwe (1999) reminds us, there remains a profound and painful relationship between perceived phenotypes (physical characteristics) and genotypes (biological and genetic characteristics). Phenotype remains the main determinant of race division and includes, but is certainly not limited to, skin colour, hair texture, and facial features. Scientists have agreed that race is a social construction rather than a biological fact. Genotype does not absolutely define one population and keep it distinct from another. Biologists argue that any distinction among human races is "but an appropriate shorthand for statistical tendencies in the distribution frequencies of some four percent of human genes over very large population samples" (Baumann 1996, 18). Thus the paradox of race is revealed: Race does not exist, yet it remains a salient feature in the public imagination. Society uses these false divisions to categorize individuals within social, political orders, which in turn determine our economic realities about power and class. These social constructions have become fully embedded in social relations, political interactions, and economic structures. Race is deployed as a shorthand for clues about a person's identity, as a central axis of social relations, and as a category of social organization central to structures, institutions, and social discourses. One's racial identity can determine "the allocation of resources, and frame political issues and conflicts" (Omi and Winant 1994, 61).

However, having emphasized the way that race is a social construction, I do not mean to imply that race is unreal. There are dangers in emphasizing the socially constructed nature of race. The seductive epistemological framework of race as a social construction emerged most consistently in geography in the 1990s, where some social and cultural geographers (among other social scientists) insisted on employing the idea that race is a social construction, without any biological adherent, as a theoretical scaffolding for their argument. The geographer Dan Swanton illustrates the limits of the social-constructionist argument by convincingly showing the failings of the tendency in geography to present race solely as a social construction. Drawing from Saldanha (2006), he insists that this framework limited the engagement of the social sciences with important questions of epistemology and interpretation (Swanton 2010). Although the social-constructionist framework was important because it illustrated the unstable nature of socially constructed racial categories, in an ironic way, it also worked to rebiologize and reduce race. A focus on social construction offered some geographers an easy way out of thinking more deeply about the work that race actually does. In my own teaching, I see the limitations of the social-constructionist argument. It is almost commonplace for us who teach about race to include a kind of "Race 101" in our classes, emphasizing to students that race is indeed an invention, a social construction. But as many of my students have asked, how does showing that race is culturally constructed do anything to ensure social and political change?

The social-constructionist argument has allowed for a particular kind of paralysis in conversations about race in geography and has worked toward a depoliticization of race. As Stoler (1997, 201) reminds us, the fact "that we who study the history of racism are so committed to documenting fluidity may have more to do with the sorts of political narratives of renouncement and thus of redeption we are intent to tell" – a point I return to in Chapter 2. Although race may not exist per se, and we can keep reminding students that it has no real biological referent, racism certainly does, and as Slocum (2008, 854) states, "fictionalizing race [can make] some of the most interesting aspects of race disappear." It is almost irrelevant whether race is a social construction when the lived reality of race is so abundantly apparent in the lives of mixed race people. I am sympathetic to Brunsma's (2006, 5) suggestion that "race is not something one is, but rather an elaborate, lived experience and cultural ritual of what one does." For me, the question "What is race?" is far less interesting than "*Where* is race?" This book tries to pay attention to how race emerges through moments and times in place, focusing on the geographical knowledges that some mixed race women impart.

In this book I ask, *What is the role of race in these women's day-to-day encounters with other bodies?* The politics of race is, in part, a competition over these socially constructed definitions, which in turn define individuals' place in the world. But this does not mean that there are no material consequences to these social constructions. As Saldanha (2006, 15, 18) puts it, "the structures of racism ... encompass much more than just mental categories ... Nobody 'has' a race, but bodies are racialized." This book is concerned with those who see themselves as being able to manoeuvre through racial categories, exploring the connections between these bodies while also citing the multiplicity of ways that these individuals see themselves as troubling race through particular actions and subjectivities. As experienced by the women in this study, the most salient points about race are that it shapes understandings of the boundaries between mixed race people and that it is always influenced by cultural identities in ways that are not easily unravelled.

Of course, the mere presence of individuals who define themselves as mixed race does not challenge racial categories. I am wary of the dangers of presenting mixed race people as "progressive trailblazers" (Elam 2011, 87), a point I return to in Chapter 3. Although some mixed race women feel they have the potential to become "race traitors" (Ignatiev and Garvey 1996) since they see themselves as defying simplistic racial classification, this stance does not mean that they conveniently escape the trappings of racism or that they automatically challenge racism simply by being. As I show in Chapter 1, specific historical genealogies employed to make sense of the mixed race experience repeatedly demonstrate the complex forms of violence enacted upon the mixed race body (Mawani 2009), but there are moments, too, when the mixed race body enacts violence. This book develops new ways of understanding the racialized and gendered embodiment of mixed race subjects by charting the acts of agency they employ to get on and get by in a highly charged, racialized world. Elam (2011, 52) reminds us of Du Bois's (1989) astute insight about the value of studying mixed race through a multidisciplinary approach, insisting that Du Bois "understood that considerations of mixed race were always grounded in an analysis of psychology, power, history, and economics." I take this point into consideration.

Terminology: Mixed Race, Mixing Races

Finally, one might well ask why I don't put the terms "mixed race" and "race" in scare quotes. It has become common practice in the social sciences to do so with the word "race" in order to indicate its arbitrary connection to anatomical features, and more often than not, the term "mixed race" is also put in scare quotes. However, I agree with feminist geographers Audrey Kobayashi and Linda Peake (1994, 231), who claim that "scare quoting gives [race] an un-natural quality, as though races could be de-constructed if only racism were sufficiently resisted." Like Montagu (1952, 284), I feel that "one cannot combat racism by enclosing the word ['race'] in quotes." Although the practice does emphasize a point – namely that whereas race is a social phenomenon, race as a biological category does not exist – I deliberately do not use scare quotes with the term "race" in order to remind the reader of the very material ways that ideas around race and accompanying racial violence continue to proliferate. I am concerned about studies that place the word "race" in scare quotes because doing so tends to allow for proliferation of the knowledge that race is a social construction without attending to its very real material consequences. Although it is indeed true that race is a social invention, I am wary of the space that such a claim creates by opening up an opportunity for "racists to reinstate biological justifications for white privilege" (Saldanha 2006, 10). Scare quotes "signal an awareness of the word's tainted history and scepticism" (ibid., 13). However, terms like "nation," "gender," and "sex" are also hotly contested, and we do not put them in scare quotes with regularity. I hope that this "Race 101" section has clarified how racial categories serve to create a social order that controls the flow of moral rights and obligations, as well as the materiality of privilege. As Maugham (1944, 219) would say, "so much for that."

Organization of the Book

The book is divided into seven chapters. Chapter 1, "Mixed Race Mythologies," attempts to critically examine the broad-ranging literature about the mixed race experience. It looks at the ways that an emerging new scholarship on multiraciality has not necessarily sparked a politicized conversation that would inform anticolonial scholarship. I argue that critical mixed race theory and its accompanying epistemological practices cannot be assumed to be politically progressive or necessarily committed to social-justice struggles. I suggest that a focus on what are seen as new forms of mixing, including the problematic appropriation of the term "New Métis" to describe multiracial identities of immigrant mixes, has strategically excluded the concerns of Aboriginal peoples in Canada and has refused to engage with scholarship on the black Canadian experience.

In Chapter 2, "Mixed Race Narcissism?" I explore in greater detail the contradictory nature of a mixed race population by introducing the participants in this study, as well as delving more deeply into my own complicit positioning as a mixed race woman conducting this research.

Chapter 3, "The Model Multiracial," begins the empirical analysis by introducing a brief history of the Canadian multicultural project. It attempts to contextualize the way that some mixed race people imagine themselves as intrinsically antiracist simply by identifying as mixed race. I make the case that some mixed race women demonstrate a particular kind of racial impotency that allows for a neutralized liberal stance and explain what role the mixed race figure played in racial formation in Toronto in the late 1990s.

In Chapter 4, "Beyond the Passing Narrative," I investigate the ways that participants positioned themselves in relation to white identity. I argue that many participants negotiated perceptions of themselves as both nonwhite and white, with subjectivity playing a crucial role in the ways that one's racialized location was allocated.

I propose the development of a new spatial metaphor in Chapter 5, "Mongrels, Interpreters, Ambassadors, and Bridges?" to examine the ways that participants contemplated the "mixed race" label to identify themselves. I also illustrate some of the more complicated affinities and alliances that participants forged with others in situations that were ridden with both racialized and gendered meanings.

Chapter 6, "Mixed Race Scanners," chronicles the ways that participants enacted complex racialized performances to disrupt constraining, oppressive, and dichotomous readings of their ethnic identity. I map out racialized performativity in the social landscape by exploring how participants often pretended to be of various ethnicities, thus demonstrating how race is a social invention.

In my concluding chapter, "Present Tense," I draw upon my empirical work to speculate about future routes in critical mixed race theory. In particular, I point out the limitations of this particular study and discuss the possibilities and pitfalls of the creation of an intellectual nexus that places at centre stage the ways that mixed race women speak about affinities, affiliations, connections, and coalitions without problematizing these stances. Finally, I explore what an anticolonial approach to the study of multiraciality would look like if we seriously contemplated producing analyses of mixed race that refused to privilege whiteness and colonialism.

1
Mixed Race Mythologies
Toward an Anticolonial Mixed Race Studies

> The mixed-race child as a harbinger of a transracial future is ... wedded to *progress*.
>
> — NYONG'O 2009, 176, MY EMPHASIS

> My father tells me that the further you get away from an experience, the deeper it roots itself inside of you. Don't fool yourself, baby, he said. Time does not heal and history is not progressive.
>
> — SENNA 2003, 212

An old adage goes, "Change is inevitable, but progress is not." This chapter interrogates the charged relationship between multiraciality and the ideal of progress. In the quotation above from her novel *Symptomatic*, Danzy Senna introduces us to her mixed race protagonist. Her father's warning to her is particularly prescient as the plot unravels. I suggest in this chapter that her father's advice may also act as a cautionary tale for mixed race scholars. I explain why I am wary of the contemporary romanticization of multiraciality that tends to permeate both popular and academic analyses of mixed race identity. It is often naively assumed that the mere presence of mixed race people augers the dawning of a new era of racelessness and equity for all racialized peoples. This myth has gnarled historical origins but is often attributed to José Vasconcelos's *La Raza Cósmica* (1925), which claimed that race and nationality could be transcended through humanity's desire for a common destiny. He proposed the ideology of a futuristic "fifth race," which would be composed of all the racialized people of the world, who would work together to produce a new civilization called "Universópolis." Similarly, but not identically, Ibrahim (2012, vii) states, "The multiracial child [has become] an icon that represent[s] the social and political horizon, a future in which the full recognition of personhood – selfhood unfettered by taxonomic restraints – would be fulfilled." In this chapter, I interrogate the mythology of a future racelessness by questioning what is actually *progressive* about the historiography of mixed race studies, tracing the multiple and different investments and agendas that have shaped the content and contours of this growing subfield. I also ask an open question: what would an anticolonial mixed race studies look like? I make the claim that colonial imperatives have governed the exploration of mixed race identity.

In the past twenty years, several new academic texts on race have made their focus the empirical study of mixed race identity as opposed to tabulating the experiences of a particular monoracial group (see Hill 2001; Parker and Song 2001; Ifekwunigwe 2004; Sexton 2008; McNeil 2010; Elam 2011; Spencer 2011; Bettez 2012; Edwards et al. 2012; and R. Joseph 2013). They are written from a variety of disciplines, including English literature, media studies, political science, and sociology. Some, but definitely not all, are penned by scholars who identify as multiracial. I map an admittedly broad epistemology of mixed race studies and inquire about its particular omissions and silences.

It is not my task here to historically detail the entire history of work on multiraciality – such a goal is beyond the scope of this project, and I am much more interested in tracing key moments in critical mixed race studies than in scrutinizing its detailed content. I ask, *How might we situate interview material gathered from some mixed race women in Canada within this particular context of growing scholarship and consider how these intellectual treatises inform and shape present and, in particular, future mixed race epistemologies in Canada?* I question how we might extend contemporary mixed race historiographies, which have emerged mostly from an American and British context (but see McNeil 2010), to develop new kinds of scaffolding that will enable us to better comprehend the specificities of the Canadian mixed race experience. I draw from the work of scholars at the intersections of critical race theory, antiracism studies, and anticolonialist approaches to race in order to shed light on the thoughts and perceptions of some women of mixed race in this study.

Toward the end of the chapter, I pay particular attention to Canada's status as a *white-settler state* and question why this context seems to be shrouded in contemporary conversations about mixing in Canada. I make the case that mixed race studies has paid far too little attention to charting the particularities of colonial histories that inform our understanding of what it means to be mixed race. A focus on the history of erasure of Indigeneity and its present resonances has the potential to radically inform and shape the study of Canadian multiraciality if we commit to an anticolonial approach to critical mixed race studies. My key point in this chapter is that mixed race people have been made intelligible in ways that maintain not only racialized and gendered hierarchies but also *colonized* ones.

As I traced my way through the intellectual work that informs the experience of multiraciality, it became obvious that one cannot examine this oeuvre without considering its attendant intellectual geographies, or the locations within which it has been produced, particularly in the global North. Where and when this work was written has influenced the epistemological direction of mixed race theory. The majority of research on mixed race identity is based in either the United States or the United Kingdom (but see Camper 1994; Hill 2001; L. Taylor 2008; Lafond 2009; and McNeil 2010). Razack (2005) has said that scholars in Canada are often overly reliant on American work on race and that Canadian academics are therefore plagued by an insufficient body of knowledge on how race operates in Canada. Thus one might say that British and American intellectual attitudes about race and, consequently, about mixed race identity have the potential to shape Canadian academic discourses on multiraciality. These attitudes are transformed through their shift from America and Britain to the Canadian context. We cannot assume that contributions from American and British scholars will provide the intellectual architecture required to understand the Canadian experience of multiraciality (but for an important engagement with this issue, see McNeil 2010).

I argue that there can be no clear agreement about what constitutes mixed race in a global arena because *mixed race cannot be pinned down to a single semantic definition. It can be understood only by relating its shifting meanings and contours to historically and geographically located processes. Transnational colonial histories, including transatlantic slavery and diasporic migrant experiences across generations, influence and alter the production of intellectual stories about mixed race people.* These ideas, theories, and knowledges travel and take shape, influencing and altering debates about multiraciality in Canada. In other words, this discussion is not and can never be a coherent or singular story.

Tracing the Epistemology of Critical Mixed Race Scholarship

Scholars studying multiraciality hotly debate how the ideas, concepts, and theories that comprise critical mixed race theory have developed (see Sexton 2008; Rockquemore, Brunsma, and Delgado 2009; McNeil 2010; Elam 2011; Spencer 2011; Ibrahim 2012; and R. Joseph 2013). While acknowledging the important contributions of others, I draw specifically from what is arguably considered the most contemporary and comprehensive anthology in critical mixed race studies: Jayne Ifekwunigwe's *"Mixed Race" Studies: A Reader* (2004). Ifekwunigwe traces the origins of mixed race research as an intellectual movement and maps the key developments in what is rapidly becoming a subdisciplinary field within ethnic and racial studies. She proposes that there are at least two ages in mixed race studies: the age of pathology, focused on miscegenation, moral degeneracy, and genetics; and the age of celebration, influenced by identity politics. This distinction is a helpful starting point for understanding the key debates in the field. Other authors have suggested similar but not identical framings – for example, Spencer (2004, 108) offers that there are two significant approaches to the multiracial idea: pathology and cheerleading. McNeil (2010, 16) cleverly critiques this charting of the evolution in critical mixed race studies, insisting that Ifekwunigwe's reader "grates the British ear ... and offers an elliptical introduction to the supposed 'evolution' of mixed-race discourse from an 'era of pathology' in the Victorian period to an 'era of celebration' and 'critique' in the 1990s." McNeil claims that Ifekwunigwe's historical schema "does not necessarily help historians interested in self-fashioning when it fails to identify how mixed-race individuals acted as active historical agents in a one hundred–year 'era of pathology'" (ibid.; see also Elam 2011).

Ifekwunigwe's conceptualization, however, does demonstrate its use by helpfully delineating the intellectual orbits through which ideas about multiraciality have travelled. The first paradigm that Ifekwunigwe explores – that of pathology – can be traced back to nineteenth-century racial science, drawing upon evolutionary anthropology to show that discourses on moral degeneration were employed to illustrate the supposed dangers of racial mixing. Mixed race people were considered to be genetically inferior and deviant examples of hybrid degeneracy. As Alcoff (2006, 267) explains,

> In cultures defined by racialized identities, infected with the illusion of purity, and divided by racial hierarchies, mixed white/nonwhite persons face an irresolvable status ambiguity. They are rejected by the dominant race as impure and therefore inferior, but they are also sometimes disliked and distrusted by the oppressed race for their privileges of closer association with domination ... the mixed race person cannot easily escape condemnation.

These ideas continued to proliferate well into the 1900s, when Charles Benedict Davenport (1917, 366-67), cited as the leading advocate of eugenics in the United States at the time, proposed that mixed race individuals suffered from emotional and mental problems: "One often sees in mulattos an ambition and push combined with intellectual inadequacy which makes the unhappy hybrid dissatisfied with his lot and a nuisance to others." These sorts of conclusions reflected an insistence on clinging to myths that equated psychological and physical superiority with white racial purity, such that culturally reductionist notions were seen as biological and natural, part of scientific inquiry. This approach resulted in a discourse that was racist in both the treatment and the definition of its subjects. As Nakashima (1992) explains, the relentless negativity surrounding the mixed race person continued into the 1930s. Castle (1926), Krauss (1941), and W.C. Smith (1939) described mixed race people as having no strength of their senses – physical, mental, emotional, or moral – and this identity, rather than environmental causes, apparently led to early deaths and the inability to produce offspring. Research on mixed race people focused solely upon individuals of combined African and European descent – those groups with the largest difference in social status and privilege in society. Early sociological theory proposed "marginal personality" disorder as a potential diagnosis of mixed race individuals (Stonequist 1937). Dover (1937, 279) claimed that mixed race people were an example of the "work of the devil, that they inherit the vices of both parents and the virtues of neither, that they are without exception infertile, unbalanced, indolent, immoral, and degenerate."

Although I have focused on literature that marked mixed race people as inferior to their monoracial counterparts, there were some who insisted that the mixed race individual was superior to monoracial individuals. Some claimed that mixed race individuals who were partially white were superior to individuals who were "full" black, "full" Indian, or "full" Asian (see Castle 1926). Park (1931) claimed that people of African European descent were genetically and culturally superior to blacks (yet at the same time, this group was seen as genetically and culturally inferior to whites). There was also a group of scientists who adopted a "survival of the fittest" mentality, claiming that mixed race individuals inherited the best features of each parent and therefore were smarter, healthier, and more attractive than monoracial individuals (Krauss 1941; Ziv 2006). These studies, with their histories woven from biological determinism, reflected a dualism that emphasized either the superiority or the inferiority of the mixed race individual. Both representations tended to emphasize her deviant status. Nakashima (1992) shows how the wilder imaginings of fiction writers reinforced the pseudo-scientific themes, where mixed race characters were envisaged as experiencing great torment because of their supposedly genetically divided selves and as suffering from low self-esteem, as demonstrated most often by their delinquent behaviour. As Ferber (2004) has persuasively argued, it is impossible to understand issues of mixed race without considering the ways that race and gender are intertwined within multiraciality. Mainstream fictional literature of the time portrayed mixed race women in particular as flighty and confused, and its mixed race characters, most often African European or Latino European, were dangerous, tormented, and pathetic (see Berzon 1978 and Nakashima 1992, 167). Women of mixed race were envisioned, even more than mixed race men, as unreliable sorts, liable to revert to the savage, primitive behaviour of the jungle (Tizard and Phoenix 1993, 20). At the same time, the mixed race person could be seen as a straightforward villain, evil incarnate, combining the worst traits of both races (Berzon 1978; Nakashima 1992). Portrayals of the mixed race woman presented her as a tragic figure, struggling between the strands of her ancestry. The mixed race woman was seen as both erotic and exotic, deviant and deceitful. Eroticizing the mixed race woman in this way provided an overtly sexualized form of racism, compounding the tragic mulatto stereotype.

Thus the mixed race body was made intelligible by a series of interwoven discourses that naturalized racist categories through what has come to be known as racial science. These categories not only impose intellectual hierarchies but also maintain political power, privileging particular patriarchal discourses. I have limited my evaluation to those clinical and literary examples from the nineteenth to the early twentieth centuries, as others have explored this terrain (see, among others, Ifekwunigwe 1999; and Olumide 2002). However, remnants of the hybrid degeneracy theory continued to spill into evaluations of mixed race identity well into the 1900s.

In 1937 Everett Stonequist, a student of Robert Park, a key figure in the Chicago School of Sociology, published *The Marginal Man: A Study in Personality and Culture Conflict* (1937), the thesis of which inferred that "the status and role of a particular mixed-blood group can be taken as an index of the larger race problem; and in turn the development of the mixed-blood class reacts back upon the general racial situation modifying it to a significant, sometimes determining, extent" (ibid., 50). The "marginal man," in Stonequist's view, suffered from personal maladjustment and clung to a victim mentality. Furedi (1998) provides an important critique of Stonequist's thesis, arguing that it provided yet another insidious underpinning for anti-miscegenation. Writing in the late 1950s, the psychologist Erik Erikson (1959) claimed that the identity process was challenging to mixed race people. Several case studies of biracial individuals have concluded that they are troubled by their status and confused about their identity and that they experience more difficulties with families and peers than others, emphasizing that biracial people are poorly adjusted (Gibbs and Huang and Associates 1989). Some studies have gone so far as to insist that it is impossible to create a positive mixed race identity:

> I believe one cannot develop a biracial identity if he or she tries to pass for White, because this requires letting go of one's biracial identity. I do not think it is possible to develop a "mixed race" or a White and a Black identity at the same time, because I don't see how a dual identity process can occur ... it is not possible to develop a positive "dual race" or "mixed-race" identity by evolving the Black and the White aspects simultaneously ... I do not think it is possible to have an identity on a psychosocial foundation that is at odds with itself. (R.T. Carter 1995, 119)

Robert Carter (ibid., 120) concludes by suggesting that a biracial person ought to become grounded in the devalued racial group as a foundation for facilitating the merger of the two racial groups. Thus even clinical psychologists have continued to reassert particular claims about biological determinism. There is no attempt within these studies to reconcile the solitudes of the mixed race person's experience, clearly illustrated through the use of terms like "biracial" and "dual identity." The mixed race individual is compared to people with supposedly stable identities, such as those who are fully black or white, as though they were actually pure-blooded.

Examinations of mixed race, largely influenced by the Enlightenment era, perpetuated the myth of racial purity and highlighted the tendency among powerful groups to view the mixed race individual as problematic, defiling, and polluting. In other words, mixed race people troubled geographical spaces merely through their presence in these locations (see also Mawani 2009).

Both the stereotype of the mixed race person as torn and confused and the ugliness surrounding the mixed race person's existence come out of a history of transatlantic slavery and a history of encounter between whites and blacks. The literature directs us to this crucial racial history, which informs and structures historical and ongoing debates about multiraciality. It cannot be forgotten, as so commonly seems to happen now, that the history of multiraciality is a history of the racism that emerged directly out of transnational slavery. This history has implications not only for those who are part black but also for those who are of other racialized mixes. These myths clearly dictate how material representations and their subsequent powerful ideologies naturalize inequalities (see Saldanha 2006) and mask the relationship between the powerful and the powerless, creating geographies of exclusion.

Celebrating the Mixed Race Subject: Romanticizing Multiraciality

> The future belongs to the impure.
>
> — S. HALL 1998, 299

Ifekwunigwe (2004) designates the second stage of critical mixed race studies as the era of celebration, or what Spencer (2011, 3) calls the period of cheerleading (see also Sexton 2008; McNeil 2010; and Spencer 2011). These studies showcase race as a social construction, emphasizing that mixed race identities can be fluid and flexible. Asserting a definitive oppositional stance against the tragic mulatto stereotype and providing a different story of multiraciality, studies in this category emphasize the agency of the mixed race subject.

Considered by many to be the pioneering mixed race psychologist, Dr. Maria Root engineered new ways to think through mixed race identity. Root asserts that the profound influence of anti-miscegenist attitudes produced conclusions that tended to reinforce static constructions of identity. Much work classified under her paradigm has been characterized by interdisciplinary collaboration and researcher sensitivity to the uniqueness of the multiracial experience. Such research has explored interracial marriages, incorporating data on courtship and marriage as well as on the stability and frequency of marriages (see Mathabane and Mathabane 1992; and C.I. Hall 1996). The focus of the literature since that time has generally attempted to recover America's mixed race history and to extend knowledge of mixed race beyond the bounds of a black-white duality. Mixes of Asians and whites and of Native Americans and blacks have been studied. Attention has been focused upon racial mixes between groups that differ the most, both culturally and socially – blacks and Europeans, Japanese and blacks, Japanese and Europeans (Root 1992; Ifekwunigwe 1999). I have previously outlined how early literature on mixed race identity substantiated the popular belief that mixed race children suffered from serious identity complexes. Research within this paradigm countered that claim by focusing upon ideological racist beliefs inherent within the environment or context of the mixed race individual. Root (1994) claims that mixed race poses no inherent types of stress that would result in psychological maladjustment; any distress related to being mixed race is likely to be a response to an environment that has internalized racist beliefs. Tizard and Phoenix echo this notion in their study *Black, White or Mixed Race?* (1993) by illustrating how mixed race children often see advantages in their situation, a finding that runs counter to the widespread belief that mixed race children suffer from identity problems. These theories emphasize the interaction of social, familial, and individual variables within a context that interacts with history and moves away from models of adjustment and identity development. They consider the complex contexts in which identity formation takes place, focusing on the role society plays rather than focusing on the "other" status of the mixed race individual.

Stonequist (1937) emphasizes that the status and role of a particular mixed group can be taken as an index of the larger race problem and that, in turn, the development of the mixed class reacts back upon the general situation, modifying it to an extent. Rather than placing the onus upon the individual to fit into the social structure, an emphasis is placed on the strategies that the mixed race person may employ, focusing upon the mixed race person's navigation through fluid, as opposed to static, social relations. Instead of concentrating on the absolute resolution of identity (as though identity is something that must be resolved), more recent studies of mixed race identity emphasize that identity is continually shifting and changing. Root (1990, 186) proposes that "the individual may shift their resolution strategies throughout their lifetime in order to nurture a positive identity." Other researchers examining mixed race identity have echoed this notion, focusing the conclusions of their research through multidimensional models that allow for the possibility that the individual may have concurrent affiliations and multiple, fluid identities with different social groups (see Root 1990; Gibbs and Hines 1992; Iijima-Hall 1992; Stephan 1992; and T.K. Williams 1992).

Root (1992, 6) applauds these studies for "abolishing either/or classification systems that create marginality." By discarding these models, these new studies reflect a defining moment in the history of research on mixed race individuals. Emphasis is placed upon the agency of racially mixed people and on their liberation from, as opposed to their confinement by, the oppressive hierarchy of racial categories. For example, Teresa Kay Williams (1992, 302) concludes that "the process of identity development is fascinating and dynamic, yet personal and complex. Each one will taste what the larger society has to offer and will spit out what does not suit him or her."

Some mixed race researchers have emphasized the importance of unravelling the ways that traditional heterosexual roles help to maintain the separation of genders and the purity of races (Allman 1996; Streeter 1996), with white supremacy and male superiority being inextricably linked. Drawing upon the work of many feminist discussions of gender roles (Ware 1992), Allman (1996) explores the Victorian domestic feminine ideal, who communicated notions of purity, piety, and domesticity; was an asexual and frail creature; and was necessarily white and class-privileged. She was also contrasted with the stereotypical image of the hypersexualized, exotic woman of colour (Collins 1990; Nakashima 1992). White, class-privileged, male identity depended upon its image as protector and keeper of white womanhood. Thus the hypersexualization of women of colour served to excuse and justify the rape of women of colour by white men (Allman 1996). Streeter (1996) explains how ambiguous racial identity conflicts with the miscegenation taboo, where in order for norms of racial purity to complement norms of heterosexuality, mixed race individuals must marry people of colour to prevent further transgressions of the colour line. These works begin to explore how the history of racialized genders, maintained through heteronormativity, continues to influence current understandings of the co-construction of race and gender as well as the role of heterosexuality in maintaining the separation of gender and the purity of race (see also R.J.C. Young 1995; Streeter 1996; and Ibrahim 2012).

Much of this research was influenced by 1990s identity politics and by the work of cultural studies scholars such as Stuart Hall, who was concerned with the critical anti-essential evaluation of the notion of an integral and unified identity (Haritaworn 2009). Drawing liberally from feminist theory and cultural studies, identity was seen as a social-historical-political construction, always in process. Of course, we are now all well aware that identities are always negotiated, rarely stable: "[Identity] is not an essence, but a positioning ... a politics of position" (S. Hall 1990, 226). Identities were also seen as rarely unified, as often fractured and fragmented, and as continually in the process of transforming (J. Rutherford 1990).

The implications of this conversation impacted scholarship on multiracial identity considerably. Mixed race identity was conceived as similarly relational, fluid, and flexible. In a progressive attempt to explore potential sites of resistance to dominant hegemonies of race and nation, some cultural theorists contemplated notions of in-betweenness and ambivalence through discussions of "cultural hybridity" (Bhabha 1994; R.J.C. Young 1995; Mitchell 1997), a term that would have significant import for studies in multiraciality. Cultural hybridity, a "construct with the hegemonic power relation built into its process of constant fragmented articulation" (Lavie and Swedenburg 1996, 10), focuses upon the process of fusion and intermingling, "involving the creation of a new form, which can then be set against the old form, of which it is partly made up" (R.J.C. Young 1995, 25). Bhabha's (1990, 211) account of hybridity as a restless, unstable, radical heterogenic space focuses upon discontinuity and the evolution of multiple forms, hybridity being "the process [that] gives rise to something different, something new and unrecognizable, a new area of negotiation of meaning and representation." Bhabha attempts to disrupt the authoritative representations of imperialist power through his notion of double displacement, which embodies various forms of cultural and political resistance. "Hybrid" is seen as a term that holds within it the potential to radically contest dualisms through the articulation of strategic subversion (Bhabha 1994, 112). Chambers (1994) also celebrates difference with enthusiasm by focusing upon fusion, hybrids, and new forms of difference that he claims are the result of global movements. In other words, hybrid and syncretic practices have been read as prescriptive models or celebrated as the only forms of resistance (Lavie and Swedenburg 1996) that allow racialized and gendered subjects to act out a multiplicity of fractal identities.

However, the term "hybridity" suggests a combination of two seemingly pure things, indicating how each is defined with respect to the other. Most often these dualisms are imagined as opposites. Yu's (2003, 1407) observation is illuminating: "Mixing is an interesting concept. It suggests a process of transformation, a taking of two previously unlike things and making something new out of them. But what are the 'things' to be mixed? To describe the process of mixing is at the same time to define the entities that existed before the mixing."

Critiquing the "Bill of Rights for Racially Mixed People"

Scholars like Maria Root offered up an interpretation of the experience of multiraciality that is much less gloomy than the pathology paradigm of the early 1900s. However, to remain caught up in the celebration of multiraciality as though mixing brings something brand-new to the table is to continue to reproduce the error of misplaced concreteness encouraged by what Zack (1992, 26) calls a "genetic logic" and Spickard (1992, 12) refers to as the "illogic of ... racial categories." A material example of the way that this discourse takes flight is Root's "Bill of Rights for Racially Mixed People" (1996a, 7). The proclamations in this bill include:

> I have the right to identify myself differently than my brothers and sisters, I have the right not to be responsible for people's discomfort with my physical ambiguity, I have the right to identify myself differently in different situations, and I have the right to have loyalties and identify with more than one group of people.

Online, the bill is celebrated, especially among mothers of mixed race children who see it as a powerful way to shatter stereotypes about their kids. For example, on the website Circle of Moms, mothers of mixed race children exuberantly post exclamations of excitement upon discovering the "Bill of Rights." A few excerpts from the website include:

> WOWWwww ... I LOVE THAT!!!! My 15 yr old biracial son would love that! He is going thru some identity issues around being african american/german/russian american; although, he looks egyptian, mexican, because of the texture of his hair and his color. People give him a bad time about his heritage. They question him all the time. I understand the BILL OF RIGHTS for people of Mixed Heritage.

> I think it should be posted on BUSES in Malls, create a FLIER for this. Send it all over the world. This empowers our children to stand up for who they are.

> Love this!!! I'm going to print this out and put it on the fridge :).

It appears the mothers on this website are drawn to the "Bill of Rights." However, the bill has been taken to task by scholars such as Sexton (2008, 76, 78), who, in a scathing critique, insists that it offers a "misleading comfort" and "assiduously avoid[s] an engagement with the ongoing struggles against racial inequality of those who are, in society's eyes, 'all black, all the time.'" The structural and material reality of racism – not to mention the historical and geographical legacies of racial privilege and marginalization – dictate that if one is perceived as black, self-proclamations like "Oh no, I'm not black, I'm actually mixed race!" will not do much to insulate one from racist acts.

Elam (2011) further points out similar limitations through her cogent analysis of Aaron McGruder's comic strip *The Boondocks,* which features a biracial girl named Jazmine Dubois. In the comic strip, Jazmine's black father, Tom, and her white mother, Sarah, are both attorneys, and thus it is assumed that they experience high socio-economic privilege. Jazmine is light-skinned and is quick to assert that she is definitely not black but mixed race. Stamping her foot angrily, she insists that she "resents racial categories!" (in ibid., 64). She regularly faces contempt from her black playmate, Huey. He showers Jazmine with disdain, claiming that she is simply suffering from a kind of racial delusion.

Elam sees *The Boondocks* as a kind of popular cultural intervention into contemporary conversations about multiraciality. Through her discussion of Jazmine's efforts to continually try to proclaim her multiracial identity, Elam illustrates how race is often problematically portrayed by mixed race advocates as an issue of individual free will. But of course not all mixed race people can occupy the category of multiraciality because there are particular phenotypes associated with identifying as mixed race, and the "Bill of Rights" cannot be understood as an antiracist blanket that protects those who are seen as racially marked subjects. The reality is that there are limits to multiraciality as an antiracist identification. The mere act of identifying as multiracial is not a politically progressive move in itself. As Sexton (2008, 35) has pointed out, "impurity and hybridity, in and of themselves, are no guaranteed challenge to the racial orders of white supremacy and antiblackness." To vacuously celebrate the existence of the mixed race individual without problematizing the very real shifting configurations of power surrounding how she is simultaneously both raced and gendered is superficial. A focus on mixing among differently racially situated peoples can celebrate difference, but the power dynamics between these differences are not fully problematized. As Saldanha (2006, 9) reminds us, "race cannot be transcended, only understood and rearranged" – not unlike deck chairs on the *Titanic*. Not all racial mixes are afforded the same freight. The reality is that "not all identities are equally hybrid, for some have little choice about the political processes determining their hybridization" (Visweswaran 1994, 132).

Antiblack Racism in Mixed Race Scholarship

Often ignored in these conversations about multiraciality is a discussion of the status of blackness. As Gordon (1997, 56) asks,

> Why is the least mixture between blacks and every other group, and the highest mixture between whites and every other group except blacks? And ... why is there such a qualitative different life in racial terms for Asians who are mixed with blacks versus Asians mixed with whites? Do we find Asians (and Latin Americans) rushing to wed blacks to uplift their gene pool, as seems to be the case with their marrying whites? Blackness, in the end, functions as a constant, underlying mark of racialization as

does no other racial designation. Its persistence suggests that the fluidity of racial identities points upward in continuing spirals of potential whiteness.

Lewis Gordon – along with scholars like Minkah Makalani (2001), Daniel McNeil (2010), Jared Sexton (2010), Rainier Spencer (2011), and Michele Elam (2011), among others – has insisted that mixed race studies has been marred by at best a reluctance and at worst a refusal to engage with blackness. In the past few years, several scholars have voiced important critiques regarding the contemporary study of multiracialism, remarking upon what they see as not only its naiveté but also its conservative tendencies and class bias. They insist that scholars gloss over the historicity of both race and sexuality (Makalani 2001; Sexton 2008), asserting that multiracial studies not only fails to pose a radical challenge to the racial order but in fact also works to support white supremacy (see Makalani 2001; Sexton 2008; and Spencer 2011). As Sexton (2008, 53) states, "The politics of multiracialism is ... properly understood only as a purely formal negation of blackness." Makalani (2001, 83) maintains that a biracial identity "has no historical basis, and would have a negative political impact on African Americans." It is implied that mixed race studies offers those who may identify as black and white a chance to opt out of blackness and further maximize the middle- to upper-class privilege that so often accompanies whiteness. The result of this discourse is at once obvious: "The multiracial phenomenon produced discourses about race that tacitly situated blackness as outmoded and multiracial as emergent" (Ibrahim 2012, vii).

Speaking of the novel *Caucasia,* by Danzy Senna, Ibrahim (2007, 155) interrogates the performance of racial difference and suggests that in the book "whiteness takes the place of a marginal racial status while blackness either disappears or loses a reality, a substitution that happens, paradoxically, to signal integration." Ibrahim (2012, 32) cuts right to the heart of the matter: "Is the dawn of multiracialism the dusk of blackness?" McNeil (2012, 2) also questions the political immediacy of multiracial studies, insisting that Sexton carefully "challenge[s] multiracial, and post-racial, environments that deny the legitimacy of African American anger." McNeil cites the work of Lewis Gordon, who argues that it is understandable that working-class and darker-skinned people would be skeptical, if not downright scornful, of middle-class and lighter-skinned people who insist that the discourse of multiraciality captures something that allows for the emancipation of black bodies. McNeil (ibid., 7) explains that Gordon employs the term "slime" to explore the superficial aims of some mixed race scholars, who "talk politely about racial transcendence while denying the facticity of their privileged position in an anti-black world." Gordon sees slime as a particularly provocative metaphor, and McNeil (ibid.) explains that it draws upon Jean-Paul Sartre's ontology of slime: "a sticky, viscoelastic material that resists ... flow and strain linearly with time when stress is applied." The violence enacted upon the black body through both the public and the intellectual iterations of multiracial discourse ensures that the specific histories of black bodies are elided and erased, repressing the realities behind the complex colonial histories that inform the ongoing success of the category of mixed race as a neopolitical, neoracial, and neoliberal identification.

Mixed race intellectual discourse has often evaded an analysis of how it conveniently props up other forms of racial oppression for some – particularly blacks and Indigenous peoples – through its claims of liberation for people who identity as part-white. Ibrahim (2012, 12) poses an important question: "What sort of multiracial politics focuses on personal experience ... cultural representation ... and middle-class status? How are these points of emphasis the outcome of a political reevaluation of normative standards, and what, exactly, was the mode of analysis that led to this reevaluation?" I return to these provocative questions in my final chapter.

Moving beyond the Pathology and Celebration of the Multiracial Subject

The unfortunate reality is that many contemporary intellectual analyses of the mixed race experience tend to assert the importance of challenging the ways that multiracial identities have been historically characterized as either pathologized or celebrated. Both positions are suffused with a particular kind of anxiety. Critical mixed race theory has not yet confronted this epistemic binary. It is only through this confrontation that a new political and progressive space for liberatory multiracial politics will emerge. Myths about multiraciality reflecting these paradigms continue to pop up with alarming alacrity in both popular and academic analyses of multiraciality. For example, multiracial counselling offers up opportunities for mixed race people to heal supposed ongoing wounds (pathology); white parents of mixed race children eagerly purchase how-to guides on the latest method to raise mixed race children with high self-esteem, as it is often assumed that they are bound to have emotional struggles (pathology); the mixed race population is intermarrying at a frenetic pace, so all racial categories will soon cease to exist, and we will be living in racial harmony because we will all be mixed (celebration); and if mixed race people promote and participate in more antiracist workshops and encourage intercultural communication, racism will disappear because mixed race people are antiracism beacons (celebration).

Twenty years ago, it was colloquially and enthusiastically suggested that the scholarship in critical mixed race theory had taken a turn for the better because it detoured from describing the mixed race person as torn and confused. This stereotype of the damaged mixed race soul might well be imagined as a passive articulation of mixed race identity. We then saw a move from the passive to the active voice – where the "best of both worlds" ideology might have been seen as offering, albeit simplistically, the multiracial subject a more progressive and active subject positioning – an opportunity to express her agency or at least to have her voice and experience heard. This kind of approach is mired in neoliberal optimism and does nothing to challenge ongoing patterns of systemic and institutionalized racism for *all* racialized people – not just those who possess the privilege to identify as mixed race. Without romanticizing the experience of multiracial individuals, how might racially mixed people who are *differently positioned* by class and other identity markers work together to challenge ongoing racial injustices for people of colour and Indigenous populations, for example? The experiences of those of different mixes are definitely not the same, yet critical mixed race scholars often seem to assume that they are. Although employed in a different context, Adolph Reed's (1997, 45) words remain striking: "The problem isn't racial division or a need for healing. It is racial inequality and injustice. And the remedy isn't an elaborately choreographed pageantry of essentializing yakety-yak about group experience, cultural difference, pain, and the inevitable platitudes about understanding." Informed by Reed's words, how might we make sense of these disparate and often competing and opposing contributions to critical mixed race studies? Without advocating an approach that dilutes all of our perspectives, does a critical reading of these discourses offer an opportunity to inform the development of an *anticolonial* perspective on mixed race studies?

Critical Absences in Mixed Race Studies: Toward an Anticolonial Approach to Multiraciality

The contestations over historical as well as contemporary representations of Canadian mixed race identity in particular are bound up with discrepancies and silences. I address these silences by making a few points regarding critical absences in mixed race scholarship.

First, many analyses of multiraciality tend to be largely ahistorical and ageographical. The histories of multiracial subjects and their parents, grandparents, and great-grandparents are erased in these analyses, resulting in a focus on the individual's personal experience of race rather than on the family's experience vis-à-vis colonial histories. The geographies of these subjects are ignored, as though what it means to be mixed race does not change from place to place, not to mention from time to time (although see King-O'Riain et al. 2014). There also tends to be a focus on the experiences of those who claim partially white descent, particularly Asian-white or black-white, rather than an investigation of why some people of racialized mixes are increasingly identifying as mixed race when they are not part white. Finally, if we are serious about decolonizing mixed race studies, we must take a closer look at both the antiblack and anti-Indigenous nature of the production of mixed race scholarship as per the critiques of Lewis Gordon, Habiba Ibrahim, Daniel McNeil, Minkah Makalani, and Jared Sexton, among others, and also recognize that we have yet to fully develop a critical space in which to explore the experiences of those of minority racialized mixes who do not claim partially white descent.

First, let me address the ahistorical quality of some studies of mixed race identity. As I suggested in the Introduction, our familial histories can be negated through use of the "mixed race" label. Ibrahim (2007, 162) suggests that "there is a problem of how to historicize mixedness or, specifically, how to provide the category with a relevance that can be usefully extended and sustained through time into a social or political critique." If critical mixed race studies is to develop an anticolonial perspective, what forms of theoretical scaffolding are required to provide for analyses of Canadian multiraciality that take the white-settler context into consideration? The stories that mixed race women shared with me in interviews were deeply informed by a Canadian colonial past that has permitted various forms of resistance and performance to take place. They saw themselves as highly mobile and capable individuals who, at times, were able to sidestep race, an issue I return to in Chapter 3. Canada's colonial past was rarely gestured to in interviews. It remained remarkably invisible. Of course, one need not necessarily speak directly to this issue, but interviewees rarely referred to their location in the Canadian polity in relation to Indigeneous voices.

Canada's history as a white-settler society influences the proliferation and dissemination of multiraciality as a popular category of identity. Whenever colonial history was gestured to in interviews, it was often relegated to a fleeting comment, related to a parent's experience in a country other than Canada, but Canada's *history as a white colonial nation-state* was not discussed in detail. Instead, Canada was repeatedly referred to as a multicultural nation – a white, liberal, democratic state – and this allowed a kind of racial privilege, or what I call a racial political impotency, to emerge among interviewees. As I explain in Chapter 2, the methodological choice to interview mixed race women may well have influenced this finding: most women spoke about their personal, individual experience of multiraciality and their day-to-day encounters with race and racism rather than reflecting upon and historicizing their experience within a complex web of historically situated racial formations. There are implications to focusing on the interview as a primary source of empirical material for multiracial study and accompanying analysis. If mixed race studies, as an area of inquiry, is going to mean anything in a politically progressive sense, we should consider what kinds of cross-racial alliances can be forged and how these alliances might be illuminated by the emerging literature on anticolonial feminist resistance *even if our empirical material might not necessarily tell this story.* I return to this idea in my final chapter.

Many analyses of multiraciality tend to look not only at the multigenerational family histories of the individuals studied but also at the history of the *place* where interviews were conducted. Obviously, what it means to be mixed changes in different national contexts over time. One need only turn to the examples of South America in order to understand the ways that people of mixed racial backgrounds identify differently (see Twine 2000a). In the case of Canada, the mixed race figure has been drawn upon and implicated in the reinforcement of the existing racial order, a point I revisit in Chapter 3. Both paradigms – the torn and confused stereotype of the multiracial subject and the "best of both worlds" ideology – are troubling because of the way they uphold traditional racial logics and maintain existing power relations within the white-settler regime.

A recurring finding in studies of mixed race people is that they "construct different racial identities based on various contextually specific logics" and that "social, cultural and spatial context are critical" in the construction of racial identities for mixed race individuals (Rockquemore, Brunsma, and Delgado 2009, 19, 21). But beyond asserting the often-heard geographical mantra that "where you are has a lot to do with who you are," which is remarkably facile, few studies have paid close attention to the actual material geographies through which mixed race identity is forged (but see King-O'Riain et al. 2014). How do state-sanctioned policies and practices influence how one identifies as mixed race in Canada versus the United States versus Britain, for example? And how does one's affiliation to one's local, urban, and regional geographies, among others, influence these experiences? Scales of belonging certainly play a significant role in one's experience of place and race.

One of the key findings in this study is that many of the women I spoke to veered away from speaking about material locations where they felt at home and instead emphasized the ways that they created a sense of place within different geographies – on the local, regional, urban, and national scales. I am curious about the conditions under which one identifies as mixed race and about when and *where* that designation shifts, a theme I explore in Chapter 5. However, I would like to circle back to a point I raised earlier: that interviewees did not necessarily see themselves as situated within the regulatory circumstances of a white-settler state. It is to this issue that I now turn.

A Colonial Response to Mixed Race Subjects: The New Métis and the Old Métis

In the rest of this chapter, I want to gesture to the ways that colonial influences, architectures, and legacies shape the experience and understanding of multiracial subjects in Canada. Contemporary scholarship in mixed race studies has displayed a serious blindness to anticolonial scholarship on the regulation of Aboriginal forms of the mixed race experience, particularly the regulation of Métis people.

Canada's colonial project has continually exterminated, denigrated, and isolated Aboriginal people. Its history is stained with countless examples of institutional regulation imposed both upon Indigenous populations and, to my point, upon Aboriginal mixed race populations (Mawani 2009, 2012; Francis 2011). The Métis are identified as people who are of Aboriginal and European descent in Canada but should be recognized more accurately as Indigenous people who have, for one reason or another, been excluded from access to legal "status" as Aboriginal people. Usually associated with the historic communities in the Red River Valley in present-day Manitoba but actually spread throughout Canada, the Métis constitute one of the nation's three legally recognized groups of Indigenous peoples: status Aboriginal people, Métis, and Inuit. This typology, however, dramatically simplifies a slippery and complex history, making it important to understand the processes of classification themselves (Lawrence 2004, 96; Teillet 2009). Although I cannot detail this history here (but see Foster 1985; Peterson 1985; Racette 2001, 2004; Lawrence 2004; Alfred and Corntassel 2005; Lischke and McNab 2007; and Teillet 2007), a brief summary of the Canadian state's role in producing different categories of Indigeneity is necessary for what follows. As Lawrence (2003, 2004) and others have argued, although the Indian Act of 1876 conferred legal status upon Indigenous people and hence required the state to address its treaty obligations to "status Indians," the act has generally operated to withhold legal recognition from as many people as possible. A key difference between Métis and status Aboriginal people in Canada, then, is that the former, in most cases, lack access to a land base and treaty rights. In contrast, those communities with status have the legal right to some controls over their land – particularly in the context of resource development and urban encroachment (DeVries 2011; Woo 2011). Thus, although all Aboriginal people are subject to artificially constructed identity categories that may have little to do with their actual heritage, Métis and nonstatus Aboriginal people are particularly likely to be seen as not sufficiently "Indian" to fit romantic or legal notions of "Indianness." Further, although most popular representations of Aboriginal peoples in Canada still portray them through romantic or degrading stereotypes, Métis people and other nonstatus people have a tenuous relationship to claims of Aboriginality.

The New Métis: How Is This *New?*

In this section, I critically analyze a 2006 article from a major Canadian newspaper to explore how representations of racialized, immigrant multiracial experience are intersecting with discourses about Métis peoples. I also speak to the ways that Canadian journalism contributes to a racial restructuring project that routinely misrepresents Aboriginal peoples.

In 2006 reporter Andrew Chung penned an article for the *Toronto Star* entitled "Are We All Going to Become Latte?" – a story on the phenomenon of racial mixing in Canada. Drawing from the stories of the parents of some mixed race children, some self-identified mixed race people, and a handful of scholars working in the field of multiraciality, Chung paints an optimistic portrait of the future of the mixed race population by focusing on the commodification of multiraciality in North America:

> The mixed-race critical mass is showing its face more and more, particularly on the Internet. Five years ago, there was one North American website dedicated to multiracial people. Now there are dozens of sites and blogs where individuals can meet, communicate, even date. Now you can buy clothes that speak to the mixed-race identity. One company, Mixed Apparel, sells its shirts by mail and Internet, with messages such as "Beautifully Blended," "Mestizo," or new terms for any mix, like "Latinasian." There are more and more books about multiracialism – not just academic texts, which have been around for decades, but children's books that talk about what it's like. You can buy mixed-race greeting cards, and interracial cake-top figurines for weddings. There are even dolls for mixed-race children.

Chung situates this desire for consumer goods that reflect the experience of multiraciality in the context of Canada's largest city:

> In Toronto, where visible minorities are expected to represent more than half the population within the next decade, we're in for a lot more blending. As one of the world's most ethnically diverse cities continues its long simmer as a racial and cultural melting pot, there will be more children ... who blend traditions that were once locked into geographical and ethnocentric isolation ... [They] are the new faces of Toronto ... They are the New Métis.

For Chung, the "New Métis" represent a new and growing demographic trend in Canada. He defines them as a new generation of latte children who hold the key to a postracial future (see Sexton 2008; McNeil 2010; Squires 2010; Elam 2011; and Spencer 2011):

> Just like the Métis, a culture is emerging around mixed-race people, with its own distinct identity – they have their own websites, books, clothing lines, even dolls. No matter how diverse their backgrounds, these individuals share remarkably similar experiences – including the feeling they don't belong in the culture of either parent.

Chung's animated take on mixed race demographics emerges through a forced delineation between the "Old" Métis, who are "born out of the miscegenation between European fur traders and Indian women," and the "New" Métis, who remain remarkably nebulous and ill-defined; at best, they are gestured to as the product of interracial marriages:

> It's instructive to look at the Métis. In the 17th century the Métis were born of the mingling of European fur traders and Indian women. They suffered discrimination, but a distinct culture flowered, as did separate Métis communities. Today, the Métis are one of three recognized Aboriginal peoples in Canada, and, at 292,310, make up the fastest-growing Aboriginal group, according to Statistics Canada ... The New Métis already outstrip them in numbers, and seem likely to exceed their social clout as well.

Chung's article raises points for interrogation, not least of which is his assumption that mixed race people apparently do not feel welcome in the culture of either parent, reflecting a disturbing and all-too-common myth about the experience of multiraciality (Nakashima 1992). The writer creates a hierarchy between the supposed "Old" and "New" Métis. Who are the "Old" Métis? And how are racialized immigrants who commit interracial intimacies accorded "New Métis" status?

Ultimately, Chung grants the "New Métis" more credibility and worth in his comparison. He relies on a temporal oppositional framework that attaches negativity to the "Old" Métis. By designating people of partially Aboriginal descent as "Old" and those of mixed racial (supposedly immigrant?) identities as "New," Chung reproduces an Orientalist divide between the past and the present and provides a flattened and reductive view of colonialism. His view of the Métis produces a representation of mixed race subjects that valorizes their identity over that of the Métis.

Temporalities of Multiraciality

In her powerful analysis of the contradictory articulations of colonial power in discussions about the relationship between Indigeneity and Asian migration, Mawani (2012) makes crucial points about the ways Indigenous peoples, Asians, and Europeans inhabit different temporalities that impact the epistemological terrain. She argues that the terms "Indigenous," "settler," and "migrant" have been temporalized by postcolonial states, suggesting that competing conceptions of *time* influence and affect both the epistemic and the political logics of colonialism (for another argument about racial time, see Ibrahim 2012). Drawing from Elizabeth Poivinelli's phrase "the tense of the other," Mawani (2012, 375) argues persuasively that inequalities between these groups were premised on time differentials: "Indians were *first but vanishing,* Europeans were *second and permanent,* and Asians were *last and temporary*" (emphasis in original). In other words, "The Indigenous were and are thought to be part of the vanishing past, Europeans comprised the past-future, and Asian migrants were 'unsettled settlers' who constituted the temporary present, here today, and gone tomorrow" (ibid., 387).

Mawani argues that the temporalization of these identities has made discussions about Indigeneity, settlement, and migration politically contentious. These distinctions in temporality also have implications for mixed race discourse, as they have reproduced the profound power differentials that exist between non-Aboriginal and Aboriginal mixed race peoples.

Lawrence and Dua (2005, 128) remind us that "Aboriginal peoples are [often] relegated to a mythic past, whereby their contemporary existence and struggles for decolonization are erased from view and thus denied legitimacy." Indeed, most Canadians' understanding of the Métis population is limited to a passing reference in grade-school textbooks to Louis Riel, leader of the Métis people on the Canadian prairies. As a result, "'Indians' become unreal figures, rooted in the nation's prehistory, who died out ... consigned to the dustbin of history" (ibid., 123). Chung's use of the word "outstrip" as synonymous with exceeding, surpassing, or outrunning is also telling. Chung assumes that the "New" Métis have greater social clout than the "Old" Métis. Does he mean social privilege? Respect? Cultural capital?

What research does he use to back up this claim? Ultimately, his article raises more questions than it answers about the experience of racial mixing in Canada. While attempting to illuminate what he sees as new patterns of mixing among racialized minority groups in Canada, Chung denigrates the Métis and places the "New Métis" on a pedestal.

The discourse produces the "New Métis" as its subject while denying them their subjectivities. I use this example to show that mixed race discourse needs to understand how it has discursively dismissed, legitimized, and actively produced and sustained social and racial hierarchies that lead to particular forms of racial and colonial violence. The Métis are refused the possibility of their own modernity through an interpellation that rejects their place in the contemporary temporal plane of existence; they are forever relegated to the past.

Chung was criticized for appropriating "Métis" as a label of identity to describe racialized mixing among non-Indigenous people. In a letter to the editor of the *Toronto Star*, dated 10 July 2006, Susan Lyndon, then executive director of the Métis Artists' Collective, wrote,

> How rude of your paper to filch the term Métis, add the word "New" – as if it is some branded item like detergent – and use the front-page headline to describe people who may well be new but are certainly not Métis. In Canada, the Métis are the constitutionally recognized descendants of European fur traders and Aboriginal women. Historically, much was taken away from the Métis; do not compound the issue by stealing their name.

Lyndon points out how mixing is commodified and focuses on filching and stealing, which prompts me to revisit the work of Lawrence and Dua (2005), who insist that immigrants in Canada ought to examine their own complicity in the ongoing project of colonization in Canada – a point I return to in Chapter 3. Appropriating the term "Métis" to define a differently positioned mixed race population shows a lack of recognition that Canadian culture is fundamentally founded on racial logics born out of an Orientalist attempt to justify the settlement of an already settled land (Goldberg 1993). My point is that critical mixed race theory has not done enough to make the regulation of nonstatus Aboriginal experience and Indigenous knowledges a foundational presence in critical antiracist analyses of Canadian multiraciality.

Lyndon raises valuable points by emphasizing that in Canada the Métis have a distinctly legalized status because "Métis," as a category of identity, is legally embedded and recognized under the Constitution Act. At the same time, this population remains largely invisible in the populist nationalist imaginary. That the Métis are not seen as a *contemporary* mixed race group but as part of a primitive past demonstrates the contradictions and incompatibility between articulations of colonial power respecting Indigenous peoples and those respecting racialized immigrant groups, even though both are so evidently shaped by the colonial apparatus.

In summary, the experiences of the Métis have been largely neglected in critical mixed race studies, reflecting the pervasive valorization of whiteness that so characterizes this subdisciplinary field (also see Mahtani and Moreno 2001). Culjak (2001) claims that it was largely the Métis population who developed a unified sense of ethnic consciousness in the late eighteenth and nineteenth centuries, which in part has validated the mixed racial formations of those who have followed. However, this history has not yet emerged as an important part of the framing of critical mixed race scholarship.

In showcasing and celebrating the "New Métis" and only superficially gesturing to the historical legacies of Indigenous mixed peoples, this article furthers a popularized colonial agenda where nonstatus Aboriginal communities and experiences are continually relegated to history, erasing the impact of present-day colonial relations in the ongoing making of practices of exclusion within and beyond the Canadian nation. It is a specific form of mixing – a non-Aboriginal mixed race identity – that is prized as new and different and is subsequently rewarded with front-page space in Canada's most circulated newspaper. Other Aboriginal mixes are seen to have less value. The Métis appear in Chung's article only when they can conveniently justify and maintain the mythical superior identity of mixed race Canadians.

A focus on this opposition has important consequences for the future theorizing of multiraciality. How do popular representations of Canadian mixed race intimacies as a *recent* phenomenon occurring between racialized ethnic immigrant groups contribute to the ongoing colonization of Aboriginal peoples? Canada's history of racism and its status as a white-settler state informs both our popular and our academic understandings of multiraciality, with certain mixes being prized and others – like the "Métis" referred to by Chung – being conveniently denigrated or disregarded. Andrea Smith (2011, 57) has insisted that "when indigeneity is not foregrounded, it tends to disappear in order to enable the emergence of the hybrid subject." Similarly, Bonita Lawrence (in S. Rutherford 2010, 11) reminds us, *"Everybody in Canada is intermarrying but nobody else is losing their citizenship as a result"* (my emphasis). Lawrence is referring to citizenship as a troubled relation between the Canadian state and Indigenous people and invoking the state's allocation of status – and therefore access to treaty rights and land – to some but not all Indigenous people.

In 1869 in Canada the Gradual Enfranchisement Act was passed, which stipulated that any Indian woman who married a white man would lose her Indian status and any right to band membership (Lawrence 2003, 7). It was through this statute that the categories of "status Indian" and "non-status Indian" were created. A blood-quantum requirement was added to the definition of an "Indian," after which time the only people eligible to be considered Indian were those who had at least one-quarter Indian blood (see Dickason 1992). Lawrence and Dua (2005, 121) point out,

> There is nothing new about racial ambiguity among mixed-bloods of any background ... For many Native people in Eastern Canada, the urbanization and assimilation pressures of the 1950s and the 1960s meant that our parents married white people. This interval also featured large-scale immigration of people of colour, so that today urban Native people form tiny, paler islands floating in a darker "multicultural" sea.

Indigenous mixed race people in Canada experience a different place in the Canadian polity in relation to the state than do mixed race people of non-Indigenous backgrounds – and here I include not only those individuals who identify as mixed race immigrants but also those who identify as mixed race people born in Canada. Although official government policies drastically limited the numbers of racialized migrants entering Canada until 1967, operating to sustain a white nation (see Walcott 2008), for those Indigenous people who were already here, the Gradual Enfranchisement Act separated Indigenous women and many generations of their children from their own communities. Mixed-race liaisons between Indigenous women and white men ensured that Indian status was not passed from the mother to her children, resulting in their legal, physical, and psychic disconnection from their land, communities, cultural and spiritual traditions, and economic base. Currently, Bill C-31, with its provision that children from the second generation of mixed Aboriginal/non-Aboriginal marriages cannot claim status, is continuing to deny Aboriginal people the benefits of legal recognition and status (Lawrence 2003, 2010).

This context of colonial violence, which has so profoundly shaped the lives of nonstatus Indigenous people (see Lawrence 2004), has typically not been engaged by critical mixed race theory; instead, the field has focused on the interaction between racialized groups who are either newcomers to Canada or the children of immigrants who arrived as a result of shifts in immigration policy after 1967. This population does not have outstanding claims on the space of the nation in relation to land and treaties, nor does it possess the history of cultural genocide in Canada that characterizes Indigenous experience. This, then, forms the backdrop for conversations about multiraciality. As a result, critical mixed race theory continues to enact a form of epistemic violence against Indigenous peoples because of its refusal to carefully and thoroughly dissect the metaphor of mixing.

It is also valuable to remember that mixed race identity in an Indigenous context is dramatically different because many mixed Indigenous people do not necessarily identify as culturally mixed; rather, they might choose to identify as Indigenous, as Métis, or not as Indigenous at all. It is not just that mixed Indigenous people have to contend with legalized forms of discrimination that are drastically different from the discrimination faced by mixed race people of immigrant backgrounds; it is also that the implications of this situation for community identity and for legal rights are compounded by mixed Indigenous people's lack of recognition by the state.

Chung's (2006) *Toronto Star* article illustrates a common tendency to gloss over and ignore Canada's racialized colonial and imperialist history in journalistic, contemporary, Canadian, multiracial discourse. Mixed race scholars are not exempt from this propensity. As many critical race scholars have pointed out, racial divides in Canada have emerged out of unequal power relations defined through processes of colonization and subsequently crystallized through pseudo-scientific racial eugenics discourses (see Razack 2002; Thobani 2007; and Mawani 2009). These categories have not only imposed spatial order, exterminating marginalized populations in particular places (Razack 2002) but have also maintained the intellectual order of existing discourses on multiraciality in Canada.

Although I am suspicious of the storytelling device invoked in this article, what popular representations of both the "New" Métis and the "Old" Métis share, if anything, is a colonial history that has sought to sustain whiteness for centuries in Canada. Canada's national mythologies or imaginaries denigrated the Métis or any notion of mixing (see Lawrence 2004) and framed the British and French as the two principal sources of the Canadian nation. The popular conversations about mixed race identity, infused by neoliberal musings, have maintained a silencing of the experiences of mixed-bloods in a First Nations context. Articles like Chung's project a national imaginary, or imaginative geography, upon the space now called Canada, one that continues to separate ideas of mixing depending on whether one is of a mixed, racialized, migrant background or of a mixed Indigenous background.

In his conclusion, Chung refers to a well-known scholar of mixed race, Reginald Daniel, who studies mixed race identity in the American context. Chung is optimistic about the future of non-Indigenous racial mixing:

> It's not clear how ready Canada is to handle this [process of mixing]. But Daniel points to one group in which there has been some success: the Métis. "Why," he asks, "do you have this group called Métis, whereas mixed blood is redefined (in the U.S.) as Native American? How do you get this category in Canada but not the U.S.?" Perhaps the path is there. It'll be up to the New Métis to take it.

Indigenous researchers like Bonita Lawrence (2004) and Jean Teillet (2009) have already carefully answered Daniel's question in their own scholarship. However, the answer is not included in Chung's article. Lawrence (2004, 6) has spoken of the dangers of conflating the American and Canadian contexts for understanding the experiences of the Métis, explaining that the boundaries of while-settler states have various meanings for Aboriginal people and that although Canadian and American colonization histories are deeply interwoven, each country has maintained dramatically different ways of regulating Native identity. Lawrence (ibid.) reminds us that "a very different discourse on mixed-blood status and Indian identity, which developed in the United States, is gaining an increasing foothold in Canada. And yet this discourse is inevitably overlaid on top of another one." Chung's article underscores the popular mythology of Canada as a racially accommodating nation. He allows an American scholar to get in the last word, without asking an Indigenous scholar in Canada to inform the reader's understanding of the nebulous path to which he refers.

There may well be ways that non-Indigenous mixed race scholarship can learn from and collaborate with Métis scholarship. However, to begin this process, it is incumbent upon critical mixed race scholars to consider the complicities of our intellectual investigations in relation to white-settler colonialism. How have we, whether intentionally or not, contributed to what Andrea Smith (2012, 69) calls "the logic of genocide," where "non-Native peoples ... feel they can rightfully own indigenous peoples' land?" Moving into this intellectual space means first ensuring that we do not conflate processes of (im)migration and those of colonialism (see Sexton 2008; and Francis 2011). It also means infusing critical mixed race thinking with sustained critiques of (neo)liberalism, multiculturalism, and democracy to ensure that they challenge colonial relationships (see Mawani 2009, 2012).

Although my project does not address the voices of those who identify as "mixed-blood" Indigenous people (see Lawrence 2004; Andersen 2014), this book questions how mixed race scholarship could benefit from a more thorough engagement with anticolonial scholarship more broadly to open up spaces for a different kind of conversation. Some Canadian conceptualizations of the mixed race body are marked by an epistemic racial violence that tends to privilege both nonblack and non-Indigenous bodies. It has become popular to insist that today's analyses of mixed race identity are progressive and thus more accurate than obviously denigrating portrayals of the past; however, I have tried to show that analyses of mixed race in both the contemporary and historical contexts can reify racial-colonial categories and can discursively burden the already highly surveilled mixed race body. My reflections are shaped by Canada's status as a white-settler nation and by my understanding that mixed race scholarship largely excludes analysis of Aboriginality and blackness, as well as analysis of the legacy of colonialism and its corresponding contemporary formations.

Canada is a country with a long history of institutionalized forms of regulation of mixed race identity, accompanied by legislation, yet contemporary scholarship on mixed race identities has not engaged with historical and anticolonial scholarship on the regulation of mixed race Aboriginal relations. This silence perpetuates other violences. Some of the current mixed race scholarship reifies colonial racial-purity logics (the same logics that have been used to attempt to legislate colonial racial hierarchies that subordinate Aboriginal Canadians, among others). Although interviewees did not directly address issues of colonialism per se, their experiences were informed by Canadian colonial racial logics that continue to be central mechanisms through which race is understood within Canada. A different kind of scaffolding is necessary if we are to move toward a truly radical critical mixed race scholarship in Canada. How can ideas about racial mixing be complicated through Indigenous critiques, paying particular attention to the role of colonial geographies in structuring definitions of multiraciality? In the next chapter, rather than focusing on what was visibly and audibly present in interviews with self-identified women of mixed race, I look at what was absent.

2
Mixed Race Narcissism?
Thoughts on the Interview Experience

> In many ways, ethnographic work into "race" is, to some extent, inevitably narcissistic.
>
> — ALI 2006, 482

> I see people two different ways now: people who look like me and people who don't look like me.
>
> — RACHEL MORSE, A MIXED RACE CHARACTER IN DURROW 2010, 9

Narcissism is a personality trait related to egoism, vanity, conceit, and selfishness. As I hinted at in earlier chapters, much research in mixed race studies has been conducted by people who identify as mixed race. In this chapter, I ask how we might more carefully consider our own identifications as mixed race individuals. What is the impact of these identifications upon scholastic endeavours in this subfield? How do our own mixed race identities influence how we do our research? Is our work inevitably narcissistic, whether we want to admit it or not? I am inspired by Stoler's (2002, 419) insistence that "those of us engaged in writing racisms' histories need to think more about the stories we tell and why we want to tell them."

I pay attention here to the myth that it can be more productive to have someone who is mixed carry out interviews with a mixed population. I also turn to the experiences of other mixed race scholars who have questioned the role of their own identities in acquiring and analyzing interview material. In particular, I problematize my role not only as an interviewer who elicited stories from participants in my study but also as a consumer and analyst of these tales.

Psychologist Albert Berstein (in Walsh 2012, 24) states that "narcissists have very little idea of how they relate to other people. They are able to pull a curtain over one part of their personality and say, 'This doesn't matter.'" There seems to be an ongoing fetishization of mixed race identity among some mixed race researchers, and I liken this to processes of narcissism. I do not provide a thorough psychological excavation of narcissism but merely gesture to the ways that some mixed race scholars and their accompanying intellectual studies (mine included) have not offered a pointed self-reflexive analysis of how the mixed race subject's experience may differ from that of the mixed race interviewee, assuming instead that their experiences share similarities. This chapter contests that prevailing belief.

So far, I have only briefly mentioned why I identify as mixed race. Here, I offer a more critical self-reflexive analysis of my participation in the acquisition of these interviews, asking some difficult questions about the social processes through which I have constructed and consumed these stories in my empirical analysis. At each moment in the encounter of the interview process, split-second decisions are made about what to reveal to the interviewer and in what language to reveal it. Crucial to my analysis is my belief that the very act of telling one's story to someone can be both empowering and debilitating.

Since I am a former journalist, I suspect my training influenced the acquisition of stories. My critical academic interpretation of these stories collides with my personal interpretations of my mixed race experiences. My readings of these personal narratives are no doubt clouded by my own sense of being in the world. Although I have been actively engaged in assembling life stories of the women I interviewed, I do not have a full grasp of their life experiences, of course. Finally, I explore how I analyzed the material I gathered through a process called "mind mapping" and point out the advantages and disadvantages of such an analysis.

In Chapter 1, I described the hypothesis that has historically governed multiraciality: the idea that mixed race identity creates marginality and must therefore lead to social maladjustment. Of course, since the late 1980s, there has been a growing recognition that the mixed race individual refuses to fit into a binary conception of self (see, for example, Funderburg 1994; Parker and Song 2001; Ali 2003; and McNeil 2010, 2012) and that people can in fact hold, merge, and respect multiple ethnic positions and perspectives simultaneously (Nakashima 1992; T.K. Williams 1996). There is also the belief that mixed race individuals can often negotiate their racialized identity and decode their ambiguity for the perceiver, depending upon the social context (Zack 1995; Twine 1996; Ali 2003). The majority of early research on mixed race identity tended to explore identity development among children and adolescents (Tizard and Phoenix 1993). I deliberately chose not to interview children and not to interrogate the impact of family dynamics on the identity development of mixed race individuals, even though scholars have indicated that the family does play a vital role in identity formation (DaCosta 2007). I made these choices because there were other issues I was interested in teasing out. One was the issue of group affiliations, parallelling Thornton's (1996) inquiry about potential future research in mixed race identity. He insists that if the mixed race identity is unique, it may be reflected "in how and with whom we bond" (ibid., 116). Thornton suggests that work in this area ought to focus upon mixed race individuals' definitions of group boundaries and how strongly they identify with ethnic and other groups. This is why I was concerned with asking how mixed race women identify within the Canadian context and with Canadian identity. Research on multiraciality has also illustrated that mixed race individuals feel that current racial categories are inadequate to describe their racialized sense of identity (Funderburg 1994; Ali 2003; DaCosta 2007). I wanted to discern how Canadian mixed race women felt about a range of aspects of their identity, not just about their racialized self, because to isolate race from other axes of identity precludes an opportunity to understand how race and other identity makers influence and impact each other. In day-to-day life, racial thinking is always accompanied by layers of meaning about sexuality, beauty, intelligence, wealth, femininity, and group alliances, all of which play a role in the manufacturing and presentation of mixed race women. I was curious to discover how participants contemplated issues of racialization in relation to their own complex identity. Indeed, I wanted to see whether there were in fact other socially constructed cleavages that contributed to identity formation and how these factors intersected with issues of race. Finally, as I hinted at earlier, since I am a mixed race woman myself, it would be false to assume that I do not have my own preconceptions about what it means to be mixed race in Canada. I admit to a certain narcissism insofar as carrying out these interviews gave me a chance to listen to other self-identified mixed race women's stories.

Moving beyond Biraciality

Identifying participants for this study was challenging. It allowed me to see how initially I used the category of mixed race as a self-evident label for analysis, which created all sorts of exclusionary effects. To further rethink the categories, definitions, and concepts used to formulate the mixed race subject, I deliberately did not focus my study upon a particular racial mix. I chose to interview a population whose identity included the awareness, acknowledgment, and affirmation of multiple racial and cultural ancestries.

It is often assumed that mixed race individuals share identical experiences (Nakashima 1992) based upon an identification of stereotypical features, with all mixed race people looking alike or looking racially ambiguous (C.I. Hall 1996). Researchers have chosen to focus upon specific ethnic compositions of biraciality, like Japanese and European (King and DaCosta 1996), Korean and European (Standen 1996), and African American and Jewish (Azoulay 1997; Zack 1997). Non-European mixes have been explored, as in Comas-Diaz's (1996) work on the "Latin-Negra," a mix of Latino and African American. However, the focus has remained upon particular biracial mixes to keep samples as pure as possible for comparison purposes – demonstrating that much of the research on mixed race tends to follow monoracial paradigms (see Mahtani and Moreno 2001). We have not yet asked the pertinent question "Which mixes matter in the study of mixed race identity?" To the best of my knowledge, few studies have chosen to analyze interviews with individuals of a variety of mixed race compositions (but see Bettez 2012). I believe this reveals a distinctly modernist as well as colonialist approach to multiracial studies, where mixed race is often seen as a mix of white and nonwhite. There is moreover a "common societal perception that the term 'mixed race' is synonymous with a black and white 'mix'" (Mahtani and Moreno 2001, 71). It is important to trouble these categories and develop new alliances in critical mixed race theory by examining the experiences of those individuals whose ancestry is mixed but may not be part white. Mixed race is also a socially constructed category, not unlike race, an idea I explore further in Chapter 5. Researching a single ethnic composition would have limited participants' definition of their ethnic identities, similar to the oppressive experience a mixed race individual faces when checking off the "other" box in statistical questionnaires. Choosing a methodological approach that explored only the identity issues of those with a specific two-part ethnic identity would have reiterated that racial designations are hierarchical, obscuring the flexibility and freedom a mixed race individual often exercises regarding ethnic allegiances. It was my hope to move away from these sorts of categorizations. I therefore did not classify individuals into biracial categories. Many of the women I interviewed clarified in rich detail their multiple lines of ancestry, with many mixed race individuals being children of mixed race mothers and fathers (such as the interviewee who had one Irish, one Native Indian, one Iranian, and one Polynesian grandparent). I chose such a wide heterogeneous sample to explore the ways that race is performed and experienced contingent upon phenotype, among other factors. I did not want to encourage marginalization within the mixed race community by focusing only upon a particular mix or just upon "black-white crossings," a term suggested by Ifekwunigwe (1998).

Why Women Only?

I chose to interview women only. I did this deliberately. I wanted to contribute to our understandings of the way that women in particular are racialized and experience race. I consider interviewing women for this project an important step toward ensuring that the voices of racialized women continue to be heard in feminist geographical inquiry.

It has been suggested that the experience of mixed race among women is unique because it is compounded by gender bias (Camper 1994). Ibrahim (2012, 17) critically evaluates Naomi Zack's assertion that it is "not an accident" that mixed race studies was developed primarily by women and that representations of multiracialism are inexorably intertwined with womanhood. Ibrahim takes Zack to task, insisting that her work illustrates a common tendency to conflate womanhood and gender but in a largely apolitical manner. She states, "I submit that this tendency to resist openly naming or explaining feminist theories of gender is a hallmark of multiracialist thought. Feminist theories of gender are the unspoken prerequisites for multiracial politics" (ibid.). In ignoring how feminist theory had the potential to radically inform a politicized model of multiracialism, an opportunity for more rigorous debate was lost in both arenas.

Ibrahim (2012, 34) further shows that many of the narratives of multiraciality have been produced by women, which suggests a "particularly maternal, or womancentric, dimension to multiracial discourse." Many critical mixed race theorists have suggested that the racialized experiences of mixed race men and women are different (see Lafond 2009). Although women of mixed race may experience less direct oppression or difficulty in countering social barriers than do men of mixed race because "non-white men ... have more social, economic, and political power than most women [and are thus] particularly threatening to [society]" (Root 1990, 196), it has been argued that women of mixed race are more likely than their male counterparts to have difficulty coping with the pervasive myths surrounding the experience of mixed race and sexuality (Streeter 1996; see also Bettez 2012), where mixed race women are read as "exotic" and sexually freer than other women (see Camper 1994). Hence I was curious to explore the multifaceted experiences of mixed race women who are simultaneously racialized and gendered. Studies are now beginning to explore the complex relationship between masculinity and mixed race identity (see Lafond 2009) – a welcome addition to studies on multiraciality. Ibrahim (2012, ix) has made an invaluable contribution to the literature through her suggestion that gender has not been appropriately acknowledged as providing the foundational logic for what she deems to be the racial dissidence between blackness and multiracialism. Although this project does not allow me to delve into that provocative and important assertion, it is worthwhile underscoring that multiracialism has suppressed its own gendered foundations, with the multiracial movement of the 1990s privileging both the sanctity of the heteronormative family and the leadership of mothers of mixed race children, an approach that had implications for the development of the movement.

Recruiting/Finding the Women

> It's a balmy May night, warm and breezy, and I'm at the Madison, a local bar, with a large group of friends drinking beer and chatting effusively. The Madison is packed, the usual twenty-something university crowd is soaking in the atmosphere. I walk to the bathroom with a friend, and while she's checking out her hair in the mirror, she does a double-take at the girl behind us. "Look," she hisses. "She's got to be mixed." I glance behind her and shrug. My friend, also a

journalist, smiles and whispers in my ear, "I bet she'd make a great interview." Before I can stop her, she goes up to her and says upbeat, "Hi, listen, I hope you don't mind my asking, but are you mixed? My friend here is doing a study on women who are mixed race, and ..." The woman is evidently taken aback and doesn't believe her. She's startled and stutters, "Ah, what did you say?" I turn bright red and realize she thinks she's getting picked up in the bathroom. I make my apologies and drag my friend out of there before any further damage is done.

The above notation from my research diary reveals much about the complicity of the researcher in shaping the data sample through the process of recruitment. Previous research on mixed race has illustrated that obtaining multiracial participants for research studies can be difficult, primarily because multiracialism is fraught with threats to validity (Root 1992). It almost goes without saying that the identification and recruitment of mixed race subjects is complex. The recruitment of mixed race individuals almost always yields selective samples. Even selective sampling techniques, such as word of mouth and newspaper advertisements, may recruit only a small number of participants. Some mixed race people may not respond to advertisements because they practice introverted racism, equating their multiracial heritage with negative status (Root 1997), whereas other multiracial individuals may not identify themselves as mixed race or biracial because, for them, ethnic or cultural identity does not factor as strongly as other identity dimensions. Advertising for people of colour also proves problematic. For one, it recruits only mixed race individuals who identify themselves as such and excludes many other mixed race individuals who successfully participate in passing for white. My initial attempt to acquire interview subjects through various advertisements reflected this difficulty. The advertisements I pinned up on billboards at universities and community centres in Toronto failed miserably. I did recruit one participant in this manner, but she ended up moving to Vancouver before I could conduct the interview.

There are obvious reasons why this method was not successful. First, I could easily have been disguising suspicious motives behind the veil of the interview request; it might have been interpreted as a pick-up attempt, for example, a point I take up later in this chapter. My insistence on not reifying the term "race" by using it in the recruitment ad might have led to readers' puzzlement about who was actually wanted for the interview. In reality, the majority of interview participants were recruited through word of mouth – by friends mentioning my research quest to other friends, colleagues, and family. As a result, the majority of participants worked in media-related fields, and although I did attempt to locate women from a variety of class backgrounds, this proved difficult. The population I interviewed reflects a very particular stance on mixed race. Participants were eager to discuss their own perceptions of their experiences and often did so to challenge and subvert existing stereotypes about the "mixed race woman." No doubt their motivations spilled over into my acquisition of the data. The importance of social networks is imperative here, as I located many of the women through either work contacts or friends.

The Politics of Recruitment

> It's a Monday morning, and I'm sitting in the office when I get a phone call. The woman on the line timidly asks for me and says, "I'm calling about the mixed race study." I ask her how she found out about the project, and she says, "Brendan told me about it." Apparently, my friend Brendan was in a bar over the weekend and approached this woman with an enthusiastic "Hey are you mixed?" which led to a long conversation about her ethnicity. He in turn told her about my study. When I talk to Brendan later, he says, "You know Minelle, this study of yours is so great. I get to go up to women in bars with a really good line. They always think I'm cool because I can say that I know a woman who is doing this study – it lends me some credibility because I can say I've got this woman friend, right? – and then not only do they agree to do the interview, but they go out with me afterwards!" I haven't licensed Brendan with this task, but he's apparently taken it upon himself to recruit participants for this study with a very insidious agenda. As a result, I'm loath to carry out the interview. However, the woman is very eager to discuss her experiences. When I finally do interview this woman later on in the month, she reveals that she has been dating Brendan since their initial meeting. She's incredibly happy, and actually thanks me, saying, "You know, Minelle, if you weren't doing this study, Brendan and I never would have met!"

This research diary excerpt reveals a series of mixed agendas. I unveil it simply because I feel we must have the courage to recognize our own complicity in others' oppression and because I want to draw attention to my own responsibility in recruiting participants for this study. Selfishly, I was thrilled to acquire yet another interviewee, and this woman's testimony turned out to be both powerful and gripping. However, I had never once imagined that my friends would use my study as a way to meet potential dates – an approach that disgusted me. Brendan's attitude also reflects the common myth that all mixed race individuals are attractive, a notion that many of the women I talked to problematized in greater detail (see also Streeter 1996). I was appalled to discover what Brendan was doing and put a stop to it at once.

Several mixed race women in this study problematized the idea that all mixed race people are beautiful and said that they had to counter this stereotype regularly (see also Mahtani and Moreno 2001). Magazine writer Cori Howard (2008, 260) states in a personal essay about raising her mixed race kids, "[My kids are] beautiful in the way all mixed-race kids are." This kind of comment imparts a racist motherly narcissism. I suggest that her comment hints at the tendency to assume that all mixed race kids must fall into (white) society's standard of beauty. The woman recruited by Brendan was undeniably pleased to have the opportunity to voice her opinion about being mixed race and was now involved in a satisfying personal relationship courtesy of the interview project. However, this does not mean that I should have excluded her from the study.

Specifics on the Interview Population

Defining the study population as mixed race did not reflect a naturalized choice in terms of "a place" or "a people" necessarily. Instead, the participants were located and defined in terms of specific political objectives that necessarily cut across time and place. Such objectives involve a number of political criteria that operate on different but connected levels (Nast 1994, 57). I chose to limit my focus to those women who defined themselves as mixed race, biracial, multiracial, racially mixed, or of mixed ethnic parentage. I preferred to give informants the space to define themselves. If they chose to identify as mixed race, I was curious about the ways that they chose this designation and about their reasons for doing so. In this fashion, I attempted not to label participants as mixed race myself. The majority of the women I chose to interview were between the ages of twenty and thirty-five, although one was an adolescent and two were over forty. I chose this age group because I did not want to interview youth and because I wanted to speak to women who were at a variety of different stages in identity construction. They were all born in Canada or had moved to Canada before their teens. By limiting my sample to women who had lived in Canada the majority of their lives, I was better able to discern how living in Canada had influenced their mixed race identity, which addresses Root's (1990) concern with recognizing that the geography of the mixed race individual plays a large role in identity formation. It was my hope that these criteria would allow for a discussion of broader questions of identity by incorporating questions surrounding identity and nationalism and therefore offer a contribution to debates about other forms of belonging. As I mentioned earlier, I chose to interview women who had lived in or near Toronto because it is considered the most diverse city in the country. Toronto also provided a practical site for interviews given that I was living and working there when I was carrying out this research.

The participants' status in the workforce was equally diverse. Whereas the majority of the twenty-four women worked in a media-related field (eight of them as television producers or film producers), the minority were students either in high school or pursuing an undergraduate or postgraduate degree (one, two, and five of them, respectively). Only three of them had not attended university, and of these three, two planned to attend soon (one was still seventeen, and the other intended to return to high school in order to get her diploma). The women were also diverse in age, class, region of origin, sexuality, family situation, and political orientation. The interviews were lengthy, with most taking from an hour and a half to four hours. Only a few required two sessions; indeed, most went straight for three hours.

It is difficult to categorize these women as a standardized group. However, there are some key similarities. Although the class categories by which these women defined themselves meant different things in different contexts, the majority read themselves as being part of the middle- to upper-class segment of Canadian society because of their educational backgrounds. As one of the participants said to me,

> Overall, the issue of race in my life has been part of who I am, but it's only been part. So ... I don't know if my experiences in terms of being a mixed race kid are reflective of what a lot of other people might have felt.

> As I said, the privilege of growing up in Toronto, you know, with parents who, you know, gave me pretty strong self-esteem and I, I didn't have much difficulty with too many things. So I think there are a lot of ways that this kind of experience could be worse. I mean certainly ... could feel more of a defining factor.

The group was more educated than I had initially expected – twelve of them had graduate degrees, and two of the women within that group had also explored issues of race in their graduate departments. Academic terms like "fragmentation," "borders," and "postmodernism" were used throughout the interviews, suggesting that these women's lives had been touched by the work of cultural theorists concerned with issues of identity. However, many of the women's descriptions of their early childhood positioned them within the lower- to middle-class bracket.

A brief thumbnail sketch of each participant follows. All names are pseudonyms. It is difficult to describe each of these women in a paragraph. I simply indicate their age and remark upon *the ways that they described their racialized identities to me,* reflecting my intent to avoid my own classification of their identity. Finally, I hope to capture some aspect of their personalities here by culling some points that participants stressed during the interview. I have tried to keep the comments on each participant pertinent while still staying somewhat vague because I feel that too much description would make them easily recognizable. Some identifying details have been changed.

Akari

Akari was twenty-two and "half-Japanese, half-white." Her mother was born in Japan, and her father was "Canadian – he's white." At the time of the interview, she was finishing a bachelor's degree. She grew up in a nearby suburban town just outside of Toronto, and her neighbourhood was middle- to upper-class. She was taking Japanese language classes and explained that she wished her mother had taught her Japanese at home. She told me that she felt like a "well-adjusted person" despite the myth that people of multiethnicity suffer from identity problems. Most of her friends were either black or Asian, and she enjoyed clubbing on the weekends. I observed Akari at the coffee shop where she was working and asked her to consider being interviewed.

Makeda

Makeda was twenty-six. Her mother was Japanese, and her father was "English, white, white, born in England." She had completed both undergraduate and master's degrees. She lived in London, England, until she was five, at which point her family moved to Toronto. Many of her summers were spent travelling and visiting family in Japan with her mother, which reflected her middle- to upper-middle-class status. She explained that she was pretty much "white identified" until high school, at which point she became involved with social justice movements. I met her at a mixed race event in Toronto.

Julia

Julia was twenty-nine and a filmmaker. Her mother was Asian from Hong Kong and her father was of German ancestry and grew up in a small farming community in northern Ontario. She spoke very proudly of her parents – "they're very very strong, amazing people." It was evident that she had a supportive family network to draw upon. Julia grew up in a Toronto upper-class suburb and skipped two grades before eventually pursuing both a bachelor's degree and a degree in film studies. She was adamant in telling me that she never felt like an outsider because she was mixed.

Naela

Naela was seventeen and the youngest of my interviewees. She told me, "My mom is from Hong Kong, and my dad is white from New York." She had strong ties with her mother's side of the family, and although she had spent the majority of her life in Toronto, she had lived in Japan for a year and a half. She spoke fluent Japanese. Although Naela came from an upper-class background, she attended a working-class public school, where she said that there were a lot of racial problems. She was attending an upper-middle-class high school with a diverse ethnic population. She told me that in her household a rift had occurred because her sister could not comprehend why Naela made "such a big deal" out of race. Naela explained that she had always been interested in racial issues and had read *Malcolm X* in Grade 6, which influenced her so strongly that she didn't speak to her father (solely because he was white) for a short period of time. Although she laughed about the incident – "things have become a lot more clear for me" – issues of race were still prominent in her life, evident through her participation in antiracist theatre productions and political activism in general.

Claudia

Claudia was twenty-nine and "fourth-generation Canadian on both sides – my father's family is Japanese Canadian, and my father was born in an internment camp, and my mother's family is British, so Scottish, Irish, and English." Although she was given an Anglicized name when she was born, Claudia tried informally to change her name to a more "ethnic" one from Grade 5 onward. She was not successful until Grade 13, when she attended school in Switzerland. After she completed her university studies, she changed her name legally. Claudia lived and taught English in Japan for three years, where she learned to speak Japanese fluently. While in Japan, she found it interesting that people saw her as a white person. Claudia grew up in a part of Toronto where there were strong eastern European communities. She admired the connections that her friends had to their cultural heritage and longed for the same. She decided to explore her Japanese heritage because people constantly asked her whether she was Japanese but never asked about her British ancestry. Although Claudia called herself "mixed," she told me that she saw herself as belonging to a different race from both her parents.

Emma

Emma was thirty-two. Her father was Malaysian and her mother "British." She held several degrees. She vigorously repudiated fitting into any one racial category and read her identity "in a way that isn't necessarily associated with a certain set of cultural values." She came from an upper-middle-class family. She told me that she didn't really think about issues of race growing up because she had lived in an ethnically diverse neighbourhood. It wasn't until she moved to the United States that she realized how salient the white-black divide was in the United States compared to Canada, and it was this subject that became the focus of our interview. In university, she found she was very attracted to Chinese culture and took courses in Chinese history. She had recently spent a few weeks in Malaysia and felt a tremendous sense of warmth for and attachment to the country.

Rhiannon

Rhiannon was twenty-nine. Her mother was born in China and grew up in California. Her father was "born in Vermont, Irish, English mix." She had lived in Toronto for most of her life. She insisted that she had unintentionally subverted the stereotype of the tragic mixed race heroine by having one of the happiest childhoods of anyone she knew, in part due to the tremendous support she received from her parents. She identified as bisexual and had two older sisters.

Faith

Faith was twenty-five and worked in tourism. Her father was a pilot, and she had travelled extensively growing up. Her mother was Polynesian, and her father was European Canadian. She spent her early childhood in Calgary, a very "white bread" place, as she put it, but also attended a variety of private schools and exclusive summer schools in France, Fiji, and Hawaii. Her family was upper-middle-class. Her extended family on her mother's side was very close. As she said, "The women rule in our family." She had one younger sister. Out of all the participants, Faith was probably the most skeptical about the interview. Although she insisted that she was ethnic, she thought my privileging of race and gender often took what she saw as political correctness to its extremes. For this reason, among others, I asked Faith to participate in this study. We had been casual acquaintances for a few years.

Shanti

Shanti was twenty-seven and working as a management consultant. She told me she was "composed of three different ethnicities – my dad is half-Persian, half-Chinese, and my mother is French Canadian." We met through a mutual friend who told her about my study, and she readily agreed to be interviewed. She told me that she had "no idea" about race growing up and was thoroughly white-identified until her Chinese grandmother moved in with her family when she was six. Suddenly, she realized that there was something "different" about her background, and she thought she might be adopted. "It was like one big puzzle," she explained. "I became aware of differences, aware that I was different from some of the other kids in my class after that." It wasn't until she was fourteen that her father told her two older brothers, younger sister, and herself that he was only half-Chinese (his father was Persian), which came as a shock to her because she had assumed that she was only part Chinese and part white up until that point. However, she also expressed relief upon discovering that she had Persian heritage, as it explained why she looked different from her family. As Shanti put it, "Finally, I understood why I didn't look like either my father or grandmother." She insisted, "It's never been an issue for me to be mixed – it's only been that I'm not completely white." She strongly identified with French Canadian culture and spoke French fluently, passed on from her strong ties with her mother's side of the family.

Darius

Darius was thirty-two and an actress who had worked on a variety of television and film productions. Her mother was third-generation Japanese Canadian, and her father was a mixture of French Canadian, Ojibway, and Irish. Darius and Claudia, another participant in this study, were close friends, having met at the "mostly white" university they attended, where both experienced feelings of alienation. After I interviewed Claudia, she suggested Darius as a possible participant. Darius grew up in Scarborough, which was then a very "white, blue-collar area." She told me that although she always felt different – "I don't look like either of my parents" – she never associated it with feelings of alienation or not belonging. Darius had significant university education, including a degree in fine arts. She had attended a number of mixed race conferences.

Shima

Shima was thirty-five and worked with a variety of community organizations developing antiracist guidelines. I heard about Shima from Makeda and contacted her to be interviewed. She identified as mixed race but insisted that she didn't always do so easily. Her mother was Scottish and her father South East Asian. She told me that race issues were never discussed growing up in her family. The first ten years of her childhood were spent in Scotland, where she experienced rampant racism. Shima explained that her father experienced internal racism and had "tried his darndest to keep us away from South Asian culture," even making up a new last name to anglicize his identity. Shima had to dig in his personal files to find out her real last name and secretly got in contact with the Indian side of her family: "My brother and I had to be detectives kind of into our own life." She "married the first blond-haired, blue-eyed guy that came along" and produced "for my father a boy, a perfect little white baby boy ... that was really important."

Rani

Rani was twenty-five and a graduate student. She was "a child of a mixed marriage between a Swedish mother and a Bangladeshi father" and had two sisters. She grew up in North York, in an upper-class neighbourhood. She pursued her first degree at an Ivy League college, after attending one of the most prestigious private schools in Toronto. A mutual friend suggested her for this study. Rani explained that she never really thought about race until she was thirteen, when people started to read her appearance as "exotic." But she didn't start thinking "politically" about her identity until she attended college, where "the predominant feeling was one of money and entitlement, mostly white. And I just didn't want to identify with that whole scene." She told me that she made a conscious decision to associate with people of colour and become involved with radical antiracist events in college. When she returned to Toronto after her degree, she explained that she had a different view of race, having lived in the United States for four years. Rani told me she read her multiethnicity as a source of strength and that it had given her a unique perspective on race issues.

Marical

Marical was twenty-seven and worked in media. Her father was a black "albino" from South Africa, and her mother was European from New Zealand. She explained that issues of race had never been discussed in her household until a few years before the interview. Countering the "usual tales" of multiethnic individuals wanting to look white, she recalled that when she was younger, she had wanted to look Asian because she thought Asians were the most beautiful. Although she identified as African Canadian, she didn't really feel that she had any strong cultural roots to draw from and thus wanted to return to South Africa for a few years to study.

Chantal

Chantal was twenty-four. Her father was from Trinidad, and her mother was "British" (of European heritage). She spent a few years of her early childhood in West Africa, where her father taught African Caribbean literature in French at university. She grew up west of Toronto, and was pursuing a journalism degree. Her first degree was in African studies. She was the only woman in my study who expressed concern that she would "throw off" my data by confessing that being mixed had caused her significant emotional trauma. Chantal contacted me after hearing about my study from a mutual friend and told me that I was doing research at just the right time because it was important to counter the ignorance proliferating about the multiethnic experience being "the best of all worlds." She explained that she was envious of her friends who had a strong recollection of their West Indian background, whereas hers was only "second-hand," as she didn't grow up in Trinidad. When she was younger, she had wished that she was white, although she told me that she had "come full circle on that" and now identified as black. She still felt residual resentment toward her father, "not because he married a white woman but because he denied that whiteness was part of my culture." Chantal very carefully problematized the whole idea of being able to choose one's racial identity by saying that the experience depends completely on how one is perceived racially.

Madeleine

Madeleine was twenty-seven and worked in journalism. Both her parents were adopted. Her father's background was "sort of like a mystery" – she believed it might be part Blackfoot and part Cherokee – and her mother's biological family was from Scotland and of European descent. Her parents divorced when she was five, and she hadn't seen her father since, as he "just took off." Madeleine had travelled extensively and had worked in Japan teaching English as a second language. She spoke fluent Japanese.

Katya

Katya was thirty. Her father was black and from the West Indies, and her mother was from Ireland. She had lived all over the world, including ten years in England, a year in Australia, fourteen in Canada, and five in the

West Indies. She lived at home, where she had a very strong and supportive relationship with her parents. Race had always been openly discussed in her household. As a child, she identified as black, but this perception changed as she became older. "At some point, it ceased to be enough," Katya explained. She had lived in "predominantly white and upper- to middle-class neighbourhoods." Katya conveyed throughout the interview that she recognized that she experienced privilege due to her extensive university education and upper-middle-class standing, although she was almost always identified as black by others.

Bella

Bella was in her early fifties and was one of my oldest interviewees. She worked in radio. I contacted her after a colleague in radio suggested I interview her. Her father was Scottish, and her mother was Jamaican, but her ancestry had a wide range of ethnicities, including Arawak. Her parents were very liberal when she was growing up, and she remembered their left-wing political leanings, not issues of race, as being what marked her as different. She remembered her father and her uncle starting up a political magazine and she spoke of celebrating Scottish folk festivals with her aunt. Many of Bella's parents' friends were Jewish, and Bella attended a Jewish school in Toronto, which may have contributed to her decision to adopt Judaism later in life. Bella had married young and believed that this constituted a strong part of her identity. She had two teenaged children.

Davy

Davy was in her forties and was of black, white, and First Nations ancestry. She was born in Toronto. She was a writer, visual artist, and women's health worker. She explained that she grew up in an "all-white" suburb of Toronto and shared several experiences of racism. Davy told me that as a child, she was not confused about her race because she "didn't know her race at all." Davy was adopted, and her adoptive parents were both white. "I was never informed by my parents that I was black," she said. Davy remembered poring over *National Geographic* magazines as a child because they featured articles about people from Tahiti. Prior to discovering that she was part black, she thought that the faces in the magazine most closely resembled her own appearance.

Sara

Sara was twenty-four and in university. She also worked part-time at a retail outlet. I met her through a friend, who had asked whether she would consent to being interviewed for this study. Her mother was Filipino, and her father was Irish. Although her mother lamented that she had "produced a white kid," Sara insisted that she's "not white but Filipino." She lived in a middle-class Toronto suburb with her parents and participated in many Filipino cultural events with her mother's side of the family. She had a younger sister. She explained that her parents had a rocky marriage and that her father patronized her mother: "He feels like he is superior and is civilizing my mother." However, her mother's extended family all lived in Toronto, so Sara had a very strong support network. Sara explained that at times she felt alienated from the Filipino community because she was "part white," even though she spoke fluent Tagalog. "I've actually had kids come up to me and say, 'It's better to be a pure Filipino than it is to be a half Filipino.' In a way, I felt isolated from that group," she admitted. Sara felt that she hadn't experienced racism because she didn't look like she was part of a visible minority, although when she was younger, people used to think that her mother was her nanny. She told me that most of her friends and the people she continued to gravitate toward were Filipinos and blacks. Although she had been identified by others as mostly Italian and Irish, she vehemently opposed being perceived as white. "I am Filipino," she said firmly, although she laughed when she recalled being called "phonky" – part Filipino, part "honky" – by friends in high school.

Kiirti

Kiirti was twenty-six and adopted. Both Kiirti's biological and adoptive parents were interracial couples. Her biological mother was Irish and English, and her biological father was a combination of French, Carribean Indian, and African. Her adoptive parents divorced when she was four, and her African father moved to Jamaica. Although she had visited him a few times, she lived with her mother and brother, who were both white. Kiirti explained that she grew up "in Toronto, in a fairly, in an all-white, fairly upper-class neighbourhood, attended an all-white school, and had all-white friends." Issues of race were not openly discussed in her household.

She told me she realized she was black for the first time when she expressed an interest in a boy and was told with disdain by a friend, "He doesn't date black girls." She had met her biological parents a few years earlier, which had a significant impact upon the way that she read her identity. "For the first time, I really had an answer for the question 'Where are you from?'" she explained, although she had not kept in close contact with either one of her biological parents. Kiirti was working as a waitress in Toronto and was contemplating returning to high school to obtain her diploma.

Zillah

Zillah was twenty-six and a journalist. Her mother was from Jamaica, and her father was from northern Ontario, although he had an Irish Scottish background. She lived most of her life in a suburb just north of Toronto in an upper-middle-class environment where few black people lived. Zillah told me that growing up, she was very white-identified, so much so that when she discovered she had an aptitude for track and field, she deliberately shied away from pursuing athletics because she didn't want to appear "too black." She remembered being called racial slurs like "jungle bunny" in high school and being puzzled, not knowing what that meant. She always considered herself unattractive, even when she was asked to start modelling for a top agency in Toronto. She added that her short modelling career further confused issues of femininity and beauty for her and that her self-esteem rose after spending a year as an exchange student in France, where she explained that she thought the men found her more attractive. Since attending university, she no longer identified as white and had explored her cultural background, wishing that she had done so earlier. She had just returned from Guyana, where she had been a freelance journalist. Most of her friends were either black or nonwhite. We talked a lot about hair during our interview, as Zillah explained that she had what would be known as "good hair" among her black friends and that her locks had been the source of much resentment from black women because they were straight and long. Zillah and I had met as students at university and had kept in touch ever since.

Asha

Asha was twenty-six and worked in the computer software field. Her mother was Armenian, and her father was East Indian Sikh. They had met at the University of Beirut. Although there was initial objection to the marriage, Asha explained that her family "came around" and that she felt close to both sides of her family. She had a younger brother and sister. Although she was born in England, she grew up in Toronto in an upper-middle-class neighbourhood. Asha said she never felt different growing up because she lived in an environment where "everyone was ethnic." Asha attended both Armenian and Southeast Asian "Sunday morning" language and culture classes growing up. She now spoke fluent Armenian. She studied math and physiology at university. Asha identified as "brown" and said that she didn't remember any racist incidents growing up. She felt lucky not to have experienced any outward hostility. Asha saw her parents as racist. They had told her that they would prefer she not date black men, which she found highly hypocritical. Asha still lived at home, despite her parents' racist sentiments. "I just do what I want," she explained. She acknowledged her own racism, as she caught herself making jokes about Chinese drivers during our interview.

Rose

Rose was twenty-two years old and a student. She held a degree in fashion design and was the president of her university's Multiracial Association. Her father was East Indian, and her mother was French Canadian. She grew up in a suburb just north of Toronto and attended French-immersion schools. She had travelled in Europe and spoke a little Italian. Although she was called racial slurs growing up, she kept it private, never telling her parents about the incidents, as issues of race were not openly discussed. She recalled wanting to look white when she was younger and even telling people that she was Portuguese instead of Indian because that made her seem "more white." She was now "really ashamed" of that, as once she got to university she began to explore various cultures in greater detail, which she attributed to her university's diverse ethnic composition. She believed that it was important for mixed race people to accept both parts of themselves rather than identifying with one over the other or restricting their marriage preference to one over the other. She also insisted that being multiethnic was more than just being "either black or white or both … There are other mixes out there which aren't getting discussed."

Zenia

Zenia was twenty-one and worked as a veterinarian assistant in Ontario. She loved animals. When asked where she was from, she said, "Well, I was born in Canada – therefore, I'm Canadian. That's how I look at it. I'm Canadian through and through. But my parents, that's another question. My father is from Sri Lanka and my mother from Norway." She spent her early childhood in Montreal and grew up in a middle-class neighbourhood in a suburb near Toronto. Zenia was vehement that people living in Canada should identify as Canadian first and place their ethnic ties in the background. Her interview demonstrated that she had an excellent grasp of Canadian history, as she would often launch into mini-lectures, explaining that too many Canadians were ignorant about their own history. She said she never resented being multiethnic or wished she were white. She spoke fluent French and Norwegian and had visited Norway several times.

The Questions

> If we would have new knowledge, we must get a whole world of new questions.
>
> — LANGER 1942, 10

For this study, I interviewed twenty-four women in Toronto who identified as mixed race. Although this number may appear small, I reiterate that this study is qualitative, not quantitative. I chose to employ open-ended questions in my attempt to give women the space to speak for themselves. I conducted a "test-run" of the interview with five mixed race women who provided useful suggestions for how to improve the questions. Their responses were not included in my final empirical analysis, and in the end, I never used all of the questions to structure my interview. In most exchanges, I used the questions as a guide. Normally, I simply asked the first question, and then the rest of the interview progressed smoothly, with the interviewee simply chatting with me about her own experiences of being mixed race. This led to many women becoming apologetic about not following what they expected to be a structured interview format, despite my reassurances to the contrary.

Each interview took between an hour and a half and four hours, was conducted face to face at a place of the interviewee's choice, and was tape-recorded. My decision to be guided by what emerged in the conversation with the interviewee reflects my interest in acquiring the personal stories of women and examining how they make sense of their experiences. Sometimes I didn't even need to ask an initial question, as the interviewee would just begin chatting. However, I would always begin the interview in the same way. I would hand the woman a copy of the questions to look at beforehand for a few minutes. If any questions seemed unfair, or if she didn't want to answer them, I assured her that we didn't have to go there.

My Own Mixed Race Status

> I have just finished my interview with Katya, and I'm sure there are crumbs all over my face from the shortbread cookies I have been scarfing down while she has been talking. It's been a really good interview, and I'm pleased with the rapport we've established. I rise to turn off the tape recorder when Katya asks me, "How do your parents feel?" I look at her and say, "About?" She smiles and says, "About your mixed race. Like how were you brought up?" I sit down again and say, "Let me turn off the tape and I can tell you about all my stuff!"
>
> — EXCERPT FROM RESEARCH DIARY

In this section, I hope to turn the tape recorder back on and explain how my own identity as a mixed race woman has complicated the material I have acquired. I already described some of my own experiences of being mixed race in the Introduction – now I want to illustrate how my mixed race identity had an impact upon the interview process. It has been suggested by researchers (Root 1992; Tizard and Phoenix 1993) that it is helpful when a mixed race individual carries out the interviews with mixed race respondents. This may diminish the discomfort some interviewees feel, as well as providing a sympathetic ear for discussion. Indeed, these experiences reflect Kobayashi's (1994, 74) assertion that "political ends will be achieved only when representation is organized so that those previously disempowered are given voice. In other words, it matters that women of colour speak for and with women of colour."

There were times when my own status as a mixed race woman did foster dialogue. Certainly, I did share commonalities and similar experiences with the women I interviewed, which was reflected through our exuberant discussions. At times during the interview process, I discovered that my own mixed race identity may have helped to diminish the fears of participants who were wary of my reasons for carrying out this study. I became very familiar with the phrase, "Oh, you're mixed, too? Oh well, then I'll definitely be interviewed!" During a pivotal point in our interview, Kiirti explained to me that she felt comfortable talking to me as a woman of mixed race:

> You see that's the sort of thing that I don't necessarily think that I would be able to describe to somebody who wasn't, and I'm going to say it again, I mean you need it for description's sake, but who wasn't of mixed race. I don't think they'd really get it.

However, at the same time, I was aware that my own identification as a woman of mixed race invoked a distinction between insiders and outsiders, creating a new set of tensions and definitions (Nast 1994). For example, a phrase that recurred throughout many interviews was, "You know what I mean, Minelle," followed by a knowing glance or smile. This sort of complicity may have created a more comfortable space for these women to tell their stories – but it also prevented them from divulging further detail, given that they thought I understood what they were not saying. As well, participants may have thought I expected the answers to my questions to coincide with my own hypotheses, carved from my own experience. Hence I tried to remain alert to the ways that I was influencing the research. I became aware that reflexivity needed to be employed throughout the processes of locating, reaching out to, and working with interviewees in this field. However, I could not assume that reflexivity on its own would ensure politicized results. It can be easily assumed, erroneously, that all people who identify as mixed race share similar experiences. This presumption of a shared mixed race identity insinuates a single, homogenous, and similar constituency. Feminists have long pointed out that there is no single analytical category of "woman" and similarly that the category of mixed race can obscure the disparate heterogeneous diversity within this label. It can be assumed that because I identify (and have been perceived as) mixed race, I did indeed share some deep commonality and bond with the women I interviewed. However, this assumption presupposes a core basis of similarity across many different identity markers. We cannot assume or expect that there will be mutual recognition among all mixed race women. As I point out in the remaining chapters, the women I interviewed held very different, often opposing, perspectives on their experiences of multiraciality. Light-skin privilege and class status, among other factors – including, of course, political mobilization in some instances – can also impact the evolution of differences between women.

Some critical mixed race scholarship offers the opportunity for the researcher to see herself in her participants. Of course, it should go without saying that I did not see myself in all the stories I was told. The experiences of some of the women were markedly dissimilar from my own experience of mixed race. I worked to comprehend the ways that all of the women made sense of their lives and described their experiences. Contextualizing their stories within their histories and remaining reflexive were obviously not enough. These women experienced very different kinds of racism based upon decisions made by others, and by themselves, regarding their phenotypes. Some of the women experienced racism on a day-to-day basis, whereas others experienced none at all because of white-skin privilege and class standing, among other factors. To insist upon the so-called similarities of experience among all mixed race women is to focus upon "notions of fixed identities which are based upon readily identifiable and socially recognized points of difference" (Song and Parker 1995, 249). In his critique of his own interviewing process, Parker emphasizes that "many dimensions of sameness and difference can be operating at any given moment. And where two people may claim commonality on one dimension, they may fall apart on another" (ibid., 246).

It is dangerous to assume that all mixed race women are "sisters" with "unified subjectivities of shared consciousness through gender" (Gilbert 1994, 92). I was separated from many of the women I interviewed through a variety of social cleavages that structure life worlds, including their ages, their life partner choices, their sexual orientation, and whether they were political activists, culture vultures, adopted or not, outgoing or shy, and childless or a mother. I shared many subject positionings and experiences with some informants, and at times my own racialized identity was only one of the axes of shared identity. As Johnson (1994, 110) puts it, "When considering positionality and the power that accompanies some situations

... gender ... ethnicity and race are only some of the structuring elements." Indeed, some of us had gone to the same college, had the same friends, and shared similar interests, and it was upon the basis of these dimensions of similarity that I was often granted legitimization, leading to extensive dialogue. My point is that in engaging in a reflexive analysis, where one confesses one's own experience of multiraciality, researchers who identify as mixed race may want to be reflexive about engaging in reflexivity, keeping in mind that it is no substitute for a lack of "connection to a larger agenda ... How we choose to change the world is a very personal matter; but the results are not" (Kobayashi 2003, 348). One needs to ask how speaking about one's position relates to larger questions of systemic privilege.

The Academic-Journalist

Nevertheless, I would like to share one aspect of commonality that emerged between me and participants, the axes of which was neither gender nor ethnicity but rather, among some women, our joint participation in the media. While interviewing women for this study, I was employed as a national television news journalist. I conducted approximately three interviews a day or more (mostly by phone but some in person) to book guests and prepare hosts for a daily news and current affairs program. My status and the news angle that I developed (along with the courses I had taken to improve my news interviewing skills) had an effect on how I conducted these interviews, particularly since interviewing women for this study made me confront issues of my own personality and professional training.

Unlike some of my colleagues in academe, I have experience approaching unknown people, either in person or by telephone, to ask them to share an experience or to tell their story. Normally, however, people will not agree to a television interview unless they have an opportunity to gain something – a rise in either popularity or political recognition – because they cannot entirely trust that their time or their words will be treated with respect. My identity as a wannabe academic (I was a doctoral student conducting interviews for my dissertation) and as a journalist at the same time was something I reflected upon many times while conducting my research.

I am drawn to the words of Vron Ware (in Blaagaard 2011, 160), who speaks about the experience of identifying as both an academic and a journalist herself:

> In terms of moving between being an academic and journalist ... they present different opportunities, I suppose. In the academic world there is an envy that journalists are in a position to write a lot and reach an instant audience. And among journalists there's mistrust towards academics, because they use long words and talk in abstractions ... The two things I consider to be really important in both professions are curiosity, having an open mind, and alertness – or attentiveness in terms of being open to things going on around you.

When I first started interviewing women in this study, it did strike me that the result could be a documentary rather than a dissertation. However, as I delved deeper into the process, I recognized that the stories that the women shared with me were so intensely personal that putting them on camera would have denied them their anonymity, and I did not want to risk that. I felt fortunate that participants trusted me enough to share their experiences and did not want to capitalize upon or exploit that trust. However, having said that, my own role as a journalist influenced the interview process. I was read as a journalist by some of the participants in this study, which lent me a credence I had not expected. Some of the younger interviewees asked me anxiously afterward for tips on how to get into journalism, consistent with Oakley's (1986) experience of being asked literally hundreds of questions by interviewees seeking information and advice. On the other hand, since many of the women I interviewed worked in media, many of our conversations reflected our joint interest in this profession. An alliance was temporarily forged that was not based upon the social cleavages of either ethnicity or gender but upon our experiences in media, as an excerpt from my research diary readily attests:

> I am sitting in the boardroom with Emma, where after several attempts, we're finally meeting to conduct this interview. Last time we scheduled, the premier announced a live press conference that day and she was called in; she had to cancel with me. But finally, we've managed to find a spare moment to conduct the interview. Emma and I have worked together very sparingly in the past – I might have called her about a special. But we've never actually talked. Now, we're half-way through the interview, and she says to me, "You know, I really think mixed race women occupy a postmodern space." I look at her and smile to myself, thinking excitedly,

"Oh my God, there's the clip!" – the sound-bite I'm always searching for when conducting my TV interviews. Almost as if reading my mind, Emma grins and says, "Isn't that a great clip?" We both laugh, as if conspiring together.

Emma and I shared a moment based upon our similar workplace experiences of constantly searching for what we call the perfect clip. This may have had an impact upon what Emma chose to reveal in the interview. She no doubt wanted to provide a good interview, and this desire may have coloured the data I received. Clearly, there are diverse motivations behind the desire to identify commonalities among women.

The Binary Paradox of Oppression and Resistance

> Oppressed people resist by identifying themselves as subjects, by defining their reality, shaping their new identity, naming their history, telling their story.
>
> – HOOKS 1989, 43

I have problematized the notion of a distinction between insiders and outsiders inherent in the research process. I am not alone in critiquing this binary; indeed, Mullings (1999) has covered this terrain. I would like to spend a little time exploring how the feminist research process has, at times, been coarsely characterized as either oppressive or emancipatory. Obviously, this is a simplification: both representations are exaggerated. I hope to examine some of the complicit complexities that emerged while I was conducting this study.

Feminist researchers, including me, like to believe that our work is emancipatory. This is often a falsehood, of course. But it can be assumed that feminist research offers a critique from the margins, where multiple positionings are valued and destabilized, challenging the perceptions of the dominant. Geography is not exempt from this aim. Sibley (1995, 184) observes, "I see the question of making human geography radical and emancipatory partly as a question of getting close to other people, listening to them, making way for them." Chouinard and Grant (1996, 171) exclaim that it is "high time for all geographers to do what they can to ensure that 'other' voices and practices are taken seriously in struggles to reconstruct 'the project.'" Similarly, I have been told by a few feminist researchers how important my work is because it attempts to produce an alternative discourse about women – particularly racialized women – for women. Indeed, many women who agreed to be interviewed insisted their purpose was to disrupt the prevailing social viewpoint that people of mixed race experience emotional difficulty and subsequently suffer due to their apparently conflicted racial identity.

Feminists have positioned women as oppressed and dominated in some research, and following from this logic, women of mixed race occupy an ironically privileged place by being further marginalized within the broader margins, or triply subordinated as women, women of colour, and mixed race women. Research on mixed race individuals has situated them within a dualistic conception of their identity. In very broad terms, either the research has tended to position mixed race people as oppressed and deviant, turning them into victims with little control over their lives while ignoring the possibility of human agency, an approach associated with the age of pathology, or it has tended to completely contradict this positioning by emphasizing the voices of individuals who insist that they experience the best of all worlds, an approach associated with the age of celebration. These characterizations construct very limited, one-dimensional identities with negative undertones. Consequently, I was congratulated on my desire to pursue a topic that would *contradict* the existing stereotypes about mixed race individuals.

Of course, the agenda is nowhere near this transparent. Such statements ignore the researcher's influence upon the acquisition of material and the choices we make in reconstructing narratives. Within this characterization, I am positioned as a progressive liberator of voices. I experience unease around this positioning.

Although I believe it is important to bring the voices of mixed race women to the forefront, I also want to acknowledge my own discomfort with the perception that surfaced among others that I was freeing participants' discourses. This would have been an extraordinarily arrogant position for me to assume! There is a social construction of the research subject as an oppressed other that sees extracting information as more valid or important than actually divulging it (Oakley 1981, 39). This view represents, as Oakley (ibid.) points out, a rationalization of inequality. It makes sweeping generalizations about the nature of the interview process as well as the interview subjects themselves, rather than unravelling the politics of research inherent in the idea that research on women is always politically empowering – because, of course, at times it is not. It obscures the development of yet another hierarchy between the researcher and the researched, the chasm widening as we construe the researched subjects as belonging to an abject population rather than as personal experts living in the mixed race community. These characterizations reveal a dualistic conception of the power dynamics inherent in the research process.

Gillian Rose (1997, 309) illustrates the divide that characterizes the "transparent reflexivity" of the feminist research process, where on one side the researcher looks "inward" at her own identity, asking what kinds of baggage she brings to her work "in the field," and on the other side the researcher looks "outward" at her relation to her research and what is described as "the outer world." In critiquing the notion of reflexivity, Rose (ibid., 310) suggests that feminist geographers are plotting a very two-dimensional map of the relations of power between the researcher and the researched, where "power relations are [charted] into a visibly and clearly ordered space that can be surveyed by the researcher: power becomes seen as a sort of landscape." Differences between the researcher and the researched, she argues, are imagined as distances in a landscape of power.

Like Rose, I believe the power dynamics between the researcher and the researched are complex. Any interaction or exchange between two people is a loaded one, with minute choices continually being made about what to reveal. These decisions are based upon momentary and split-second reflections on the situation by each individual present. However, these dynamics, although almost impossible not to recognize, are difficult to cite in detail. I prefer to see the interview as an encounter of infinitely complex social choices, reflecting a vision of research as a process of constitutive negotiation based upon Butler's (1993) notion of performativity. I performed my story as an interviewer and as a mixed race woman, just as the women I interviewed were charged with the task of telling their stories and making their meanings, thus providing and producing a performance in space around their experience of mixed race. These interviews ought to be envisioned as the product of a personal exchange of information – merely a snapshot of a place-specific process of resistance to oppression and the play of differences within a particular site at a particular time.

Happy-Go-Lucky Multiraciality

I want to delve deeper into this idea that some mixed race scholars may be heard as liberating voices. When I first started interviewing mixed race women, I was told (mostly by white feminists) that my work was critically valuable because it produced an alternative discourse about women – for women. Other mixed race scholars and students approached me excitedly, telling me that my work offered up a "voice for the voiceless" (a problematic phrase – are mixed race women voiceless?) because they said that they saw their own experience mirrored in academic work for once. Thus I was congratulated on my desire to pursue a topic that was seen as supposedly confounding the existing stereotypes about mixed race people as torn and confused about their racialized identity, which is what I believe Root's "Bill of Rights for Racially Mixed People" (1996a), discussed in Chapter 1, ultimately attempted to accomplish. These kinds of responses require further critical investigation.

A number of scholars of mixed race theory have insisted that some academic supporters of multiraciality have too readily "assume[d] ... roles as scholarly cheerleaders ... swept up in the unreflective emotionalism of the ambiguity avalanche" (Spencer 2011, 3). There has been a tendency to see mixed race research, particularly between 1990 and the current day, as offering an enthusiastic, but ultimately politically vacant, critique from the margins, challenging the perceptions of the dominant historical account of multiraciality. Through people's congratulatory gestures, my approach to multiraciality was valorized. Although I believe it is important to bring the voices of mixed race women to the forefront, I also want to acknowledge my own role in supposedly giving flight to their feelings and thoughts.

Since conducting my study in the mid-1990s, I have come to see how my own reading of the historiographies of mixed race epistemologies at the time influenced the acquisition and analysis of my interviews. I can see how wedded I was to ensuring that my work contradicted the stereotype of the mixed race person as torn and confused, with no place to call home, primarily because most of the research that I encountered emphasized a sombre tale of multiraciality. The icon of the tortured mulatto figure stubbornly preyed on my mind throughout the research process. I was determined not to make this figure the subject of my research. Although it is true that many women of mixed race who agreed to be interviewed insisted that they wanted to disrupt the prevailing social viewpoint that people of mixed race experience emotional difficulty due to society's perception of them as conflicted and confused, others did, in fact, describe their trauma growing up as mixed race – particularly those individuals who grew up outside of an urban area. These stories, although admittedly rare, did not become the focus of my analysis. I recognize now that I was much more interested in hearing and, in particular, sharing stories about strategies – paying attention to the high walls that women sometimes managed to climb over in order to challenge various forms of racism. But when I voiced my concerns to some of the same people who congratulated me, I was met with bewildered stares. What's wrong, they argued, with telling a happier story about the experience of multiraciality? Did I want to drain all the "happy-go-lucky" stories of multiraciality out of my analysis?

Ahmed (2008) urges us to critically consider the relationship between multiculturalism and the promise of happiness by contemplating two figures. The first is the kill-joy feminist: "[Does she kill] other people's joy by pointing out moments of sexism? Or does she expose the bad feelings that get hidden, displaced or negated under public signs of joy?" (ibid., 127). The second is the figure of the melancholic migrant, "the one who is not only stubbornly attached to his difference, but who insists on speaking about racism, where such speech is heard as labouring over sore points. The duty of the migrant is to let go of the pain of racism by letting go of racism as a way of understanding that pain" (ibid., 133). The feminist kill-joy and the melancholic migrant are both anchored as angry and unhappy figures – if only they would just "get over it." Both are chastised for complaining about racism and sexism – they would be much better off, it is argued, if they would just choose happiness because, like racial categories for some mixed race people, apparently happiness can also be a choice, exempting it from any systemic or institutional analysis, which is a profoundly neoliberal stance.

Ahmed's (2008) work strongly resonates with me. In the euphoria over multiraciality as celebrated in the popular press (see Squires 2007), there is a pervasive belief that racism has, to use the vernacular, left the building – and that because interracial mixing is occurring (not skyrocketing, despite prevalent claims to the contrary), we will see fewer incidents of racism. This myth is insidious and powerful. By celebrating the myriad ways that mixed race people seemingly effortlessly choose to liberate themselves from the shackles of racism, leaving their pain, melancholia, and unease at the door, these representations of the experience of multiraciality do not challenge social narratives of racial injustice or intervene in processes of systemic racism. In fact, they can work to do the opposite. Such interpretations, whether unconsciously or consciously, can provide a troubling, conventional, and colonial form of social hope (Ahmed 2008).

It has been suggested that contemporary approaches to multiraciality allow for "gross historical amnesia and acute political naïveté" (Sexton 2008, 51). The prevalence of recent research that relies on the myth of racial choice (see Spencer 2011) means that we need to shift our focus away from small sample sizes of in-depth interviews with people who identify as mixed race and toward approaches that are historically and geographically situated, refusing to be caught up in the wave of rapture that so often surrounds the multiracial subject this millennium – as Senna (1998, 12) ironically reminds us, it is "strange to wake up and realise you're in style." It is not enough to simply ask mixed race people to share their stories because there are a range of factors that limit the stories we hear from them, and as researchers we make choices about which stories we give airplay. We are not always transparent about these choices. I revisit this issue in the last chapter.

We also need to pay greater attention to the focus on family dynamics in discussions of experiences of multiraciality (for illuminating analyses, see DaCosta 2007; and Ibrahim 2012), and I believe that we need to broaden the scale to include not only an interrogation of the varied histories of state racism that inform these narratives but also an account of the specific historical transnational geographies that intersect with the ongoing commercialism and global commodification of mixed race identity (DaCosta 2007).

I have tried to stress that it is important to unravel the politics of research inherent in the myth that research on mixed race people is politically empowering or antiracist because, of course, it is not. Ten years ago, we might have said that among the biggest dangers for researchers to watch out for in critical mixed race studies was the tendency to construe the researched subject as belonging to an abject or deviant population or perhaps to assume that she belonged to a distinct, homogeneous group. But I suggest there are new, more pernicious undercurrents here that may work to reinforce pernicious forms of neoliberal racism, despite (or because of!) our best intentions. Being seen as mixed race kill-joys or melancholic researchers is the least of our worries. Unearthing those historical and geographical precedents that inform the contemporary experience of multiraciality may offer what Ahmed (2008, 135) calls an "alternative social promise."

The Partiality of Stories

> I am at home, eating macaroni and cheese in the company of my best friend in my television workplace. She's always been interested in my interviews and asks me how my interview with Emma has gone. Taking a sip of red wine, I reflect for a moment before I answer the question. My friend knows Emma intimately on both a personal and professional level, but I'm well aware that the interview is confidential. I say guardedly, "Well, she told me a lot about her dad in Malaysia," thinking that wasn't divulging a great deal. Anita looks at me strangely. "That's odd. Her dad died a year ago. Did she tell you that?" I'm stunned because Emma referred to her father all the way through the interview as if he was still alive. I change the subject, but my mind is whirring. Just how much did Emma tell me, and did she in fact keep other important details from me, knowing that I am her work colleague and she wants to guard her privacy?

I want to mark the very real dangers of attributing a particular value to these stories. I hope that this discussion reveals the limitations of acquiring the story of multiraciality from participants. Certain reflections were told at particular social moments, and my own participation in these interviews played a role in the process of acquiring data, where I performed the multiple parts of coaxer, counsellor, confessor, and compassionate colleague or friend. These stories do not begin to capture the ways that the body tells a story. There is often so much that is not expressed due to the limits and constraints of the interview process. Emma deliberately chose not to focus on the death of her father during the interview, referring to him instead as though he were alive, in the present tense. This reminds me of Clifford's (1986, 7) insistence that "ethnographic truths are ... inherently *partial* – committed and incomplete" (emphasis in original).

Of course, no story is complete. Instead, stories are always subjective, revealing part of reality but not all of it. What we divulge when we narrate tales of our experiences depends upon when and where we are doing the telling, on the ways that we rework the stories of our lives, and on modifications that we make due to our mood, the place, or the time of the narration. We are engaged in a constant process of readjusting our stories in response to the context of the storytelling, not to mention the presence of a listener. The lives of the women I interviewed and their subsequent discussions of their multiple identities were diverse, active, and layered, so it is valuable to consider the multiple ways that they told their stories and the role of the interview in shaping the content. These interviews may be understood as simply patchworks of sound-bites, reflecting a playfulness within the retellings of life stories. There are many ways to tell the story of a racialized and gendered existence, and in the tellings, "a supermarket of possibilities [pervades], with endless choices potentially available ... Old linear narratives ... break down" (Plummer 1995, 139).

Conclusion: Beyond Redemption?

I have suggested that some of our approaches to studying mixed race experiences may be understood as narcissistic. It is no coincidence that the majority of scholarship in mixed race studies is conducted by individuals who identify as mixed race and that in our zeal to show that mixed race people aren't torn and confused, there has been a zeal to attach racial discourses about mixed race people to supposedly progressive ones. I am reminded of Stoler's (1997, 187) words: "That those who study the history of racism are so committed to documenting fluidity may have more to do with the sorts of political narratives of renouncement and thus of redemption we are intent to tell." The intentions behind our narratives are worthy of further analysis and require us to take a harder look at how we decide what constitutes a mixed race community, among other questions. Some of the participants in this study expressed a desire to build diverse and pluralistic communities, whose members at times are ironically at radical odds with one another yet manage to coexist. The material garnered through these extensive interviews offers a highly complex portrait of attitudes toward mixed race. This material is explored in greater detail in the next four chapters.

3
The Model Multiracial
Propping Up Canadian Multiculturalism through Racial Impotency

> I should be the new symbol for Canada! I am one big melting pot of stuff! I'm a stew! A big Canadian stew!
>
> — KIIRTI, INTERVIEWEE

> [The multiracial movement] seem[s] to take for granted that *the state is neutral,* that citizens seek neutrality as an ideal, and that the ideal of neutrality is the only available theory of justice.
>
> — IBRAHIM 2012, XXVI, MY EMPHASIS

I begin this chapter with a comment from Kiirti, one of the participants in this study, who enthusiastically told me that she worked from her individually identified body to the national body politic, seeing herself as an ideal emblem for Canadian identity. I found this statement to be provocative yet at the same time discouraging, as I explain in this chapter. McNeil (2010, xvi) encourages us to "ask critical questions about the symbolic roles of mixed-race bodies," and I take his invitation seriously. How does the state ensure that some mixed race bodies (as opposed to other, so-called monoracialized bodies) are able to proudly call the nation their own? What does the figure of the multiracial body in Canada do to support neoliberal conceptions of the state, thereby excluding other racialized bodies, particularly black and Indigeneous bodies? And how does the freight of Canada's colonized racial legacies inform the ways that multiracial bodies are able to be employed as figures that maintain the state apparatus?

Consider these words by poet Wayde Compton (2004, 16):

> ... oh all
> my fellow mixed sisters and brothers let us mount
> an offensive for our state. surely something
> can be put together from the tracts, manifestoes,
> autobiographies, ten-point programs, constitutions,
> and historical claims.

Compton's call to arms haunts me. In his poem, he calls upon his fellow mixed race brethren to "mount an offensive for *our* state" (my emphasis). I am struck by his use of the pronoun "our" instead of "the" in front of "state." It made me want to explore the specific conditions under which some mixed race people choose to ally themselves with the nation. When and where do they think about themselves as Canadian? Clearly Kiirti saw a connection, if the above comment from her interview is any indication. This tendency is not exclusive to mixed race people in Canada. Similarly (but not identically), Michael Pellegrini (2005, 531), a mixed race scholar based in the United States, says the following about his own personal racial historiography: "In truth, I do not really think much about race, period. We are Americans and individuals." Pellegrini is swift to describe himself as American. Although he identifies as an American citizen, his argument pertains to the Canadian context. How does identifying as multiracial allow for a particular kind of affinity with the nation-state? Who is awarded this ability and privilege, and when?

In my research, I found that some interviewees expressed great affection for Canada as a state, country, and nation. Those who felt differently were in the minority and explained that an affectionate identification with Canada would be anathema to their racial politics. How might we make sense of these disparate positions?

I suggest that for some mixed race women, identifying as mixed race means carefully not referring to a race politics at all. A particularly depoliticized, sanitized, and neutral view of multiraciality emerges, where multiculturalism and liberal multiracialism are conflated. Diversity is celebrated without recognition of a power politics at play. Their mixed race bodies are deployed as normative cultural models of racial democracy and liberal tolerance. Ibrahim (2007, 155) tells us that the mixed race body can be understood as a "rhetorical emblem of successful integration," and McNeil (2012, 7) reminds us that conversations about postracialism in the United States seem to be disinterested in shifting the discourse away from one that favours examples of black performativity and toward one that would recognize the ways that the multiracial discourse props up a black other to "delegitimise expressions of black anger in the American public sphere." He goes on to ask a very important question: "Why [would] 'people of colour' ... organize politically when they have been offered the opportunity to commodify black rage and become respectable citizen-consumers in a land of multicultural diversity?" (ibid.). Some mixed race people commodify hybridity and mixing, as though the combination of two, three, or more is much better than one.

In this chapter, I explore how discourses of multiracialism adhere with ease to apolitical tenets of the diversity discourse. I unveil through interviews the way that some mixed race women choose to adopt a racially impotent stance. I concur with Makalani (2001, 94) that "what has been identified as a broader outlook on race is actually a color-blind ideology that slights the continued salience of race and racism." Multiculturalism in particular had different meanings for the women I interviewed: it was understood as a coarse description of their personal geographies and dwelling places, but it was also seen as providing some women with a space of entry and acceptance into Canadian society. Many of the women interviewed chose not to reject this sense of belonging, a stance that ensures the ongoing success of state multiculturalism, which people of colour must buy into if it is to appear successful. Furthermore, another notable aspect of the depoliticized nature of multiraciality is the various ways that some mixed race women reflect the broader tendency among non–First Nations people to elide Canada's colonial racial legacy.

I begin by providing a critical reading of multiculturalism, emphasizing the differences between multiculturalism and multicultural policy. I then explore how some mixed race women articulate their relationship with multiculturalism and multicultural policy. Finally, I introduce the idea of the *model multiracial,* insisting that some mixed race people unwittingly reproduce and maintain the economy of white supremacy through apolitical and neutral affiliations with the nation-state.

Multicultural Policy: A Critical Overview

This section attempts to sketch out a meandering history of the development of multicultural policy. The aim is to deconstruct representations of multiculturalism that confuse "multicultural" as an adjective with the goals and aspirations of a multicultural project. Too often, questions of supposed factual demographic diversity are conflated with issues of potential and cultural representation. The term "multicultural" refers to the multiplicity of the world's cultures and to the coexistence of these cultures within nations, in a strictly literal and indexical sense. What distinguishes Canada beyond its status as a multicultural country is that the multicultural project has been enshrined in its Constitution and through its laws, reflecting the project's salience in the social and political context of Canada.

Multiculturalism as policy emerged in part because of perceived challenges posed by the influx of ethnically diverse immigrants into Canada (Elliott and Fleras 1990). Canada was established as a dominion in 1867 through the British North America Act, which inaugurated a relationship between individuals of French and British backgrounds, otherwise known as the charter groups (Kobayashi 1993, 211). At the time of Confederation, Canada identified itself as 90 percent English or French (Ley 1984). Only 8 percent of Canada's population was not of British or French origin at the time of Confederation (Kalbach 1992). After 1881 immigration by both non-British and non-French migrants grew to significant numbers, as the population density was dropping noticeably in Canada. Chinese immigrants were recruited to build the Canadian Pacific Railway. The number of immigrant source countries grew to include those in eastern Europe and Asia (Kobayashi 1993). Between 1896 and 1914 up to 3 million immigrants, most of them from central and eastern Europe, arrived to settle in the western provinces (Elliott and Fleras 1990). Assimilation into the cultures of either of the two dominant groups was the major objective of immigration policy at the time (Palmer 1975). The government response to this wave of immigrants is referred to as a policy of "Anglo-conformity," and its goal was to make immigrants British in all respects – language, culture, and ideology included (Hudson 1987). In 1907, 20 percent of the immigrants entering Canada were from central and southern Europe, and by 1913 this figured had reached 48 percent. Although immigration had been a response to national needs, the arrival of 3 million immigrants between 1896 and 1914 evoked racial tensions.

It is critical to point out the exclusionary racist nature of immigration policies at this time. The completion of the railway in the 1880s released a large and inexpensive workforce in British Columbia, and the Chinese were believed to be a threat to the jobs of white workers. When business and labour felt threatened by competition, the government responded with discriminatory policies, and anti-Chinese sentiment thrived. In the 1880s Prime Minister Sir John A. Macdonald "subscribed to the theory that [the Chinese] were sojourners who might be rented, as one might rent a machine" (Roy 1981, 152), and Baureiss (1974, 3) explains how in 1892 a local newspaper in Calgary proposed to its readers that "although the Chinese had a legal right to be in Canada, law-abiding citizens should implement a law to make their stay illegal, and boycott the Chinese by not giving them employment." In 1885 a head tax was levied upon each Chinese individual entering the country. No other group received this type of restriction. The head tax steadily grew from $100 in 1900 to $500 in 1904, the equivalent of a year's labour wages (Baureiss 1985). In 1923, due to mounting pressure, the Chinese Immigration Act, or what has become known as the Chinese Exclusion Act, was passed; it virtually brought Chinese immigration to a standstill. Until its repeal in 1947 (in part spurred by the fact that it violated the United Nations Charter of Human Rights), only forty-four new Chinese immigrants were allowed to enter the country (ibid.).

Due in part to these concerns, and to the subsequent pressures from charter groups and First Nations peoples, there was opposition from federal and provincial governments to immigrants from specific source countries. This led to the creation of the 1910 Canadian Immigration Act, which prohibited the entry of "immigrants belonging to any race deemed unsuitable to the climate or requirements of Canada" (Malik 1996, 118). The Immigration Act of 1910 set the tone for immigration until the 1960s. A class of immigrants was created that was

> deemed undesirable because of climatic, industrial, social, educational, labour or other conditions or requirements of Canada, or because their customs, habits, modes of life and method of holding property were deemed to result in a probable inability to become readily assimilated. Selection would also be carried out on the basis of whether applicants belonged to "preferred" or "non-preferred" countries. (Malarek 1987, 11)

Canada's immigration policies have been discriminatory, reflecting the internal pressures within the nation's society. Between the Immigration Act of 1910 and the Immigration Act of 1952, the list of preferred countries underwent some adjustments, but the inherent basic discriminatory logic remained unchanged. Admittance continued to be prohibited on the basis of nationality, ethnic group, occupation, or class. This trend continued for several decades. From 1945 to 1962 Canada's immigration regulations were explicitly selective of Anglo-Europeans and largely excluded non-Europeans. Canada has historically had a tradition of recruiting immigrants from the United Kingdom, northern Europe, and the United States, while restricting those from Asia and the developing world. Perhaps in an attempt to divert attention from such blatantly racist policies, Canada's immigration policy of 1962 (formalized in 1967) was the first in the world to abolish all quotas or preferences on the basis of race, national origin, religion, or culture. Ethnicity and country of origin were replaced with education and training as the criteria for entry into Canada, which allowed for racialized immigrants of a higher class status to enter Canada. These new criteria were set in place to deracialize the selectivity that had previously characterized the immigration program. This supposed race-blind immigration policy employed a point system that established criteria based on personal attributes. Many non-Europeans from developing nations were encouraged to come to Canada. These immigrants tended to be better educated and from more urban backgrounds (Kobayashi 1993) than their predecessors, and they came from largely racialized nations, such as India, Pakistan, and countries in the West Indies.

Evident at this time, therefore, were dramatic changes in the composition of ethnic diversity in the country. Between 1945 and 1971 the majority of immigrants arrived from Europe – over 4.3 million individuals (Elliott and Fleras 1990). As the demographic shift quickened, the social landscape of the country, especially in the urban areas, began to change. The increasingly visible political actions of many noncharter ethnocultural groups, such as the Canadian Jewish Congress and Ukrainian Canadians, who worked to develop an "ethnic" political base (Yuzyk 1967), led to the coining of the term "third force." This referred to the sizable portion of the population that was neither French nor British.

In the light of this increased ethnic diversity and subsequent demands for cultural protection and social equality among ethnic groups, the Canadian government began to reappraise its relationship to ethnic minorities. It established the Royal Commission on Bilingualism and Biculturalism in 1962, originally in response to growing dissatisfaction and friction between the English and the French, without specifically setting out to explore ethnic relations in Canada. The commission was directed to approach its task in terms of one country, two languages (English and French), and two cultures (British and French), while acknowledging some vaguely defined contribution by the "others" (Hudson 1987, 63). Its goal was to identify a uniquely Canadian identity (Weinfeld 1985).

There remains considerable debate regarding the creation of the Royal Commission. In 1962 there was already a political movement in Quebec "actively seeking independence," which showed "the very fragile nature of Canadian Confederation at this time," so "providing additional fuel to an already simmering issue was avoided at all costs" (Ujimoto 1991, 138). Peter (1981, 81) argues that the very heart of the Royal Commission's report "obscured the French Canadian challenge to political power and deflected it into linguistic and cultural directions." He suggests that the policy of multiculturalism was used to legitimize the continued dominance of the ruling British-speaking elite at a time when its position in society was threatened by Quebec's claim to political power and by the economic and cultural vitality of other ethnic groups (ibid.). However, others illustrate that the Royal Commission provided an opportunity for ethnic groups to "force their issues onto an agenda designed to redefine the country. They were fundamentally challenging the idea of the French/English construct as the main contradiction ... and therefore the main plank on which the country should be redefined" (C. Joseph 1995, 27).

The political climate in Canada at this time was marked by the awareness that ethnic independent movements were active throughout the world. Quebec was already caught up in growing nationalism. As the Royal Commission carried out its task, it appeared to the Canadian government that "visible minorities" (a highly contestable term I will examine later in this chapter) should also have rights and government funding (Rex 1996). The commission gradually altered its focus as it ran into hostility in the western provinces, where second-, third-, and fourth-generation Ukrainian Canadians emphasized that they continued to be denied equal respect and opportunity because of their cultural heritage. As a result, the commission's mandate was extended to include the contributions of the other ethnic groups. These concerns of the commission were revealed in its report.

After tabulating its responses, the commission recommended a major extension of bilingualism to help alleviate the disharmony in English-French relations, conceiving of a bilingual framework within which other ethnic groups could prosper. Although the commission agreed to keep bilingualism as a national goal, it "modified its own terms of reference from biculturalism and argued for a multicultural policy" (Hudson 1987, 63) within a bilingual framework. It attempted to establish an ongoing dialogue between the government and minority groups, placing the participation of those groups on the political agenda. A contentious policy emerged that was designed to fit minority cultural differences into a workable national framework.

1971 Policy Statement on Multiculturalism

In 1971 Prime Minister Pierre Elliott Trudeau gave a speech to Parliament in which he outlined his government's responses to the commission's report:

> It was the view of the Royal Commission, shared by the government and I am sure, by all Canadians, that there cannot be one cultural policy for Canadians of British and French origin, another for the original peoples and yet a third for all others. For although there are two official languages, there is no official culture, nor does any ethnic group take precedence over any other. No citizen or group of citizens is other than Canadian, and all should be treated fairly ... adherence to one's ethnic group is influenced not so much by one's origin or mother tongue as by one's sense of belonging to the group ... the individual's freedom would be hampered if he were locked for life within a particular cultural compartment by the accident of birth or language. It is vital, therefore, that every Canadian, whatever his ethnic origin, be given a chance to learn at least one of the two languages in which his country conducts its official business and its politics ... a policy of multiculturalism within a bilingual framework commends itself ... as the most suitable means of assuring the cultural freedom of Canadians. Such a policy should help to break down discriminatory attitudes and cultural jealousies. National unity, if it is to mean anything in the deeply personal sense, must be founded on confidence in one's own individual identity; out of this can grow respect for that of others and a willingness to share ideas, attitudes and assumptions. A vigorous policy

of multiculturalism will help create this initial confidence. It can form the base of a society which is based on fair play for all. (Canada, House of Commons, *Debates,* 8 October 1971)

The official promotion of multiculturalism has been heralded as a turning point in Canadian history (Fleras and Elliott 1992). Trudeau (in McLeod 1981, 13) stated, "Canadian identity will not be undermined by multiculturalism. Indeed, we believe that cultural pluralism is the very essence of Canadian identity. Every ethnic group has the right to preserve and develop its own culture and values within the Canadian context." The policy recognized the political significance of those people who were not of British or French heritage. Multiculturalism, within the framework of official bilingualism, accentuated the need to maintain the cultural heritage of all groups within a multicultural population. It also established the right of members of "visible minority" groups to equality with members of the two charter groups of British and French ancestry. The dichotomy between language and cultural identity was emphasized. The cornerstone of the 1971 policy was, as Trudeau put it in his speech, "multiculturalism within a bilingual framework" – essentially what the Royal Commission had advised. Trudeau outlined four key ways that the government would implement its multicultural policy:

- Resources permitting, it would seek to assist all Canadian cultural groups that had demonstrated a desire and effort to continue to develop, a capacity to grow and contribute to Canada, and a clear need for assistance;
- It would assist members of all cultural groups to overcome cultural barriers to full participation in Canadian society;
- It would promote creative encounters and interchange among all Canadian cultural groups in the interest of national unity; and
- It would continue to assist immigrants to acquire at least one of Canada's official languages in order to become full participants in Canadian society. (Canada, House of Commons, *Debates,* 8 October 1971)

It is worthwhile to discuss some of the controversy surrounding Trudeau and the development of multicultural policy. As Gwyn (1996, 118) illustrates, "Today's Canada is Trudeau's Canada. Multiculturalism is his creation, reinjecting back into Canada the hyphens ... Trudeau seduced us ... [he] made his personal agenda the national agenda." Allan Smith (1994, 174) notes that "[multiculturalism] cannot be understood without some reference to the prime minister himself ... Trudeau's move to imbed the multicultural idea in federal policy thus reflected a strongly held conviction that the public power could not allow itself to become identified with promoting the interests of a particular segment of society." Ironically, any talk of multiculturalism is conspicuously absent from Trudeau's memoirs, whereas he devotes lengthy discussion and debate to questions of national unity. His imagining of multiculturalism insisted that the state indeed had a place in preserving the cultural heritage of its citizens. In fact, the development of official multiculturalism has been envisioned as a political ploy on the part of Trudeau to ensure another term in office by designing an attractive policy to lure in "the ethnic vote." In effect, the policy reflected his persona: charismatic, alluring, and magnetic. As Gwyn (1996, 183) argues, "The program only became real ... when looking for votes after his near-defeat in the 1972 election, Trudeau abruptly tripled multiculturalism's budget to $10 million. At the same time, his government started advertising heavily in ethnic newspapers."

In an effort to put these principles into practice, the government established several programs during the 1970s. There were courses to teach English and French to newly arrived immigrants and programs for Canadian ethnic studies in schools and universities. Multicultural grants were issued to support the development of various cultures and languages. Specific initiatives for language and culture maintenance received substantial government funding – reaching nearly $200 million between 1971 and 1990 (Elliott and Fleras 1990). A Multicultural Directorate was established within the Department for the Secretary of State in 1972 to promote social, cultural, and racial harmony. The Ministry of Multiculturalism was set up to monitor government departments, and the Canadian Consultative Council on Multiculturalism was devised in 1973. Five Canadian provinces eventually endorsed multiculturalism as official government policy with a variety of programs geared toward cultural awareness. Provincial and federal efforts to improve the access to and responsiveness of services for ethnic minorities resulted in a restructuring of various social institutions within education.

To aid in the elimination of discrimination, the Multicultural Directorate worked to enhance "intercultural and interracial understanding and the cultural integration of immigrants" (Peter 1981, 81). In 1973 federal government expenditures amounted to $10 million distributed to nearly 500 ethnic groups. Programs were designed to fund the development of voluntary ethnocultural organizations where groups could "celebrate" their diversity through folk festivals and the like. A cultural enrichment program was devised where individuals were encouraged to learn and retain minority "nonofficial" languages through heritage-language programs. Financial aid was channelled through the Department for the Secretary of State to particular ethnocultural groups in order to further the aims of the multicultural policy.

In general, multicultural policy encouraged individuals to voluntarily affiliate with the culture and tradition of their choice, supposedly without fear of discrimination or exclusion. Cultural differences were endorsed as imperative components of a national mosaic rather than being dismissed as incompatible with national goals. Ethnic differences were to be forged into a workable national framework (that of unity within diversity). This focus upon difference as unity was seen as a remarkable divergence from the conventional strategies of nation building. As Gwyn (1996, 187) notes, "For most Canadians throughout the 1970s and 1980s, multiculturalism became a synonym for tolerance. Since this by now had become central to their self-image, they supported the policy enthusiastically. Canadian nationalists often cited official multiculturalism as one of the characteristics, along with bilingualism, that made Canada distinct from the United States." In 1972 the number of immigrants allowed into Canada was 122,006. By 1973 this figure had risen to 184,200 and by 1974 to 218,465, the highest level ever (Elliott and Fleras 1990). Various reasons have been proposed for the increased immigration flows to the country. It has been observed that Canada, with its aging population and decline in birth rates (especially in Quebec), relies upon immigrants to ensure a steady population growth (S. Smith 1993). By 1981 the countries of origin of newly arriving immigrants had altered significantly. No longer predominantly European, 43 percent of immigrants entering Canada originated from Asia. The early 1980s witnessed further changes in immigration policies and restrictions. Due to the recession of the mid-1980s, the Canadian government decided to limit immigration levels, but wealthy immigrants were not refused entry if they were seen to be readily prepared to invest in the nation's future (ibid.). However, by the mid-1980s, immigration levels were actively increased in light of the evidence that fertility levels were below replacement value. From a low point of 85,000 admissions in 1985, immigration levels were projected to rise to over 175,000 by 1990 (ibid.). However, immigration figures have not yet reached the level they were for the first few years after the multicultural policy was announced.

Between 1981 and 1988 multicultural developments assumed an even higher profile in redefining government-ethnic relations (Elliott and Fleras 1990). Since 1971 only a statutory framework for government policy had existed. By 1988 Canada had developed a legislative base for multicultural initiatives, the Multicultural Act of 1988, which sought to promote cultures, reduce discrimination, and accelerate institutional change in order to reflect Canada's multicultural character. The Multicultural Act of 1988 attempted to recognize "the diversity of Canadians as regards race, national or ethnic origin, colour and religion as a fundamental characteristic of Canadian society and is committed to a policy of multiculturalism designed to preserve and enhance the multicultural heritage of Canadians while working to achieve the equality of all Canadians in the economic, social, cultural and political life of Canada" (Canada, House of Commons, *Debates,* 1988). This policy reflected a more radical critique of power relations, and legislative reform was intended to provide the basis for social change. There was an expansion of government spending in support of ethnic activities, and research funding was also significantly increased: in 1983-84 national grants amounted to $2.6 million (Hudson 1987). The Canadian Ethnocultural Council, founded in 1980 as an umbrella organization representing the political interests of over thirty organizations, played a significant role in redrafting the multicultural policy. This led to the Multicultural Act of 1988, which encouraged a shift from heritage issues to equality-rights issues (Kobayashi 1993). The Special Committee on Visible Minorities in Canada also made important recommendations, tabling its responses in the report *Equality Now!* (Canada, House of Commons 1984). Its eighty recommendations included a new framework for immigrant language training, increased funding for ethnic and racial organizations, and continued government support of multicultural sharing events (Hudson 1987).

In 1984 the parliamentary Standing Committee on Multiculturalism was formed to evaluate the policy's past achievements and future needs. In 1987 this committee made several recommendations, documenting the need for a strengthened policy. In essence, the committee emphasized that the [policy of 1971] is clearly insufficient and out of date ... The cultural industries and government programs are not doing enough to preserve and enhance our multicultural reality ... Multiculturalism can only be seen as something of a marginal policy ... The mainstream of Canadian society and institutions have yet to be "multiculturalized." (Canada, Standing Committee on Multiculturalism 1987)

The committee also recommended the creation of a separate Department of Multiculturalism and division of the Canadian Race Relations Foundation. The Standing Committee on Multiculturalism identified racism as a serious problem in Canada (Henry and Tator 1985) and recommended numerous ways that antiracist policies might be adopted (Kobayashi 1993). In 1988 the Race Relations Directorate was re-established and given directives to fund programs in the community, working with businesses, the police, and various forms of social services and government organizations.

To summarize, then, official multiculturalism has been promoted for a variety of social and political objectives, ranging from the elimination of discrimination to educating the public regarding the merits of cultural pluralism. Canada has transformed a descriptive fact and normative idea into an official ideology, as reflected in its government policies, programs, and practices.

Critiques Levelled at Multicultural Policy

> The limits of the policy overwhelm.
> — MCKITTRICK 2011, 1

Many insist that multicultural policy is not, and never will be, a substitute for antiracist legislation, despite the fact that it has often been seen as such. In reality, issues of ethnic inequality and racial discrimination have significant political and economic roots gnarled in the history of social institutions in Canada, going far beyond what multicultural policies can address. As Henry and Tator (1985, 329) argue, "Cultural solutions cannot solve non-cultural problems." Programs that support cultural retention will not successfully achieve racial harmony and equality. Despite the insistence that the present policy ought to go beyond the contradictions already institutionalized in the past, the Canadian government has not successfully moved beyond recognizing Canada as constituted of a diverse ethnic population. There is no firm commitment to bringing about antiracist objectives. The policy ignores the "more distressing image of racism occurring as a social relationship of dominance and subordination, created by and engendering structural inequality" (Kobayashi 1993, 222). Most disturbingly, policy documents refuse to clearly define the term "race," which illustrates how much more needs to be done if the processes of racial discrimination are to be fully understood. As Kobayashi (ibid., 221) argues,

> Nearly all [Canadian] government documents continue to treat "race" as an unproblematic category, naturally given rather than socially constructed. The objective, therefore, becomes that of overcoming discrimination, fostering equality regardless of "race." Such an objective only perpetuates the separation of human beings according to arbitrary phenotypical characteristics, instead of addressing the social processes by which races are created through an ideology of physical (or cultural) difference as the product, not of nature, but of racism itself.

Critics of multicultural policy insist that to address racial and ethnic justice, the policy must consider making some fundamental changes to the structures of society. As Kobayashi (ibid., 205) insists, the policy encourages a "symbolic" multiculturalism, where government programs recognize and promote multiculturalism without a firm commitment to bringing about its objectives. Racism cannot be eradicated through specific cultural retainment programs. These sorts of projects, which advocate an increased awareness and tolerance of racial diversity, imply that racism is simply a matter of attitudes rather than unveiling the systematic nature of discrimination. As a result, it is taken for granted outside of the country that in such a diverse nation with such a strongly funded multicultural policy, racism should be on the decline. However, as Barrett (1992, 199) states, "Racism in Canada has been institutionalized ... Racism in this country is as deeply rooted as that in the United States ... It remains puzzling how Canadians have been able to maintain a reputation for tolerance and harmony. What has characterized Canada has been an ostrich-like denial that a significant problem of racial hostility exists at all." One of the participants in this study, Makeda, provided an apt analogy in comparing American and Canadian race relations:

> [I have heard it said that] racism in this country is like a marshmallow ... which means if you try to hit and strike back, your fists and hands keep melting back into the mess. Whereas in the States it's kinda like a brick wall – you can feel it, all the time, and you know what you're striking.

I found this metaphor comically appealing, providing a shorthand to understanding how race works in Canada. Thompson (2010, 263) tells us that Canadians "are fundamentally uncomfortable with the notion of race. Our democratic conceptions of equality, social justice and citizenship demand that the superficial morphological and physiological characteristics used to distinguish supposedly distinct races matter not; the self-evident truth of the liberal ideal is that all are created equal." Thompson (ibid., 266) goes on to say that Canadians "avoid all language of race, preferring instead to use the kitten-hugging terminology of 'visible minorities' and 'multiculturalism.'" Thompson rightly points out that Canadians cling to a kind of moral superiority over the United States in refusing to admit that racism exists in Canada. As a policy, multiculturalism expresses the ideology of the nation as a unity of human difference, without unravelling how tensions arising from this difference can be managed (Malik 1996). In other words, there is a strong contradiction between multicultural policy's desire to celebrate difference, which represents an ideological commitment to equality, and the persistence of structural racism as a practical reality among Canadians. As a result, the perception of racial differences continues to arise out of the persistence of social inequality (ibid., 7). Dei (2007, 58) puts it another way: "Multiculturalism works with principles of symbolic equality at the expense of material and cultural equity."

If power is discussed, it is in relation to the notion of *visible minorities*. It ignores the fact that not all ethnic minorities are visible, encouraging the separation of some minority groups from others. Equally, one might be defined as a "visible minority" in some spaces and not in others. Notably, many other minorities not included in the concept are also visible, namely chronological minorities, such as the young and the old, and those who are clearly impoverished, not to mention those marked by gender differences. It is assumed that all members of a visible minority face the same experiences of racism, where differences are homogenized under the "visible minority" banner. The phrase defines visibility in terms of its relation to the invisible majority. However, ethnic identity is not limited to visibility, as it is also a matter of divisive politics. As Makeda pointed out,

> I think a large part of the pain are the problems that, you know, some or many mixed race people experience are not ... inherently the result of being mixed race but are the result of living in a society that makes that, in some cases, a hard thing to be.

McKittrick (2011, 1) puts it succinctly: "The policy in fact disavows race ... A national origin narrative emerges, with Canada firmly tied to a colonial framework wherein narratives of European settlement produce the conditions through which diversity is made possible." June Jordan (1992, 165) reminds us that "there is difference and there is power. And who holds the power decides the meaning of difference."

Some have called for the abolition of multiculturalism as official government policy, reasoning that it only encourages the ghettoization of ethnic groups, permitting immigrants to "indulge their nostalgic love for their mother countries ... far too fancy a piece of window-dressing for a government to get rid of" (Philip 1992, 186). Others have insisted that "it designates official, largely cosmetic government programs designed to placate the Quebecois, native Canadians, blacks, and Asians" (Stam 1997, 190). These sorts of critiques reflect public sentiment about the policy (Bissoondath 1994), and by 1998 the Department of Multiculturalism had merged with the Department of Canadian Heritage, the budget of official multiculturalism having been cut back significantly.

This section has attempted to clarify the ways that the Canadian government has processed multicultural ideals through a state-operated apparatus. The next section situates readings of the policy within the context of the lives of informants, examining multiculturalism as "a web of complex social relationships, a multiplicity of powers and constraints, [and] a shifting composition of cultural representation" (Kobayashi 1993, 223-24).

Despite the proliferation of research on particular ethnic groups in Canada, comparatively little research has been conducted on the Canadian public's perception of the multicultural policy. This is a deficiency because multiculturalism forms the backdrop against which much of the current research in ethnic studies becomes meaningful. Although several studies have explored the multiple meanings of multicultural policy among particular ethnic groups (see Bienvenue and Goldstein 1985; and Cryderman, O'Toole, and Fleras 1992), I chose to examine the meanings of multiculturalism for participants in this study. Given that these women were positioned as "ethnic" by the rules of the multicultural policy and, at the same time, often considered to be of European or French origin by virtue of their own mixed race backgrounds (many of the women were, for example, partly European and partly Asian), I was curious to unpack their readings of the policy in order to explore how it has provided a social framework within which individuals contemplate their own ethnic and national allegiances.

Some Mixed Race Women's Readings of Multicultural Policy

For some women in this study, the policy had produced discursive and material social spaces through which they negotiated both their ethnic and national alliances. They insisted that the policy compartmentalizes fluid and flexible senses of place and identity. I foreground the more opaque instances of exclusion subtly encouraged by the policy. Women in this study defined the Canadian "multicultural" project in very specific ways, demonstrating that although the term connotes nuances of diversity and equality, as a cultural representation, it carries a series of contradictions inherent in institutional processes in general. Although I did ask questions about multicultural policy, I soon discovered that multiculturalism was discussed only infrequently in the interviews. Conspicuously absent from the women's discussions were explorations of multicultural policy, especially as an antiracist mechanism. Instead, if the policy was discussed at all, it was described as an institutional project that funds and promotes staged ethnic representations, supporting the expression of and deliberation upon private forms of difference through food, family, and religious conventions. Many informants indicated that these events did not communicate any sense of the daily realities of their lives.

Naela, for example, made the distinction between the multicultural composition of Canada and the multicultural project through her clear distaste for the term "multiculturalism":

NAELA: I hate the word "multiculturalism."
MINELLE: Okay. Tell me why.

NAELA: Well to me, it's sort of like this government-created term to like make Canada into some pathetic attempt at patriotism, a way for people of colour to be able to look at Canada in patriotic ways? All I can see is this cheesy commercial with kids of different colours, holding hands? It just brings up this really kinda fake, superficial, "let's dance for each other, and make each other spring rolls to show how much we love each other!" sort of idea?! So I think that, but I don't feel that, I think that I really enjoy watching dance performances and eating food from different cultures, I mean I love it as much as anyone else does, and it's interesting. But that doesn't, that doesn't do anything in terms of racial biases or prejudices. It doesn't break any stereotypes or barriers. Like if anything it just perpetuates them because it sort of minimizes entire cultures! Into the dance and the food. So in that sense I hate it. But I do think multiculturalism, in terms of getting people in communities to live separately but as part of a larger society, I mean I agree, I can't imagine how else people would be able to do it. To be able to live?

Naela emphasized that multicultural policy, driven by an inauthentic celebration of heritage and tradition, is not successful in eradicating racism in Canada. Inequality of opportunities and stratification continue to be tolerated, endorsed, and promoted on the basis of racial and ethnic origins through government-funded celebrations of cultural traditions. Policies that aim to offer equality regardless of race often actively perpetuate the notion of natural racial difference, from which racism and discrimination take their moral and intellectual force. As Naela suggested, the celebration of particular stereotypical snapshots of ethnic cultures sanitizes cultural differences. By preserving these differences in the form of segregated ethnicities, the Canadian cultural mosaic of multiculturalism preserves biases by assuming that each and every ethnic group is a monolith of particular views and interests. In other words, some participants found themselves essentialized in racial and national terms.

Chantal too contended that we are a far cry from witnessing the prospects for a true multicultural society. She insisted that we are seeing just the opposite: a disturbing trend toward ethnic and regional fragmentation, which again points out the contradictions between multiculturalism as a project and what she described seeing on the streets of Toronto:

> I don't see a lot of multiculturalism here. I see a lot of different people here. But people ultimately gravitate and keep to themselves. So it's kinda fraudulent. I think it's a nice idea, I think it's a theory, I think it's something that is often attached to Canada, but we're not living it – because I don't socialize with Chinese people, I don't socialize with a lot of different people, even though they're outside my door. Right? It's a misconception that that is a fact that we have here. Because the term implies people living amongst each other, coexisting, it implies an integrated society. And we do not live, and that's why you have Chinatown, Little Italy. And you have. You know, that's not multiculturalism. That's segregation. They're different things. And I don't think we're learning from living among each other. Because we're not. So in other words, Chinatown can be down the street, and I also go to Chinatown because I can go in, quite freely, and I go to Kensington Market, and go to the fish market, or whatever, I'm not learning. My mind isn't being opened. I'm not learning about Chinese culture [just] because Chinese families live there. And to me, multiculturalism implies that it's the sharing of information, and that we're all made more aware? Because we live amongst each other? But that presumes that we do in fact live amongst each other. And we don't. We don't socialize that way, we don't ... It's a lie, basically. (laughter)

Chantal saw through the superficialities of celebrating cultural diversity and went on to argue that multicultural policy can serve to camouflage underlying racial animosities. Both Chantal and Naela perceived the government policy of multiculturalism as reinforcing crude cultural stereotypes. They doubted that the policy had had an impact upon decreasing racism in Canada.

Marical also addressed multicultural policy, explaining her political reservations with it:

> As an official policy? I mean oh I don't know. I mean multiculturalism is just the way people live in this city. People just try to get along and you know whatever you look like, or poor, rich, I mean if you go to borrow a cup of sugar from the person next door, they might look at you weird and not understand you or try to figure out what language ... but you know they'll lend you the cup of sugar and then they'll try

to figure out whose turn it is to shovel the front lawn and you know that kind of thing. People just try to get along. So that to me is what multiculturalism is. And when you start defining it by politics and ... I'm wary of that because that becomes power, and it becomes in people's interest to, you know, to get everybody identifying with a kind of tribalistic mentality, sort of beating from the same drum. And that just encourages tradition, I think, rather than unity. So official multiculturalism? I mean I like the idea that Canada promotes it so that it's seen as something that is a good thing. So encouraging, encouraging respect for cultures, I mean all cultures, I think is great. Whether ultimately it could be a policy that should yield some sort of political end at the end of the day, other than everybody just getting along, I, I, you know, I worry about that. I don't think it should be used as an end to anything. It should just be about getting along or learning more about each other's culture.

Apart from these three women, very few participants specifically addressed the policy of multiculturalism, even when questioned outright. Of course, we can't expect that all participants were familiar with the specifics of the policy per se. However, any question that I posed about multiculturalism invariably led to extended debate about how some participants found themselves positioned outside of national discourse, despite the project of multiculturalism, which insisted on bumper stickers like "Together, we're better!" National and racial discourses were inextricably intertwined in interviews in complicit ways. Women in this study voiced exasperation with the difficulty of identifying as Canadian. This was due partly to the emphasis that multicultural policy placed upon their ethnic allegiances.

Multicultural policy focuses upon ethnicity as a primary aspect of identification. Although this may have reflected the experience of those who immigrated to Canada decades ago, the majority of participants in this study grew up alongside the emergence of this policy and saw ethnicity as only one of the many factors that framed their sense of self. Ethnic identity, especially among mixed race women, is complex and incorporates many components, including parental heritage, racial and cultural affiliations, and religion. Their situationality and locality become key sociopolitical signifiers of their "ethnic place" in the Canadian landscape. As Zenia said,

> I was born in Montreal; therefore, I'm a Montrealer. That's how I look at it. You know, my parents, my mom's from Norway and my dad's from Sri Lanka, and they're twentieth generations of Norwegian and Sri Lankan respectively, you know. But that doesn't make a difference because that doesn't ... That's not who I am.

Zenia read her identity as more than the sum of her ethnic parts. The specifics of her identity did not mould neatly into a form suitable for multicultural display. As Bissoondath (1994, 211) argues, "multiculturalism effectively stultifies the personality, creating stereotype, stripping the individual of uniqueness." With its emphasis upon ethnicity, multiculturalism reduced Zenia's identity to her ethnic constituency. The experience of occupying a doubled space in two ethnic cultures complicates any simplistic reading of ethnicity within multicultural policy, as mixed race women have a vast array of ethnic allegiances. I suggest that mixed race women in this study often shrugged off the chain-like restraints of ethnicity as defined by the multicultural policy. Their experiences of ethnicity tell a far more complex story.

Marical, for example, suggested that multicultural policy confused questions about her many ethnic allegiances:

> You know, is your history your family? Or is it, you know, are you a product of your family history or are you just your geography or how you were educated or what your immediate values are? Like how much of your past is part of you? I guess that's the question.

Multicultural policy's focus on an individual's ethnicity places emphasis upon the importance of the past. In Marical's case, her identity was defined by her parents' origins rather than by her own current set of ethnic allegiances. There are myriad factors that contribute to an individual's sense of ethnic identity, which changes over the course of a lifetime and through various geographical spaces. These identifications are rarely static – but multicultural policy would have us believe that they are.

Moreover, multicultural policy constructs socio-spatial boundaries between the identifications of "Canadian" and "non-Canadian." I wish to remind the reader of Trudeau's statement that "every ethnic group has the right to preserve and develop its own culture and values within the Canadian context" (in McLeod 1981, 13). The phrase "within the Canadian context" is cause for concern. Multicultural policy advocates a strangely paradoxical position. On the one hand, it insists that all Canadians deservedly have the right to preserve their ethnic heritage. On the other hand, this liberal notion tends to veil the assumption among citizens that there is such a thing as a discrete "capital-C Canadian" society that exists more or less independently of ethnic groups and to whose development ethnic groups are encouraged to make their various contributions. This concept was illuminated through many narratives around the theme of who is considered a *real* Canadian (see Mackey 2002). If I did ask a question about multiculturalism, it inevitably led to discussions about the difficulties of identifying as Canadian in what participants read as their own country. According to the women interviewed, an "authentic" Canadian is still based on the centrality of British and French stock – those "real" Canadians who are part of a "capital-C Canadian" society. Both of these identities are read as white, or European. Subsequently, mixed race women continue to be positioned as outsiders, excluded from the national discourse, despite the goals of the multicultural project. The process of control in the form of multicultural policy is manifested in the exclusion of individuals who are deemed marginal. Racism subtly penetrates the national discourse, where those who are positioned as ethnic as designated by the policy are thus recognized as outside of Canadianness. Julia summarized the issue as follows:

> I mean "Canadian" is very much a white definition. I mean that's why people question me when I say I'm Canadian and they don't see me as being white. If they don't accept that as an answer, then they're not seeing me as white, and I guess the Canadian definition is very much a white one. Look at who's in power, look at who's running Bay Street. It's all white guys. How many people of colour are there in the House of Commons? How many women are there in the House of Commons?

Julia's narrative reveals the ubiquitous nature of racism (not to mention sexism) and how it bleeds into dominant readings of the national rhetoric. I am reminded here of the work of Eisenstein (1996, 15), who insists that "no nationalism can fully include a multiracial/woman-specified democracy." Those with particular phenotypes – or those categorized under the rubric of "visible minority" status – are excluded from the dominant discourse of Canadianness. In other words, you're "not quite [Canadian] if you're not white" (Kondo 1997, 93). As noted below, Julia further explained how the underpinnings of the question "Where are you from?" assumed her foreignness. This question is a loaded one for people of mixed race identity. Hill (2001, 173-77) provides a humorous yet insightful commentary on what he calls "The Question":

> Canadians have a favourite pastime, and they don't even realize it. They like to ask – they absolutely have to ask – where you are from if you don't look convincingly white ... Do you suppose that ... strangers will ask an indisputably white Canadian with a traditional Anglo-Canadian accent where he is from, where he was born, or where his parents were born? Absolutely not. Strangers will assume that he is a true Canadian, and leave that part of his identity unmolested. The offence-causing kernel at the heart of this interrogation is its implication: "You are not white, you don't look like me, so you're clearly not Canadian." It also suggests "Since you're clearly not Canadian, and I am, I am within my rights to ask you just exactly where you're from."

In a country where ethnic differences between citizens are always racialized, it becomes increasingly complicated to identify as Canadian when you are mixed race. As Julia explained,

> I've gone to the point where I feel like when people ask me if I'm mixed and they're not happy with the response or they ask me where I'm from and they're not happy with the response "I'm Canadian," I feel like turning around and asking them, "Well, what the hell are you? Are you Canadian? What makes you more Canadian than me that you would question the fact that I'm Canadian?" Because that's obviously not the response they were wanting. But you know it's like, well, you asked me a stupid question, I'll give you a stupid answer.

Julia was understandably resentful because she was excluded from the discourse of the state, where forms of national identity are exclusionary, homogeneous, and unitary. When Julia told others, "I'm Canadian," she discovered that her response was interrogated, her identity distanced, and her phenotype exoticized as different. For her to identify as Canadian seemed insufficient and almost unacceptable to her interrogators. In the process of deliberately identifying herself as Canadian to deflect the question "Where are you from?" Julia refused to conform to prescriptive racial categories, creating new meanings of nation during social interactions. However, Julia still had to struggle to assert her desire to identify as Canadian and was vigorously interrogated, frequently challenged, and often rejected when she did so.

Finally, I further problematize how ethnic and national positionings in Canada are entangled by looking at how the multicultural policy produces spaces of distance through the hyphen. As I mentioned earlier, multicultural policy advocates that immigrants in Canada should privilege their ethnic identity and make their individual contribution to the Canadian mosaic. As Gwyn (1996, 234) asserts, "The absurdity here is that no one from Italy, say, or Somalia, comes to Canada to be an Italian or Somali. They come here to be Canadian. As soon as they landed, though, their new state in effect tells them that rather than becoming Canadians they must remain Italian-Canadians, Somali-Canadians, and so on." These hyphens of multiculturalism produce spaces of distance that position ethnicity outside Canadianness – not only as an addition to it but also as an exclusion from it. In contrast, the American melting pot ideology discourages hyphenation. The metaphor of the melting pot suggests various immigration groups blending together with the existing culture to form a new and different culture. The idea that each cultural group has an effect on the end product encourages the adoption of an all-American national identity. This is not to assume, of course, that racism is successfully eradicated as a result.

Akari suggested that it becomes impossible to position oneself as solely Canadian without announcing one's exoticized ethnic identity:

> I wouldn't just say I'm Canadian and that's it. Because I mean just the fact for me to even say when someone's asked me, what are you, the fact that if I say Canadian, that doesn't satisfy them. That just tells you right there, like you know what I mean? It's not possible to be just Canadian and no race. Like I couldn't realistically live in Canada and think that way.

Akari found it difficult to claim a national identity without being required to declare her ethnic allegiances. The policy of multiculturalism is reassuring to those who vigilantly patrol the borders between ethnic and national belonging. In effect, the state encourages the maintenance of an apartheid form of differentiated citizenship. The burden of hyphenation, where one is seen as not solely "Canadian" but "Canadian and fill-in-your-ethnic-background," is especially heavy for women of mixed race, who further trouble the hyphen by employing and intermingling two or more ethnicities in their own definitions of their identities through the coining of labels like "African-Persian-Cherokee-European-Canadian." The mixed race person resists the occupation of a single ethnic space. This stance makes the process of self-definition lengthy and exhausting, requiring a whole geography and history of explanation. Faith commented,

> I think that's why sometimes I hate discussing it when people ask [where are you from] because I can't just say one thing. Like you can't just say you're Canadian and have people understand, oh you're Canadian, or whatever. I always have to go into this lengthy explanation about Chinese, Polynesian, and then British. Then there's the whole thing about oh well where were your parents born? And it's like Fiji, and then that goes into that whole Fiji thing. And no, I'm not Fijian. But you're from there. No, my mother was born there physically, but it's like. Which brings me, if I think about it, full space to here. Well, I was born in Canada, so I am Canadian, but what is Canadian? AAARGH! It drives me crazy! And it's just like this whole, long – I'm not just one simple thing.

The hyphen marks a distance from potential claims to nation. It is a troubling symbol that refuses to admit the possibility of the commingling of ethnicities and national citizenship, compounding difference as a "property marker, a boundary post, a knot, a chain, a bridge, a foreign word, a nomadic, floating magic carpet" (Wah 1996, 60). This study's participants inhabited this space of the hyphen, where difference is continually expropriated. The hyphen holds a particular tension, articulating a union of contradictions, each word symbolizing the inverted contradiction of the other. Consequently, the hyphen marks places of ambiguity and multiplicity. More attention needs to be paid to the hyphen itself rather than to the words – and subsequent places – on either side of it.

Kiirti further demonstrated the frustrations and paradoxes inherent in the desire to identify as Canadian, pointing out the problematic nature of attempts to do so:

> I mean I hate the fact that people ask me where I'm from. And I'll say I'm Canadian. And they say, "No no no no no, but where are you FROM?" "I'm from HERE." "No no no, but where are you FROM?" And I'll say, "Fine, you want to know? I'll tell you." And I'll tell them

ALL the different places my parents are from, and then they'll say, "Oh, so you're Canadian." They DO! And it's like, "GO AWAY!"

Kiirti's comment neatly encapsulates the messy contradictions of assuming a Canadian identity. The very constituency of the social fabric of Canada is a reflection of its diverse ethnic population, which has been read as intrinsically "Canadian" outside the country (see Elliott and Fleras 1990). However, it becomes impossible to identify as Canadian within the country, in spite of the country's diversity, given that when one questions national borders, one also questions the boundary markers of race. Thus it is repeatedly revealed that hegemonic national discourses do not take kindly to those who inhabit marginal spaces – especially mixed race women, who might be seen as "the double foreigner, the double stranger ... held up to the phantasmic and found doubly wanting" (Eisenstein 1996, 41).

I believe that racist ideologies underlying dominant discourses about the nation further confuse ideas around the nebulous nature of Canadian identity. Indeed, reverberating through many of my interviews were inquiries into who Canadians *really* are and what binds us together. This question is one that we visit and revisit, reflecting the ebb and flow of Canadian national being in the shadow of the Americans, who seem absolutely certain of who they are. The conception of citizenship suggested by multicultural policy demands a model of homogeneous people that is not representative of the complex and diverse ethnic composition of the country. In the next section, I show how informants challenged and contested socially constructed categories of Canadian identity outside of the "two solitudes" (C. Taylor 1993, 1) by developing new constitutions of cultural citizenship. I then point out the privilege that comes from being able to identify in this way through a discussion of what I call the *model multiracial*.

The Model Multiracial: Moving from Individually Identified Bodies to the National Body Politic

> Don't you know who I am? I am an individual!
>
> — OBAMA 2004, 100, WHERE BARACK OBAMA MOCKS A MIXED RACE WOMAN AND PROVIDES A SCATHING INDICTMENT OF HER, SUGGESTING THAT SHE AVOIDS BLACK PEOPLE (SEE ALSO McNEIL 2010)

> Whether multiracial identity, consciousness and organization will seriously subvert or merely reinforce racial hierarchy ... remains very much an open question.
>
> — OMI AND WINANT 2012, 312

This section of the chapter attempts to address how mixed race women in this study imagined themselves as part of the Canadian nation-state. For many women in this study, questions of national belonging still figured predominantly. I am reminded of Philip's (1992, 16) powerful words:

> I carry a Canadian passport: I, therefore, am Canadian. How am I Canadian, though, above and beyond the narrow legalistic definition of being the bearer of a Canadian passport; and does the racism of Canadian society present an absolute barrier to those of us who are differently coloured ever belonging? Because that is, in fact, what we are speaking about – how to belong – not only in the legal and civic sense of carrying a Canadian passport, but also in another sense of feeling at "home" and at ease. It is only in belonging that we will eventually become Canadian.

How is there a seductive pleasure of belonging within and affiliated to the nation-state for some mixed race women? Clarke (2011, 55) proposes, "I think it would be healthy for Canada to declare itself to be, not only multicultural, but a nation respecting hybridity, I mean, métissage – the intermingling and intermarrying of people of many different cultures and backgrounds ... It would emphasize that we are, in every way, a 'rainbow' people, further dethroning the current ethnocentric leadership." I unravel how informants thought "affectionately" (Said 1991, 116) about the politics of national allegiances by trying to capture some of their explanations of their everyday experiences of the nation. In their minds, these affiliations confounded the dominant definition of the national narrative. Informants offered their own alternatives to the dominant national constructions. Some women of mixed race read their own mixed race status as compatible with contemplations of national identity. For some mixed race women, a futuristic reading of Canadian identity would move beyond definitions based on European or French descent. For them, this would displace and shift the terms of a nationalism linked to European and French origins. By opening up the term "Canadian" to scrutiny, participants reformulated the conventional meanings associated with the phrase. As Makeda said,

> I think that "Canadian," as a term, has a certain reference to a certain kinda person. And I'd LOVE to have that category opened up. So that people can say "Canadian" and imagine all sorts of different people. Right? I'm not making a bid for an amnesiac Canada that can suddenly embrace its own diversity and forget its past transgressions. I think they both have to occur. Canada has to come to terms with, and it doesn't have agency, but all those things that comprise Canada, the stories have to be able to address all those people and those histories. And I think that I want to be part of that project. Because it seems to me to feel very exciting? It feels very exciting when someone like Shyman Shulvydera [Shyam Selvadurai], who wrote *Funny Boy*, wins a prize, not because he's winning the prize but because he can stand up and say, "I want to say something about refugee policy because now I wouldn't even be able to come into this country," right? So as you're lauding this cultural contribution, think of all the other cultural contributions they're disallowing by setting up these prohibitive reform policies. Right? So I think that in that way, I would like to be part of redefining Canada. I think Canada is a country that can continually open itself up to new people.

As Makeda explained, the act of claiming a Canadian identity for her would have meant the occupation of a distinctly contradictory space, where one can both embrace a sense of country and unveil the exclusion of specific histories of oppression and resistance. This transformation of the term "Canadian" would include an unpacking of the embedded racist history of the country. Makeda's thoughts on the subject are in line with S. Hall's (1997, 184) suggestion that appropriating the term would include unmasking the hidden histories of the majority, and "histories without the majority," in an "attempt to snatch from the hidden histories another place to stand in, another place to speak from." Thus this tortured past would become part of the present, informing and playing a part in the creation of Makeda's sense of national identity. In reading the present in terms of the past, because the past has never been fully transcended, Makeda proposed the occupation of a space where she could finally be proud to belong. The voices of the marginalized are actively centred as part of a reimagined citizenship. McKittrick (2011, 2) states, "Waiting for our multicultural future must include those practices of racial violence that have provided, and continue to provide, the grounds through which we anticipate a different future."

Marical also explained that a new identification of Canadian would include a diverse range of racialized voices beyond a government-institutionalized program of multiculturalism that funds superficial celebrations promoting "sari and samosa" stereotypes:

> I think that in Canada there is hope to be like "I am Canadian" means not just like multi-culti-folklorama crap. Okay, not just like, you know, Heritage Canada a minute, you know, or whatever the hell it is. But some kind of genuine recognition that this country is made up of a lot of different people and a lot of different-looking people, you know.

Although Marical was skeptical about belonging as constituted within national categories, some informants read their own mixed race identity as a model for an optimistic Canadian citizenship where their ethnicities were not necessarily compartmentalized. As I have mentioned, multiculturalism in Canada confuses issues of ethnicity and nationalism by treating ethnicities as clearly divisible, dichotomous, and nonoverlapping categories outside of Canadianness. However, some mixed race women continually experience ethnicities as overlapping layers. Some women see themselves as being in an excellent position to take on the additional challenges of developing a multicultural identity seemingly compatible with Canadianness by challenging assumptions about racial and ethnic purity. For Darius, questions about her mixed race were influenced largely by her own sense of nationalism and vice versa, with her own mixed race being read as a positive position from which to experience the nation:

> I think being Canadian, Canada is really on this frontier of racial miscegenation, so I don't really separate [my ethnic and national identities]. I see myself as being Canadian and being mixed race. A lot more than someone perhaps that see themselves as monoracial, someone who was full-blooded Korean, and their parents were from Korea, and they lived in Canada, but they grew up speaking English all the time, I think it's probably even more of a challenge for them. To me, for me, being Canadian and being mixed race, and the issues around identity there, are not at odds with each other. They are related in a way. If I had stronger cultural experiences, it might be more difficult.

Clearly, for some mixed race women, being mixed race is not necessarily incompatible with Canadian identity. What conditions do the discursive practices of multiculturalism produce that allow this perspective to flourish? Walcott (2008) helps to elucidate this issue by pointing out that the 1960s and 1970s offered an opportunity for the nation to rethink questions of race in both the United States and Canada, with a different outcome for each: "While the racial tension relinquished somewhat [in Canada], what came into its place was a skillful selection of *individual persons as representatives* for the Black community in a newly re-imagined multicultural Canada; these persons' selection was never sustained, nor were they the route or the mechanism to serious avenues for advancement, so that others might have similar opportunities" (my emphasis).

Many of the women interviewed intrinsically saw themselves as part of the Canadian polity – as instructive representative symbols for an optimistic Canadian citizenship. Darius explained that she identified as "Canadian" more than she did as any of her multiple ethnic parts. The term can be used to evoke images of home, which are often associated with the familial. She asserted herself as part of the dominant national discourse:

> See, I know I'm Canadian, there's no question about it. Whereas my mom, who is Japanese, full-blooded Japanese but third-generation Canadian, comes from a group of people that were interned in the war because they weren't Canadian, but had never necessarily been to Japan, you know? So maybe it was more of a difficulty and challenge for them to ask the question "Am I Canadian? What is Canadian?" For me, it's never really been an issue because I was born here, I have always lived here. I don't feel Japanese, and like I say I don't feel Japanese, or Native, or white. Really. Canadian to me is like a nationality. It's like where you were born. And that's really clear to me. It doesn't have anything to do with my racial identity ... Race isn't just blood quantum or skin colour. Or nationality. Or parentage, or experience. It's like something else, it's something more than all these other things! And who knows where it comes from!

Rani read her mixed race identity as harmonious with her national ties and insisted on calling herself mixed, which for her encapsulated not only her ethnic identity but her sense of citizenship as well:

> I think "mixed" is a flexible enough word. That it can catch a lot of people in its net. "Mixed background," "mixed heritage," I find most useful. I don't know why. But it is my heritage. And it's more than just ethnicity. It's the fact that I'm Canadian too. Kinda thing. It's all mixed up. Together.

Women of mixed race are used to names, labels, and categories imposed upon them by others. However, as Minh-ha (1989, 141) reminds us, "despite our desperate attempts to mend and maintain, categories always leak." To counteract this compulsion of classification, many mixed race women decide to identify as Canadian. However, it does not necessarily follow that in choosing this identification, they blindly follow the rules as advocated by the policy. Instead, for them, it seems to reflect their very real experience of growing up in Canada. Some mixed race women I talked to did not feel any particular kinship with any of their ethnicities, and many of their parents were second- or third-generation Canadian, having been born in Canada as well. The histories of their parents' racial legacies were not necessarily part of their experience.

Of course, it is impossible to deny the obvious cultural capital permeating these interviews. Walcott (2008) tells us that multiculturalism in Canada provided both a "promise and an interruption. The promise resided in a desire[d] recognition and a belief that equality was possible, especially as signalled through the inclusion of some singular and sometimes exceptional [Black] figures. The interruption located itself in the stalled and still stalemated desire to forge a Black national coherent community across the regions of the nation."

I want to be careful here not to conflate the black community and the mixed race community, as such a comparison is intensely problematic and erroneous at best. However, I see similarities in the way that some mixed race women are able to become symbols of the promise that Walcott discusses through their embodied presence in the Canadian social landscape. Participants believed that they deserved and were able to exercise their right to choose their own ethnic allegiances. Identifying as Canadian reflected social decisions on their part through a clear redefining of their own allegiances to nationhood. Yet it also reflected a political impotency that I explore in more detail in the next section.

Emma delineated her own definition of Canadian identity, revealing that she experienced both her national and various ethnic selves as constantly ephemeral and shifting on a day-to-day basis, depending upon her location:

> I was born in England and then we moved to Canada, which added a whole new layer of mixed race on it. So I always sort of like to quote a friend, who described herself as a salad of racial genes, you know, because she's just a little bit of everything. And in a way, that's maybe uniquely Canadian. There are so many people here that come from so many different cultures and especially in Toronto, which is where I grew up, that it's just, it's kind of typical of who we are. We're an immigrant country with an immigrant culture. [In Canada] you can define yourself however you want in a way that isn't necessarily associated with a certain set of cultural values. So my [national] identity has been just a mixture of all those factors.

Emma compounded questions of race and nation by insisting that moving from England as a mixed race immigrant imposed another layer of mixed race upon her identity. Some women of mixed race are active participants in shaping their own identities by altering others' perception of their place in Canada. But this only reasserts Canada as a diverse place, not as a place that truly welcomes newcomers. Emma wrote herself into the national discourse in particular ways, recalling a time when she deliberately chose to identify herself as Canadian in order to defy existing stereotypes related to her phenotype, a stance that reflected a defiant reappropriation of national identity:

> I remember in Washington a cab driver saying, "So where are you from?" "Oh I'm Canadian," I said, and then it went, "Where are you really from?" "Well I was born in England," I said, just to stymie him further because what he wanted to hear me say was, "Yeah my father's half-Chinese." He wanted to be able to identify me with a racial group. Which I just refuse to be identified with – like either-or, you know? The closest I want to be identified to these kinds of cultural stereotypes is to say I'm Canadian, which defies pretty much all stereotypes because there's nothing really identifiable about it.

Emma employed the term "Canadian" as a foil when describing herself in this situation, forcing another to think about his racist assumptions about what defined a real Canadian. By refusing to be identified with a racial group, Emma resisted definitions of ethnic identity that reinscribe conventional notions of traditional culture. Her version of national allegiance refigured "Canadian" as a more useful "catchall" phrase because it is nebulous, recognizing that one need not be European to be Canadian. However, there is another way of reading this experience, which I explore in the next section. Similarly, Shima also reappropriated the term "Canadian," reading it as a label that reflected her multiple identifications:

> I feel Canadian. I think that I'm certainly more Canadian than – I don't feel Scottish. I feel like I have some connections there. I did live there. I also feel like I have connections with India. It's not romanticized in a way that I think I'm going to go there and find acceptance. I think when I was younger I might have thought that. But I do feel Canadian. I think Canadian is about struggling with these questions.

For Shima, being Canadian meant constantly struggling to negotiate her various identities, reflecting Pierre Elliott Trudeau's comment that "national unity, if it is to mean anything in the deeply personal sense, must be founded on confidence in one's own individual identity" (Canada, House of Commons, *Debates,* 8 October 1971). Being Canadian, for many mixed race women in Canada, means questioning any notion of a coherent, stable, and autonomous identity – either national or ethnic. As Sara suggested,

> I think [being mixed race] is very typically Canadian. I mean, all I've seen of Canadians are different racial groups. So I think that it's only natural that there would be a very big mixed population. So I think it typifies being Canadian. That's perfectly in tune with that.

The social and ethnic constituency of Canada paralleled Sara's own mixed race identity. Identifying with nationalism did not necessarily mean the subsequent adherence to ethnic stereotypes as dictated by the policy of multiculturalism. These women's interpretations of what constituted difference were constantly shifting, socially constructed, and geographically diverse. They pointed out the popular misconception that being Canadian means being solely of either European or French descent by designating their Canadian identity as a site for the recognition of complex national and ethnic allegiances, acknowledging the wide variance within ethnic groups.

For Faith, claiming Canadian status meant going beyond the legalistic definition of possessing a Canadian passport. It meant experiencing a sense of home:

> I have a very weird hang-up about [being asked, "Where are you from?"]. When they ask, it's like, I'm from Canada. Like, where was I born, where do I fit, what is my country of affiliation? It's Canada. Absolutely. And that's another thing that really irritates me about the whole thing about Canada, when people say where we're from, people respond, "I'm from Czechoslovakia." Well, no you're not! You have a Canadian passport, you're Canadian, with Czechoslovakian heritage. Like I HATE that. Like I'M Canadian. Yes, I have a variety of roots! But like my experience is Canada. Like I HATE this whole thing, all these people who think they're other things. Especially if you're born here. I'm sorry, but you're Canadian.

Faith had a clear sense of home and belonging in Canada and her identity was closely linked to questions of national identity, marking the connection between geography and culture. This connection between home and identity is not just an attachment to the abstract concept of nation. Kiirti, who was adopted, revealed how she felt when she discovered her parents' individual ethnic identities and expressed how that had an impact upon her own sense of country:

> I mean once I knew, once I knew where everybody was from, whatever, and there was massive mix, not only that mix, how could I then deny the people that I had grown up with? And all of the experiences that I had had, and I was such a mixture that truly WHO WAS I? I am Canadian, this is where I am born, this is the culture that I know, and my mother forever and my father forever telling me how CANADIAN I am, and my accent, and, my Canadianisms, and God forbid, I say "eh?"! I mean, they're ON me! (chuckle) I am ... It's like that commercial! I-AM-A-CANADIAN. That's what I am. And how could I possibly be anything else? I couldn't. Too many things to choose from. And this sounds so patriotic, but that is what makes Canadians. And, and. Sort of my God! Alright! Well, now I'm decided! I should be the new symbol for Canada! I am one big melting pot of stuff! I'm a stew! A big Canadian stew! (laughter)

Kiirti read her mixed race identity as a model for Canadian citizenship. She explained how her body was marked by her own sense of Canadianness, reflected in her accent and her "Canadianisms." She refused to renounce her Canadian identity in the name of a compartmentalized ethnic identity, given the variety of her ethnic mixes, and emphasized the salience of her own experiences growing up in Canada. In the excerpt, Kiirti was referring to a series of Canadian beer commercials, where the viewer is bombarded with numerous Canadian icons, including the maple leaf and prominent Canadian road signs, over a soundtrack of Canadian rock music. At the time of the interview, these commercials were inundating the airwaves. I draw the reader's attention to Mukherjee's (1994, 72) insistence that "when we non-white Canadians watch beer commercials, we never fail to notice our absence there." Yet Kiirti drew a comparison between her own sense of nationalism and these commercials, despite the lack of a nonwhite presence in the advertisements. As I gestured to in the introduction to this chapter, Kiirti's commentary stressed neutrality, and as Ibrahim (2012, xxvii) tells us, "the appearance of neutrality is required to produce particular forms of racial visibility."

Is the Model Multiracial Progressive?

> Do mixed race persons symbolize positive political values or problematic ones?
>
> — ALCOFF 2006, 265

How might we more critically contextualize these optimistic commentaries among some mixed race women who see themselves as quintessentially Canadian? It is worthwhile revisiting some of their comments before embarking upon a different reading. Let me return to their interviews briefly to refresh the reader's memory:

> Being Canadian and being mixed race ... are not at odds with each other. They are related in a way. *If I had stronger cultural experiences, it might be more difficult.* (Darius, my emphasis)

> [In Canada] you can define yourself however you want *in a way that isn't necessarily associated with a set of cultural values.* (Emma, my emphasis)

> See, I know I'm Canadian, *there's no question about it* ... It doesn't have anything to do with my racial identity. (Darius, my emphasis)

> "Mixed" is ... most useful ... It's the fact that I'm Canadian too ... *It's all mixed up. Together.* (Rani, my emphasis)

> The closest I want to be identified to these kinds of cultural stereotypes is to say I'm Canadian, which defies pretty much all stereotypes because *there's nothing really identifiable about it.* (Emma, my emphasis)

> I think [being mixed race] is very typically Canadian. (Sara)

> I'm a stew! A big Canadian stew! (Kiirti)

Some of the women spoke passionately about seeing a relationship between identifying as mixed race and identifying as Canadian. Although some of the women imagined themselves as embodying positive and progressive political values, we must ask whether these values can also be seen as problematic. Alcoff's question on the previous page reverberates. How is the mixed race body deployed in the Canadian context to allow a form of *neoliberal multiculturalism* to thrive? In the excerpts above, what struck me most plainly was the social and class privilege threaded throughout them. In turn, I am reminded of Andrea Smith's (2012, 75) words: "The consequence of not developing a critical apparatus for intersecting all the logics of white supremacy, including settler colonialism, is that it prevents us from imagining an alternative to the racial state."

In this section of the chapter, I suggest that a complicit relationship emerges between multiculturalism, neoliberal diversity (as a mechanism of both urban and national governance), and the mixed race body. I borrow heavily from the work of McNeil (2012, 1), who suggests that "transnational intellectuals in their critique of forms of neoliberal multiculturalism ... privilege the multicultural American citizen as a subject more universal and legitimate than even the multicultural world citizen." Whether used to name a concept or used as a description, "neoliberalism" remains a rather slippery term (see Roberts and Mahtani 2010). McNeil (2012, 3) explains that neoliberalism "can be deployed to address a period decisively shaped by a cultural, political and economic project based on the idea that the free market is capable of acting as a guide for all human action and protecting a minimal package of minority cultural rights."

Neoliberalism tells the story of a self-sufficient, autonomous person who can conveniently detach from historical and cultural precursors to pursue a self-interested project of unencumbered freedom, options, and opportunities. In the Introduction I remarked that a particular form of experiencing multiraciality relies upon a kind of strategic forgetting. Many of the women interviewed seemed to be able to disconnect from historic racial matrices in order to focus on their own individualized experience of history, drawing from their personal pasts to envision an optimistic and progressive future of racial harmony. Significantly, few of the women, apart from Makeda, made reference to Canada's imperializing and colonizing racial formations. Although they shared their own personal and varied experiences of racism, few participants made mention of Canada's history as a white-settler society, and Indigeneity was rarely mentioned. These women did not necessarily see themselves situated within socially and historically colonized and racialized matrices but preferred to locate themselves within the state-prescribed structures that allowed some of them to identify with embodying the nation. How did this come to pass? I suggest that neoliberal influences on both the national and urban scales affected the gathering of interviews, encouraging a mainstream mode of subjecthood.

Mackey (2002, 101) reminds us that the diversity of cultures is often what is seen as making Canada unique, yet these differences are "framed as freedom of *individual* choice" (emphasis in original). This is a quintessential neoliberal quality. That some of the participants made a link between their individually identified bodies and the national body politic was perhaps not altogether unsurprising, given that the interview was meant to make space for them to reflect on their own individual histories. However, that some of them insisted on making a link between multiraciality and an optimistic model of the nation-state was curious to me. They saw the mere experience of identifying as mixed race as a progressive gesture toward building a new and improved democratic state apparatus.

Elam (2011, 9) suggests that "people who identify as mixed race are held up as self-evident physical testimony that the glorious post-race apocalypse is a natural evolution of the *democratic* experiment" (my emphasis). In a similar but not identical vein, McNeil (2012, 2) reminds us that "metaphors of infantile and commodified mixed-race objects are invariably present in texts that support and critique corporate visions of multiculturalism." As I suggested in the Introduction and in Chapter 1, the progressive qualities of identifying as multiracial are more apparent than real (see Makalani 2001). They do not speed up the demise of racism, despite their attempts to transform what have been regarded as cultural defects (the era of pathology) into cultural virtues (the era of celebration). McNeil (2012, 4) states, "Some scholars who announced the dawn of critical mixed-race studies in the late twentieth and early twenty-first centuries challenged forms of neoliberal governmentality that repressed discussions of institutionalized racism and eradicated all explicit discussions of race in public." The voices of mixed race women tend to follow a similar pattern of submerging questions of antiracism and forms of institutionalized racism.

Let me draw from Kiirti's story to make my point clear. By seeing herself as a new figure for Canada, Kiirti saw herself as a kind of racial trailblazer. She offered her mixed race body up as a quintessential model for Canadian identity, without the messy and fraught politics that can accompany antiracism. In this way, the mixed race person can occupy a uniquely paradoxical position of being saturated with racial dimensions while maintaining a particular racelessness, what we might call a racial impotency. She is able to identify as a kind of poster child for Canada and multiculturalism. She articulates her own individual sense of empowerment "within and through the rhetoric of possessive individualism" (Elam 2011, 13). It is easy to see the mixed race person in Toronto in particular as the model Canadian citizen. Signifying multiple cultural and linguistic competencies across racial divisions, she is a multifaceted cultural ambassador for our times, a signal of lucrative transnational market competitiveness and success (see DaCosta 2007). But this exalted status (Thobani 2007) is available only to certain racially identified mixed race bodies – individuals who present a particular phenotype as racially ambiguous. Elam (2011, 24) suggests that those who look racially ambiguous are the most successful poster children for multiraciality: "People who wish to self-identify but do not appear ambiguous – or ambiguous enough ... are less suited to serve as political representatives [of the multiracial movement]."

Toronto as the Neoliberal City

I want to return to situating participants' stories historically and geographically. In particular, how did circulating and deployed state discourses about national multiculturalism intersect with formally and informally circulating urban discourses about neoliberalism and diversity? I switch scales – from the national to the urban – to ask about the cultural cues these women took from living in Toronto.

One cannot discount the role that Toronto played as the dwelling place for these women. State policies of multiculturalism developed around notions of liberal inclusion in the 1970s were reconstituted to signal neoliberal market competitiveness in the 1990s and were articulated at the city level. The political context in the city during the time of the interviews – the mid-1990s – was fraught with neoliberal influences. Toronto is understood as one of the most diverse cities in the world, and diversity is its official doctrine (Boudreau, Keil, and Young 2009). This diversity storyline was capitalized upon in the early 1990s. With approximately half of its population made up of immigrants, Toronto continues to be seen as a transnational metropolis. Boudreau, Keil, and Young (ibid.) insist that Ontario in the mid-1990s was governed by a provincial bureaucracy that advanced an aggressive form of neoliberalization. In their view, manifestations of this neoliberalization included amalgamation and lean government, a global city strategy where Toronto bid for the Olympics, growing bourgeois urbanism, a rescaling of the urban imaginary through urban sprawl and suburban subdivisions, and new social disparities that were the partial result of cuts to welfare and workfare programs.

Although this book does not delve into the details of this dissociated form of governance, the government in power at this time and its accompanying policies on diversity provided a discursive context for the interviews. "Diversity" – as a buzzword, a tourist-trap advertising call, and a factual aspect of the city – offered a "rallying identity" (Boudreau, Keil, and Young 2009, 34) in a postamalgamated City Hall and in the city more broadly. The new amalgamated city employed a promotional motto, "Diversity: Our Strength," which was scrawled on bumper stickers and seen readily protruding from any city cab. Boudreau, Keil, and Young (ibid.) persuasively claim that commodifying diversity in this way not only allowed the city to consolidate a postamalgamation identity but also provided a way for the city to empower itself within a global metropolitan scene, giving it traction in international economic and geopolitical spaces. Thus the city's diversity was sold as a major competitive international advantage around the world. Under this veneer lay a city divided by ongoing and increasing demographic racial rifts and socio-economic inequalities. Yet for many of these women, given their advantaged class positions, which reflected Canada's post-1960s immigration policy, these socio-economic divides did not necessarily touch their lives.

McNeil (2012) cleverly explores what he calls the "sly civility" between neoliberalism and neocolonialism. He refers to David Theo Goldberg's (2008) analysis of the 2008 presidential race in the United States, which "deployed mixed-race metaphors ... to talk about mixture as a virtue considered to fuel commercial intercourse," and cites Paul Gilroy (2000, 21), who borrows from Frantz Fanon in speaking about the "perils of childlike mixed-race faces being sold as translators or exotic objects." Toronto has adopted many neoliberal tenets, and in some ways some mixed race women model aspects of this neoliberal identity, becoming de facto neoliberal ambassadors. A few participants, but not very many, addressed how they felt at home in Toronto precisely because they saw it as diverse. However, although I expected them to speak in detail about the pleasures of living in this city, they tended to speak about belonging in national terms rather than speaking about their urban identities or urban belonging. When some did speak affectionately about their place in the city, national and urban belongings intermingled, particularly for Sara:

> But I think when I left Canada, I guess I was looking to find a place where I would fit in and be accepted, and I got to Japan and I felt accepted and supported, but I didn't find, feel that it was my place either. I felt more Canadian and I didn't feel Japanese. And then as I was travelling back through Asia and through Europe, I didn't find any places that I felt entirely comfortable with. I felt, I felt pointed at, stared at, whatever, in every place that I went to, and when I got back to Toronto, I just was so relieved, I felt like I was home. And I felt like I didn't mind it any more, people asking where I was from 'cause, because I felt that everywhere I go in the world, people will do that. But there's a bit of a difference between being asked that question, which I get asked everywhere, and all the other things that sort of are around in my life, and I know that I can build in Toronto and I can have anonymity in Toronto. That's a real luxury. You know I can't have that in Scotland, I don't feel that in Glasgow, I don't feel that in, you know, India, I don't feel that in so many other places.

Zenia, too, explained that living in Toronto informed her sense of national and personal identity:

> I know Toronto really well. I feel very connected to Toronto, and a lot of that has to do with the fact that it is multicultural, in the sense that you have many cultures existing. And I really like that. I really like that about the city. Um, that would be how I would define the city. Not necessarily exactly the way that Toronto is made up, but under the same basic idea that you've got people from around the world all living together, or all living in the same city. In their separate compartments. A lot of the time. I don't mean it like that so much. Like I said, there are times when I've gone out, with a group of my friends, to do something, and the crowd is mixed. People from different ages, different ethnic backgrounds, different religions. And we're all there because we enjoy the same type of music. Or because we want to be together. I like that. That's where I feel at home. On a geographical, emotional spatial level.

Marical also shared with me the complex relationship between nation, city, and identity, insisting that although her personal geography remained relatively stable, the way that she was defined racially was always subject to radical change:

> I live in Toronto and I'm going to live in Toronto next week and I'm going to live in Toronto like three weeks, you know, from now and probably for the rest of my life, if I live in Toronto. There's a stability within that geography, like the geography doesn't necessarily change, whereas race does change. And I suspect that's why more people cling onto the idea of like nationality because that's something that is a lot more stable than what race is, I think. I don't know. Especially if you're a mixed race, you just can't, like it doesn't – it doesn't fit, you know.

Some of the women may well be imagined as part of what Florida (2002) uncritically calls the "creative class" – individuals who are seen as contributing to the vitality and vibrancy of the city's cultural core. As I mentioned in an earlier chapter, many of the women were employed as journalists or worked as artists more broadly (Florida himself does not engage in an anti-racist critique, but see Catungal and Leslie 2009). Of interest to me is that some of these women had grown up in middle- to upper-class environments and that this context, combined with the reality that some of them were seen as racially ambiguous or possessed an ability to identify as mixed race, provided an excess of cultural currency that gave them access to predominantly white spaces. They had access to the benefits associated with white networks. One cannot assume that by simply seeing mixed race and Canadian identity as compatible (Darius) or identifying as embodied models for the nation-state (Kiirti), these women actively challenged or undid institutionalized systems of race inequality. Spencer (2011, 3) claims that "racial ambiguity, in and of itself, is no guarantee of political progressiveness, [or] racial destabilization." Some mixed race women are co-opted into acting as the ultimate poster children for an ongoing apolitical Canadian multicultural project. Their mere presence in the social landscape superficially signals to those less politicized that multicultural policy has apparently been successful. It is problematically assumed that if interracial mixing has occurred, as evidenced through the presence of multiracial people, then racial integration has been achieved. Of course, this is a naive claim but one that is readily welcomed.

In other words, a steadfast clinging to liberalism animates these sentiments. At racial liberalism's core lies a ubiquitous, globalizing, sanitizing narrative about race, one that is exemplified through the embodiment of the racially ambiguous individual. This narrative insists that the mere presence of mixed race people in the social landscape somehow guarantees a more racially tolerant world. Increasing numbers of mixed race people in Canada can be seen as establishing the moral legitimacy of Canadian global leadership and are embodied as *symbols of progress*. But how, exactly, is this progressive?

Mixed race people are drafted into and shape multicultural narratives, reinforcing racial hierarchies. Mackey (2002, 88) has critiqued the idea of national progress in terms of its role in Canada's historical amnesia: "Cultural difference has been reconfigured and appropriated to strengthen national identity – to create a unified (although hybrid) narrative of national progress ... It is through the presence of others, through highlighting the *reconciliation of difference,* that historical and present-day violence is erased and Canadian national character is produced as innocent and 'tolerant'" (emphasis in original). Unwittingly or not, some of the mixed race women in this study saw themselves as a symbol of tolerance and a modernizing agent of a new multicultural world order (Elam 2011). This construction was produced against the backdrop of a national identity, one produced through and by the state, and it emerged from and in response to the peculiarities and particularities of their social, political, historical, and economic contexts.

Some of the women spoke eloquently about difference, but it was an apoliticized form of difference that skipped or glossed over Canada's history of colonial and racial injustice. Elam (2011) has suggested that this elision supports a colour-based status quo that does little to discourage commercial and political co-optation of mixed race, limiting self-reflection at the expense of darker-skinned people.

Although I saw some self-reflection among participants, there was little conversation in the interviews about redefining the terms of engagement with what it means to be Canadian against a backdrop of ongoing colonial inequities, particularly for blacks and Indigenous populations. Ibrahim (2007, 158) astutely observes that mixed race discourse "allows the [mixed race person] to speak in the place of strangely silenced others, in the name of resistance but somehow without resisting" – a definitively neoliberal stance.

I suggest that some mixed race women may well be defined as *model multiracials*. They marry racial liberalism to a benign form of Canadian nationalism (as though nationalism couldn't be anything but benign). Some racially ambiguous bodies are celebrated as exotic racial trailblazers. Some mixed race bodies that are employed as an upbeat symbol of integration exemplify ideas that proliferated with the inauguration of 1970s multiculturalism: openness, diversity, and, of course, tolerance, but not necessarily acceptance.

Brown (2006), focusing on the United States, articulates how neoliberal multiculturalism incorporates a form of supranationalism, privileging the multicultural American citizen as a subject more global and legitimate than even the so-called multicultural world citizen (see also McNeil 2012). In some ways, the model multiracial might be understood as an even more universal and legitimate symbol of the success of globalization than the quintessential world citizen of which Brown and McNeil speak. Excerpts from interviews suggest that the mixed race person can become a pawn in the multicultural game. She can play a complicit role in underpinning colonial national rhetoric because of the potential evacuation of antiracist and anticolonial engagement. As Walcott (2011, 26) reminds us, "One of the triumphs of neo-liberal ideology has been its very effective management of the imagination, alongside the management of the economy, institutions, [and] populations."

Conclusion

> Although there is always an entertainment and encouragement of cultural diversity [within multicultural policy], there is always also a corresponding containment of it. A transparent norm is constituted, a norm given by the host society or dominant culture, which says that "these other cultures are fine, but we must be able to locate them within our own grid."
>
> — BHABHA 1990, 208

> [The] anti-racist struggle has been appropriated and I think it might have to do with the discourse of multiculturalism being used to ... bind [immigrants] to the state as Canadians. It can turn a fight against racism into a fight for racial equality within a settler-state.
>
> — BONITA LAWRENCE, IN S. RUTHERFORD 2010, 12

In this chapter, I have attempted to show how the policy of multiculturalism both impeded and facilitated senses of belonging for mixed race women in this study. Elam (2011, 94) claims that "mixed race is not a modern palliative to the 'race question' but, instead, a palimpsest of national anxieties and ambitions involving race." These national anxieties were on performance in interviews, being evident in conversations about national affiliations.

I have endeavoured to illustrate how the imaginations of identity inherent in discourses of Canadian multicultural policy offer overly static representations of ethnic representations and nationalism. Although many Canadians still read multicultural policy as an inclusive vision of humanity, the narratives of Canadian mixed race women in this study suggest the need for a more critical reading of the policy's goals and aspirations. On the other hand, some of their articulations of mixed race agency underpinned and further re-entrenched liberal multiculturalism, propping up the colonial project. A kind of racial impotency emerged in those interviews, where mixed race women saw themselves as racially progressive, forward-thinking, unique, and different without necessarily adopting a position that would involve the articulation of an anticolonial politics. Doing so would have meant eschewing their particular brand of racial privilege.

Some mixed race women see themselves as naturally attuned to being antiracist and may be influenced as much as their so-called monoracial counterparts by the myths and stereotypes about the experience of multiraciality that pervade popular culture. Ibrahim (2012, xix) shrewdly tells us, "No man is an island; rather, one is the outcome of a series of events that occurred at some point elsewhere." Although Ibrahim employs this idea in a different context, I draw from it to illustrate how some of this study's mixed race subjects were implicated in the mythologies of multiraciality. Identifying as mixed race provided an opportunity for some to imagine themselves as the quintessential model multiracial – an exemplary symbol of equitable global citizenship – which I argue was shaped by the particular neoliberal climate of the city of Toronto at the time interviews were gathered. Conflating multiraciality with the apolitical narrative of Canadiana is dangerous because it is impossible to extricate definitions of what it means to be Canadian from a tortured history of racialized hierarchies, imperialism, and white-settler colonialism.

The next chapter explores the solitudes of blackness and whiteness. I critique discussions of "whiteness" as defined in academic writing by drawing upon more stories from women who identified as mixed race.

4
Beyond the Passing Narrative
Multiracial Whiteness

> If you want to talk about what it means to be white, you've got a paragraph. If you want to talk about what it means to be black, you've got a library.
>
> — KATYA, INTERVIEWEE

In several critical mixed race literary sources, "passing" emerges as a predominant theme (Spickard 1989; Spencer 2011; Dawkins 2012). Passing as white when one sees oneself as mixed race can be either a passive or active process depending upon other people's perceptions of one's racial background. However, "passing" in most texts refers to the process of passing as white only. It is often assumed that mixed race people commonly choose to identify as white if they can do so. This chapter attempts to shift the passing narrative by asking how whiteness was constituted among some mixed race women in this study. In interviews, did they speak about efforts to embrace or renounce a white identity? What did attempts to reject whiteness mean to them? Were there attempts, in fact, that promoted a multiracialism that worked "to dismantle and not fortify the privileges of whiteness" (R. Joseph 2013, xvii)?

It can be erroneously assumed that a white identity is available only to individuals of exclusively European ancestry (but see Twine 1996). This chapter discloses the currency of whiteness while paying attention to the myriad ways interviewees refused it. Missing in the literature is an understanding of how contemporary mixed race women conceptualize a desire to renounce whiteness while still recognizing its accompanying privileges. In this chapter, I hope to show how we might understand the experiences of some mixed race women and their relationship to blackness.

I show how meanings of whiteness shifted in particular contexts by unveiling interviews where whiteness was viewed as a fluctuating political category rather than an unyielding and desired site of privilege. As Dei (2007, 57) states, "Race occupies more than one space at a time." What does occupying white space mean for these women? I address a particular aspect of the missing discourse of whiteness by considering the ways that some of the women in this study, through their own very distinct class privilege, worked hard to renounce occupying space within whiteness because they saw whiteness as a site of racial privilege.

Revisiting White Studies

> How can it be that so many well-meaning white people have never thought about race when so few blacks pass a single day without being reminded of it? ... White people just didn't *know*, had just never *thought* about it.
>
> — P.J. WILLIAMS 1997, 27, EMPHASIS IN ORIGINAL

The scholarship on whiteness emerged in the academic sphere in the 1990s (Frankenberg 1993, 1997; Bonnett 1997; Delgado and Stefancic 1997; Fine et al. 1997), with whiteness being "dragged out into the foreground after the [silhouettes] of 'Blackness' [were sketched]" (Wong 1994, 136). Whiteness is something that is difficult to describe but almost impossible not to recognize. Its power and presence are continually felt, yet it has the paradoxical ability to remain shrouded within a veil of invisibility, ensuring its transparency while asserting its centrality and dominance in multiple ways (ibid.). Mirza (1997, 3) defines whiteness as

> [an] unchallenged hegemonic patriarchal discourse ... which quietly embraces our common-sense and academic ways of thinking ... a powerful place that makes invisible, or re-appropriates things, people and places it does not want to see or hear, and then through misnaming, renaming or not naming at all, invents the truth – what we are told is "normal," neutral, universal, simply becomes the way it is.

To address this troubling tendency toward one-sided discourse, feminist theorists have addressed their own problematic stance in relation to whiteness as a site of privilege and power, often in conjunction with their own contemplations of male privilege and largely influenced by the critique of whiteness by women of colour. Some of the early dialogues about whiteness and privilege were conducted by white lesbians (Bulkin, Pratt, and Smith 1984) who analyzed how race had largely influenced their lives and offered suggestions for a movement to create spaces where differences within and between women could be negotiated and discussed (Wong 1994, 135). Feminist writers such as Peggy McIntosh (1989), Maureen Reddy (1994), and Jane Lazarre (1996) have illustrated through autobiographical work how whiteness confers membership within a social group and the importance of contemplating this social positioning as a way of being in the world. McIntosh (1988, 10) was one of the first feminists to begin to critique the notion of "whiteness" by unpacking the term, writing about the "knapsack of white privilege" that accompanies white skin. Although now seen as somewhat ancient, it is worthwhile to quote a lengthy passage from her groundbreaking essay "White Privilege and Male Privilege: A Personal Account of Coming to See Correspondences through Work in Women's Studies" (1988):

> As a white person, I realized I had been taught about racism as something which puts others at a disadvantage, but had been taught not to see one of its corollary aspects, white privilege, which puts me at an advantage ... I have come to see white privilege as an invisible package of unearned assets which I can count on cashing in each day ... like an invisible weightless knapsack of special provisions, assurances, tools, maps, guides, codebooks, passports [1-2] ... Some of the daily effects of white privilege in my life [include:] ... If I should need to move, I can be pretty sure of renting or purchasing housing in an area which I can afford and in which I would want to live ... I can turn on the television or open to the front page of the paper and see people of my race widely represented ... I can talk with my mouth full and not have people put this down to my color ... I can do well in a challenging situation without being called a credit to my race [5-7] ... In unpacking this invisible knapsack of white privilege, I have listed conditions of daily experience which I once took for granted, as neutral, normal, and universally accessible to everybody [10] ... It is an open question whether we will choose to use unearned advantage to weaken hidden systems of advantage, and whether we will use any of our

arbitrarily-awarded power to try to reconstruct power systems on a broader base [19].

McIntosh's knapsack includes "unearned assets," things to which everyone should be entitled but which are in fact awarded to particular racialized groups. White privilege requires social reinforcement and maintenance, so an important component of this privilege is the invisibility of the mechanisms that reinforce it. Drawing from McIntosh (1989), Frankenberg (1993) offers one of the first empirical studies of how white women think about race. In her analysis of forty interviews, Frankenberg illustrates how race shapes white women's lives. Most white feminists cited personal reasons for exploring whiteness in relation to their own relationships to status. Frankenberg's desire to explore whiteness grew from her dissatisfaction with the limited repertoires of responses available to white feminists when charged with racism. According to her, sites of multiracial feminist dialogue "deteriorated into [places] where racial tension and conflict seemed to [fester]," and she "found herself straddling two sides of a 'race line'" (ibid., 3). Frankenberg explores how the women she interviewed read their whiteness as something they chose not to think about, as a naturalized state of being, as normal, with anything else being positioned as "other." She repositions the voices of these women to assert her claim that the world is constituted out of relations of power and privilege and that in the social landscape, whiteness as privilege plays a major role. Frankenberg sees whiteness as a position of structural advantage, associated with privileges of the most basic kind. She also claims that it carries with it a set of ways of being in the world, often not named as white but looked upon as either normal or invisible. Through her empirical analysis, Frankenberg illustrates how racial denial tends to mask a disingenuous innocence, reflecting a refusal to acknowledge the oppressive constraints of whiteness.

After Frankenberg's ground-breaking book was published, many more texts in feminist and cultural theory critiqued the notion of whiteness. Those who had experienced white privilege were able to talk about issues of race and identity without fear of offending those who had originally critiqued their passive position. Theorists have argued that the challenge for contemporary cultural analysis is to make whiteness viable as a culturally constructed, ethnic identity contingent upon the violent denial of difference. Fine et al. (1997, viii) hope to "pry whiteness ... in all its glistening privilege ... open ... and wedge it off of its unexamined centre," insisting that it is necessary to study whiteness as a system of power and privilege because it wages symbolic violence through its refusal to name its defining mechanisms. These writers have begun to counter the "unmarked marker" status of whiteness (Frankenberg 1997, 1) and to colour the transparency of white positionings by pointing out the accompanying privilege and power that often accompany white skin.

Although Frankenberg's (1997) exploration of the multiple intersecting experiences of race and place has made one of the most explicit references to the spatial diversity of white identities (Bonnett 1997), some scholars have pointed out the limits of work on whiteness. Ideas about race and racialization do not spring up out of a vacuum but have particular cultural precursors, and several historians (e.g., Roediger 1991; Ignatiev 1995) have revealed how contemporary definitions of "whiteness" originated. They note the excesses of white consciousness and glorification and show how white supremacy was strengthened during periods of turmoil and economic competition, construing whiteness as a product of American capitalism and labour organizations (Bonnett 1997). Critical whiteness studies have marked an important departure in studies on "race" and ethnicity for many contemporary theorists, inviting whites to examine themselves "more searchingly and ... behind the mirror" (Delgado and Stefancic 1997, 4) by looking at their complicit role in contributing to oppressive systems of privilege and power. Studies have recognized how whiteness constitutes not only systems of government, law, and economy but also a whole discursive terrain through which ideas, institutions, forms of representation, and modes of knowledge production are created. I applaud these writers' desires to explore the "extent to which the stakes in whiteness impassion so many of our race rituals" (P.J. Williams 1997, 27).

I am interested in examining how whiteness is understood not only by people who claim a white identity but also by people of mixed race identity. When and where does whiteness shift for multiracial people? How do individuals who are seen as white in some places and not white in others challenge perceptions of whiteness? In particular, I argue that much work on whiteness has reflected a hierarchical and oppositional approach to race, obscuring the diverse range of experiences of whiteness, or what Arat-Koç (2010, 148-49) calls "'cracks' along the colour line."

To demonstrate ways that we can make whiteness visible, I turn next to the voices of my informants, who explored their own complex processes of racialization with me. Before I begin, however, I would be remiss if I did not explain why I refuse to speak in depth about passing among mixed race people. Of course, as I alluded to earlier, passing is a recurring theme in the literature about multiraciality. This chapter has been written precisely because so many of the women I spoke to eschewed their ability to pass. I have made a deliberate choice in this book not to focus on the ways that mixed race people pass as white. The reasons are epistemological. As Spencer (2011, 72) states, "Racist fantasies of American mulattoes dreaming of whiteness are a function solely of the white imagination." Indeed, there remains a recurring trope around the experience of multiraciality that assumes that mixed race people would want to pass as white if they could choose to do so. The myth, according to Spencer (ibid., 54), is that "American mulattoes naturally despise their connection to blackness, naturally aspire to whiteness, and this is a constant, natural reality for them." What Spencer does well is explore the issue of motivation in relation to passing. In an analysis of the ways that American mixed race novelists have written about multiraciality, he indicates that "the decision to pass as white is based on the achievement of some practical goal. In no case does the melodramatic red herring of divided-blood psychotrauma play any role whatsoever in any character's decision to pass as white, whether temporarily or permanently (ibid., 67). What this chapter attempts to do is extend Spencer's thesis from one that examines novels about mixed race themes prior to the "marginal man" thesis, discussed in Chapter 1, to one that situates an abolition of this myth through the stories shared by mixed race women in this study. At the same time, however, I do not want to propagate the myth that in renouncing whiteness, mixed race people successfully move toward occupying a nonwhite space. Such a claim would be not only naive but also overly optimistic. As I emphasize throughout this book, cultural capital matters. By virtue of their educational and class backgrounds, these women experienced an ability to articulate their vision of abandoning whiteness, yet they were still very clear that this option was often available to them only because of the class privilege they held. Ibrahim (2012, 122) tells us that "whiteness as a category can be disavowed once it is disarticulated from class and gender analyses."

I address the ambiguous and contradictory spaces of whiteness through some women of mixed race who negotiated impressions of themselves as both white and nonwhite. The mixed race women in this study refuted the idea that a white identity is available only to those of exclusive European descent. Instead, they acknowledged the myriad ways they were racialized. In determinations of who is permitted to be white and who is marked as black, a fluctuating categorization is at play that asserts both the temporality and the spatiality of whiteness. How is white identity constructed, enacted, and challenged by women who are mixed race? How are mixed race women raced as white and as nonwhite? How do racialized dualisms play themselves out in the day-to-day realities of mixed race women? I attempt to answer these questions by demonstrating how attributes generally associated with whiteness, particularly skin colour and privilege, were understood by some of these women. There was a shifting nature to whiteness for participants, with identities being constructed within the spaces of "difference" and at the same time being a matter of rich and complicated negotiation. In particular, I share stories from participants who insisted that although they were half-white, they were not white, and I explore the spatialities of whiteness, looking at participants' acknowledgment that processes of racialization took place within physical contexts rife with complex social relations.

"I'm Half-White, But Not White"

> Be white be white be white, they say
> But I'm not good at being white
> Being pushed to be white only made me a ruin
> When they say I look white, I say
> "you're half-right!"
>
> — BOMBAY 2010, 257

> Of course, no one is "all white." I am submitting here to the cultural fantasy of white racial purity not because it is real or possible, but because it is widely accepted. Most seem to believe that a child could be all white, and that he or she should be raised as such if physical characteristics permit.
>
> — MORALES 1996, 49

In this section, I hope to unravel the complexities of whiteness among participants through a discussion of the statement "I'm half-white, but I'm not white," which emerged several times in the interviews. Several women made the distinction between the two categories. Although the phrase at first sounds paradoxical, I argue that to be "half-white" and "not white" at the same time is to represent two separate entities of existence, a positioning that requires a further disentangling. For example, Makeda emphasized the ways that whiteness has been reified when she explained that she voiced her own racial identity in a strategic manner by telling people she was half-white:

> When I get asked, "Where are you from?" I'm always tempted to say, "Well, I'm half-white" and just leave it at that, because it's impossible to be half-white, right? Like racism and white supremacy disallows that. So, to say you're half-white is meaningless, within the, you know, racialized context. So you can say, "I'm half-Japanese," and somehow that is intelligible? As a statement of identity?

By calling herself "half-white," Makeda tried to short-circuit the (ill)logic of racial categorization. Makeda suggested that for her, it did not mean anything to be half-white because whiteness was equated with invisibility and cultural neutrality in her eyes. Makeda also recognized that racialized identities are asymmetrically based on descent: "whites" are not supposed to have any "nonwhite" ancestry (as Makeda said, it's disallowed), whereas blacks and Asians can have some "nonblack" or "non-Asian" blood and will still be classified as black or Asian. Of particular interest is Makeda's insistence that white supremacy disallows the possibility of identifying as "half-white." The one-drop rule played a significant role in informing Makeda's understanding of the ways that whiteness governs racial identity. The one-drop rule emerged in the late seventeenth and early eighteenth centuries as a means of increasing the number of slaves in the United States (Davis 1991). It incorporated a legal standard that designated individuals with any black ancestry as black, thus blocking access to claims to whiteness (King and DaCosta 1996). The production of whiteness is read as both an embodied experience and a social construct, shaping desires and the possibilities for belonging and acceptance. As Akari explained,

> There was this Korean girl and I remember it got me really mad when she said to me, "I just thought you were totally white." I hated hearing that, I remember, and it made me even more mad, the fact that she was Oriental and saying that. "How could she not see that I'm half Oriental?" I remember thinking in my mind. I don't know, I really didn't like that,

like, even though yes I'm half-white, it's like, but I'm not a white person, living in this world you know. I just have the general feeling that it's easiest to be a white person living in our society. I mean, in terms of like race, you know. That's what I mean by all this majority/minority. But I know I'm definitely not a white person. I am part of like half of that, but if you categorize me now I get really upset because I'm not fully white, and therefore I'll never be white. But at the same time, like white people don't look at me, I'm sure they don't look at me and think, oh I'm not one, you know when they're talking to me. I'm sure that's not their perception. They think I look exotic.

The legacy of the one-drop rule was echoed here as well. Akari made a distinction between being of half-European ancestry, which she deemed to be white, and whiteness as a place of structural advantage, privilege, and power. She claimed a point of difference between being "fully white" and "half-white," constructing whiteness as a biologically pure category (Frankenberg 1993). It's clear that the word "white" takes on multiple meanings. Akari explained that she was affronted when someone assumed she was white. Even though she acknowledged that she was sometimes the recipient of white privilege and that she had been welcomed "into the club" (Morales 1996, 44), she did not identify as white herself because of its connotations with class and privilege.

Chantal made it clear during her interview that she did not think her experiences in life were the same as those of someone who identified as white:

> MINELLE: How do you feel about the term "biracial"?
>
> CHANTAL: It doesn't imply a full identity – it means you're half of something and half of something else? Which even though that is what you are, to me it has some sort of implication that doesn't imply fullness, or wholeness. A whole identity. And that's what I don't like about it.
>
> MINELLE: How do you feel about people saying, "You're half-white, half-black"?
>
> CHANTAL: Hate it! (laughter) Hate it! Hate it because it doesn't define or describe my experience. HERE. Doesn't mean anything. And that would be, like what do you mean? You want to talk about my genetic

makeup, I can talk about that no problem. That is my genetic makeup. But that is very different, though, than my life experience. And in terms of validating my life experience.

Chantal rejected the label of "half-white, half-black." Chantal's phenotype is troubling to the enforcement of strict racial boundaries because she generates social uncertainty about what those categories mean. Chantal problematized the whole notion of being "half and half," a theme that emerged prominently in this study and that was discussed with much disdain by the majority of the women. Chantal stressed the value placed on having a whole or unitary self, raising the assumption that someone who is mixed race cannot possibly have a whole sense of identity. She saw herself as a whole person, not simply the sum of her parts. Chantal further made a distinction between her phenotype (her physical makeup) and genotype (her genetic makeup). She was quite comfortable with discussing her genotype in terms of European and black heritage. This background represented, in her words, her "genetic makeup." But it did not socially or personally explain her own life experiences as a mixed race woman who was classified by others into awkward racial slots. Chantal explained that she was not racialized in the same way as those who identified as white even though she did share European descent.

The Spaces of Whiteness

Many women interviewed for this book challenged the notion that racial identities are fixed, natural, and unmalleable. For them, whiteness was not a stable and clearly defined space but was constantly changing, depending upon the time and place. The women talked a great deal about their ability to move in and out of whiteness. There were different degrees of whiteness at play in their experiences – they could be white, half-white, or not white at all in different arenas. For example, Marical demonstrated that the category of whiteness is rarely concrete and is constantly shifting and changing:

> Being mixed just recognizes a multiplicity of identities. It recognizes that fluidity. It recognizes the fact that somebody might think I'm white, somebody might think I'm black, but you know that, that there is like a sort of, there's nothing definite about things ... I get that all the

time, "Are you white or are you black?" you know, and it took me a while to get there but I always [say now], "I'm not, I'm both, I'm not either. I'm mixed race."

Marical recognized that racialized categories are socially created and transformed through particular spaces. To assume that the mixed race person will identify with how she looks is "presumptive, but pervasive" (Root 1990, 197). Just as Marical was perceived differently by different people, she refused to locate herself as either white or black. Although others located her as either white or black in particular spaces, she defined herself as mixed race to position herself outside the oppositional discourse of race. Mixed race places like that claimed by Marical become important socio-political signifiers of racial production and resistance. Teresa Kay Williams (1996, 199) claims that "by the time one has become an adult, one's racial membership within a hierarchically structured, racialized society has been concretized." This notion is problematic for describing mixed race women in this study. For them, racial categories were rarely stable but instead fluid and flexible, continually shifting and changing. Those who were deemed to be white in some places were not always seen as white in others. Williams's notion becomes even more complex for mixed race women because their phenotype cannot be neatly placed by the race border guards. Makeda explained that others relied on physical markers to classify her racially:

> It really depends on everything. It's funny because I think that race is very obvious, sometimes. And yet, there's so much, it's so slippery? Right? For me, it depends on the time of year, where I am, how long my hair is, whether I'm wearing makeup, whether I'm not, what kind of clothes I'm wearing, like I run the gamut, of kinda ... People identify me as all sorts of different things.

It is a constellation of circumstances, among which skin tone is only one, that creates the potential for racial identity. Within the potential range of identities, a mixed race person can experience and adopt various racialized identities in multiple formations. Makeda explained that the intricacies of cosmetics, hair, clothes, time, and space played a role in the ways that she was raced, problematizing the polarities normally associated with racialized identities by accentuating the multiplicity and mobility of social positioning.

Racial classifications are not only slapped upon mixed race women like a "peel-on, peel-off label" (Jones 1994, 14) but are also chosen by them at various times and places in their lives. Of course, it would be naive to presume that the mixed race woman always experiences an unopposed freedom to choose how she wishes to be perceived racially. There was a very real fluctuation in the ways that women in this study were racialized, as I explore in greater depth in the next chapter. Informants enacted crucial relationships between individual agency and the categories of whiteness and blackness. Although cultural representations of race are indeed powerful, these women were not simply passive recipients of "social inscriptions" (Streeter 1996, 308) of these categories. They experienced a wide array of racialization processes. Naela, for instance, pointed out how whiteness is dependent upon place, people, and context:

> There are moments I feel dark, and I like it. There are moments that I like it. And then there are moments that I feel really really like, WHITE. And it really depends on my mood. The way I look at the colour of my skin. Depends on who I'm with. When I'm around white people, I feel distinctly darker than them, and different, even though some of them might have skin the same colour, I just feel darker? But then, when I'm around other people, I feel very white.

Naela made the important distinction between "feeling white" and "being white," highlighting that racial identity is about not only skin colour but also the individual's feelings and thoughts associated with skin colour. She shifted being white from an external definition to an internal feeling. Naela choreographed a very complex dance of tensions through her discussion of multiple racialized selves. Her own sense of her racial identity changed within the context of particular situations, indicating the perpetual relational aspects of a white identity. Whiteness is neither constructed nor exists within a cultural vacuum. As Fine (1997, 58) remarks, "Whiteness and colour are therefore not merely created in parallel, but are fundamentally relational and need to be studied as a system; they might ... be considered 'nested' rather than coherent or independent variables." Clearly this was the case for Naela, whose colour appeared more or less strongly, depending upon the place and company she was in. Saldanha (2006, 18) has noted that race needs to be understood as a contingency chain, such that connections are not taken for granted but are "made viscous through local attractions ... There is no essence of whiteness, but there is a relative fixity ... in all the 'local pulls' of its many elements in flux." Racial identity is geographically and temporally specific, so perhaps we need to ask new questions. Instead of continually asking "Who am I?" we ought to contemplate "Where am I?" This question would shift the focus from a politics of identity to a politics of location (Probyn 1990; Bondi 1993), exposing context as a key factor in racial identity shaping. The interview participants acknowledged that processes of racialization occur in sites of competing and complex social relations.

I have demonstrated how racial identities are capable of shifting, which shows how race is a social construction and not necessarily associated with skin colour. In the next section, I illustrate that meanings associated with whiteness, particularly privilege and power, shift as well. Although the categories of whiteness and blackness have been weighed down with sociohistorical meanings (to explain and justify social inequality and injustice), I argue that there are ways to envision these categories outside of the seemingly inevitable affiliations. I counter claims that whiteness is normal, invisible, or a secure site of privilege by citing excerpts from my informants.

I have illustrated the various degrees of whiteness and how whiteness can shift in different arenas. Whiteness can mark you, and being read as white can be difficult, different, or dangerous in some contexts. These markings are neither natural nor neutral, and in the next section I show how participants took up these markings and how they played with their whiteness. I address a particular aspect of the missing discourse in works on whiteness, namely the unproblematized constitution of whiteness as a site of privilege and power.

Whiteness and Privilege

> Charis is stuck with being white. A white rabbit. Being white is getting more and more exhausting. There are so many bad waves attached to it, left over from the past ... like the killing rays from atomic waste dumps. There's so much to expiate! It gives her anaemia just to think about it. In her next life she's going to be a mixture, a blend, a vigorous hybrid, like Shanita. Then no one will have anything on her.
>
> — ATWOOD 1993, 85

Most of the literature on whiteness has focused on the advantage and privilege accompanying white skin (Reddy 1994; Scales-Trent 1995), and I agree with Reddy (1994, 141), who stresses that "much work needs to be done in order to make visible and undermine white culture and its ties to domination." Others have charted arguments insisting that whiteness is produced as an advantage through pedagogy and the economy, and although not dismissing the very real existence of these associations and the powerful ways they shape social relations, I propose that these characterizations encourage the myth of racial superiority by ignoring the complex interweave among culture, class, and individual experience in different contexts, as well as the structure of privilege within and outside of racial categories. If we take it as a given that white supremacy structures the lives of people of colour irredeemably, what does it mean to explore the ways that mixed race individuals attempt to shift away from places of white privilege? Whiteness studies have often obscured the multiple subjectivities of identities, assuming that racial classifications remain undifferentiated by the dimensions of class and gender, among other dynamics. The links between whiteness and privilege are often overlooked in these readings, supporting the ideology of white supremacy by not dismantling the hierarchical relationship between whiteness and nonwhiteness that upholds white privilege. There is a particular evolution of the meanings attached to whiteness, too.

I also want to flag that the privilege of whiteness has never insulated white women from the brutality and misogyny of some men. The "white women in these theories miss a lot of the reality of white women in the practice of male supremacy, revealing a trivialization of the white woman's subordination implicit in the discussion on white women and privilege" (MacKinnon 1997, 301). By asserting the privileged status of whiteness time and time again, we are emphasizing a clean, coherent division between the privileged and underprivileged, making it difficult to contemplate potential zones of alliances across charged political lines of difference. Issues of power, privilege, and prestige are much more complex than the literature currently envisions them to be. I consider other states of existence by revisiting the social landscape of whiteness through the voices of informants, recognizing that they experienced domination and subordination through the grid of whiteness and blackness but outside of the grid, too.

I suggest that whiteness as a category needs to be interrogated, especially in critical mixed race studies. Spencer has pointed out that the pervasive and tenacious persistence of whiteness must be the target of all successful antiracist efforts, and this imperative is crucial to the development of an invigorated critical mixed race theory. It is useful to unpack the varied dimensions of whiteness in order to understand how class, gender differences, and sexual orientation, among other dimensions, have altered white experiences. I believe there are other ways of contemplating whiteness outside of its links with privilege and power. I have already discussed how whiteness is pitted against blackness within oppositional discourses. To follow from this premise, then, whiteness is positioned as a place laden with advantages, and colour is thereby disintegrated to embody deficit or lack. I hope to conceptually subvert this notion by citing some specific examples where whiteness was not seen as a site of privilege and power.

Some informants chose to contest the dominant representation of whiteness by challenging the notion of whiteness as a site of privilege and power, reconfiguring power relations between whiteness and blackness. In the rest of the chapter, I attempt to unveil the particular characterizations associated with whiteness.

The literature on whiteness stakes a great deal of its legitimacy upon the status of whiteness as an oppressor identity, reifying it as an essentialized category. The existing discourses on whiteness position subjects in terms of a relationship between power and disempowerment (Anderson 1996). Many participants in this study who were raced as white experienced privilege and prestige. As Naela wryly noted,

> Well, I think a lot of people look at white as cultureless. That's the first thing if you're white. And you don't really have culture. But you have power. So do you want power, or do you want culture? Which do you want, which is more important to you?

However, they were also quick to point out alternative circulations of power, defining other sorts of discourses and promoting other subject positions for racialized subjects by exploring multiple mappings of power. There are many layers of privilege at play for women who are seen as both white and black in particular places. What appears to undermine privilege in one domain can be reframed and reread as the enactment of privilege in another.

Consider Marical, for example, who lived the ironies of a racist society. She dislodged the perception that those who are seen as white always experience privilege. Indeed, although she was read as white in particular places, the perception of her phenotype as someone who was white could be detrimental:

> It doesn't work for me to just have black or white as categories. You know, it doesn't – you shift, I think, you, your identity's always, you know, change depending on where you are. And the thing is like, this is just such a, such a thing that I'm slaughtered for saying or will be slaughtered for saying, but it's not only those categories that indicate where you are in your life. Like I think in the greater society certainly, white has privilege, middle-class has privilege, straight has privilege, and male has privilege, and I would never argue that. But in specific communities, it doesn't necessarily work like that, I don't think. And in a specific context, in a specific community of black people, I feel really isolated and really not that I have a lot of privilege. And I will [notice] my privilege when I step out of that community into the greater world, and I know that people will probably listen to me more because I am, you know, I'm fair and this and that and the other. So it's such a difficult terrain to negotiate in terms of power because you know, power means different things in different contexts. But I don't want to, I don't want to diminish what power means in a greater social context or, or you know, challenge the idea at all that this world is basically a white, middle-class, male-dominated world. You know, I do not want to, don't want to challenge that at all. But I just think it's not always, always like that. You know what I mean? And difficult.

Marical explained that she had experienced alienation from the black community for not looking "black enough" because of her partially European heritage. Although she could experience white privilege, she had at times been stigmatized within the black community for being mixed race. Other mixed race writers have commented on this experience. As Hill (2001, 111) notes, "Some of us feel that we have to involve ourselves actively in the community to prove that we belong. It is as if we expect, at every turn, some person to challenge our identity or our right to be there."

Some participants who were of European and African mixes frequently experienced a series of paradoxical tensions engendered by colourism in black contexts (Streeter 1996). Because a white phenotype is valued within some black communities, those participants who were light-skinned experienced privilege – albeit in insidiously heterosexual ways (Twine 1996) in the form of hypersexualized attention from black men and hostility from black women. Marical's narrative suggested that the danger lay in *making assumptions regarding the values attached to racialized categories and ranking oppressions associated with those categories accordingly.* Marical was discussing the particularities of oppression, which I argue can be unravelled only through an indexing of particular place-specific encounters with the racialization process. Marical's narrative documented multiple intersections and spaces between disadvantage and privilege, pointing out some of the contradictions of being read as both white and nonwhite in various spaces. Although she admitted that her light skin tone was read as white in some places, she also insisted that her fair skin could be read as a liability.

The notion that there is something called the "white experience" that can be described independently of other aspects of social life, like class and sexual orientation, is untenable because it assumes that whiteness is a distinct category, the impact of which can be neatly separated. The stories of mixed race women are rife with contradiction and paradox. Racial identities are not essentially or rigidly fixed, contrary to what is often thought. Rather, race operates as a field of power on multiple levels, where whiteness is not always associated with privilege. It also works on the basis of many other variables that disintegrate and recompose depending upon time and space. We need to develop more nuanced understandings of whiteness that take into consideration how race, class, and gender are simultaneous social processes that shape all social relations where multiple positions may privilege, subjugate, and dis(empower) all at the same time. Mixed race women in this study troubled the seemingly consensual understandings of domination, power, and privilege arising from one-dimensional race analyses. Attributing hierarchical social values to the dimensions of blackness and whiteness did not necessarily hold for Marical. She acknowledged her position of power as a woman who could be seen as white in particular places. At the same time, she refused to see these views as normalized. Instead, they were problematized and recognized as containing a series of ideas about social hierarchies.

These women imagined race and power very differently, revealing new sorts of contemplations of power systems and privilege. Next, I unveil the invisibility of whiteness by showing how whiteness literally "marked" participants. Whiteness was contemplated as a site of disadvantage by informants, and I demonstrate how they moved away from whiteness in particular places.

The Public and Private Dimensions of Whiteness

In this section, I address Bonnett's (1997, 199) concerns that we need to stop finding whiteness normal and unexceptional by dislodging the presumption that whiteness is "mainstream, non-exotic, and boring." I do so by uncovering the invisibility of whiteness and pointing out how participants clearly acknowledged the *public* privilege that can attend white skin. However, in their day-to-day *personal* lives, they deliberately took pains to disrupt others' readings of them as white.

It is important to note that there are many other stories that could be told here about the experiences of whiteness. I have chosen to focus upon only the ways that women in this study disrupted perceived readings of their light skin – if they could in fact "pass" for white – which of course was not always the case. Indeed, some of the women interviewed explained that in their adolescence, they could often "pass" as white and that it wasn't until they were older that they decided not to identify with the dominant group. I suggest that many factors play a role in how women choose to identify, and I refer the reader to Twine (1996) for a provocative analysis of factors influencing racial identification choices among mixed race girls in Berkeley, California. I also touch upon many of these issues in the next chapter.

Women in this study employed innovative coping strategies to negotiate and subvert racial and cultural membership, transforming their social ambiguity into complex identities. For example, Naela recounted having to navigate carefully through people's perceptions of her as a white woman in a situation where multiple perks did not necessarily attend white skin:

> Last summer I worked for this theatre group doing popular theatre, like social-justice work. And every time we would talk about a white system, like systems of power, people would like sorta, look at me? Or whatever, or if anyone made a comment about a white person, they would all look at me and see my reaction? And even though I told them about my background, what it was, and they knew how I felt, they still thought there was an element of spying in what I was doing there? And also, or they thought I was about to burst into tears, because it's like, "Hey, I'm partly white! Don't say those things!" So I had to make it VERY clear, like one day, finally, I just got so sick of it. Because everyone was just sitting there staring at me, anytime anyone said the word "white." Like

literally, everyone would just stare at me. So I just said, "Listen. I understand what you're talking about. I'm not, like don't look at me like that!" (laughter) I can deal with this. You're not offending me personally. And I don't feel that, I don't identify as white. And it was really complicated. And I felt, I still feel odd about the whole situation. And then, so it really affects the way I perceive things and the way I can work with people? Like it affects everything.

Naela's participation in the antiracist theatre group abruptly challenged and precipitated a shift in the way she constructed and thought about her racial identity. At the same time, however, she experienced resistance and hostility from this politicized community of colour when she tried to claim a nonwhite racial identity. When she was not encouraged to embrace and assert a nonwhite identity because she was perceived as white, or racially neutral, she enacted her own strategy by explaining to the group that she did not personally self-identify as white. Naela's encounter with the antiracist theatre group demonstrates how those mixed race individuals who look white will at times face difficulty in gaining acceptance by people of colour, given the attitudes and feelings that are projected upon them because of the oppression that white skin symbolizes to people of colour (Root 1990).

Whiteness in this arena meant being associated with people who were in positions of structural advantage and privilege – and being void of ethnicity. Naela wanted to dissociate herself from those notions. She saw herself as being marked not as a person of colour but as someone who might be seen as being racially neutral within this arena. She challenged the prevailing viewpoint among members in the group by voicing her desire to, in her words, combat systems of power. Naela rallied against the notion of racial neutrality and the importance of assigning everyone a place in the deconstruction of racism – for surely it would be ridiculous to assume that everyone who is white colludes in the production of oppressive power relations or to say that every person of colour resists hegemonic discourses. Naela clearly echoed these ideas:

In the last ten years, [I've tried] to separate myself from whiteness? Whiteness is something I've sorta conditioned to see as something not part of me? In a sense? It also means to be more, part of the structure or the system. And who controls the government, and the business, and the city in this country? Actually another one is definitely like colonizer.

Naela countered her own white privilege and the systems that created and offered it to her by conditioning herself not to see it as something that was part of her. Ignatiev and Garvey (1996) might designate her a "race traitor," someone who is normally classified as white but who defies the rules of whiteness so flagrantly as to jeopardize her ability to draw upon the privileges that often accompany white skin. Naela deliberately opposed the race line, repudiated her own race privilege, and jeopardized her standing in whiteness in particular situations. By doing so, she contributed to the process of destabilizing the construction of whiteness upon which society relies in order to preserve the current system of racial subordination. I am reminded here of the words of Alexis Kienlen's (2010, 43) powerful poem entitled "why i don't say i'm white," where she explains why she denounces whiteness:

> to say i'm white
> is to deny the many truths of who i am ...
> if i say i'm white
> i deny so many facts of my history ...
> saying i'm white
> means turning my back on my ancestors,
> an entire nation ...
> my meaning of home.

Some women in this study did not choose to fit their identities into prescribed racialized slots like whiteness when they could, in fact, pass. Naela disrupted the assumption that mixed race individuals who are part European and can pass as white will be very likely to strive for this racial identity in order to have maximum social power to escape the oppression directed toward people of colour. I argue that these participants could choose to move away from whiteness but that these decisions were largely influenced by the ways they were privileged through other social axes, like class, since the majority of women interviewed were well educated.

Like Naela, many informants *publicly* acknowledged whiteness as a site laden with privilege, echoing the ideas of feminist theorists. However, *privately*, they read their whiteness as disadvantageous, a site they wanted to move away from personally. As a result, they had developed particular strategies to dissociate themselves from whiteness. They acknowledged the power of hegemonic discourses while insisting on the possibility of resistance, creating a space where difference was tolerated, even celebrated, as a position of privilege. These women made a political choice not to align themselves with whiteness.

I now demonstrate how informants employed strategies not to be seen as white in particular places. I challenge Appiah's (1997, 79) claim that "nothing you do to change your appearance or behaviour can change the past fact that your ancestors were of some particular origin." I explore some of the ways that these women employed specific markers – both visual and verbal – to appear less white in particular places. Although they were often perceived as white in some situations, they deliberately dislodged this perception by adopting certain visual cues – either by dressing up in a particular way or by changing their name – to appear less white. Clearly, whiteness is only partially about skin colour because these women were seen as nonwhite in particular places. As in Davy's case, this fact was illustrated by the diverse forms of racism they experienced:

> MINELLE: What does it mean to look mixed?
>
> DAVY: It just means that, it means a lot of different things. It depends on where you live, and what your culture is. And for me, it's just meant that there's been issues of confusion, sometimes on my part, and sometimes on other people's parts. It means that I don't get some of the reaction that people who are fully black get, that I do get privilege because I don't look that dark. Or that black. There are things that I don't see, or that I don't experience, that other people do. But I've experienced a lot of very blatant racism and discrimination in my life.

Davy, like Marical, explained that as a mixed race individual, she experienced privilege on a fluctuating plane. At times, she experienced privilege that attends white skin. Yet at other moments, she was racialized as a black person. In certain contexts, informants in this study appeared as white, and they dealt with this strategically, developing ways to appear less white by adopting particular cultural signifiers. As Ali (2003, 13) reminds us, "People have difficulty in placing 'mixed-race' individuals and will often rely on erroneous visual signs to guide them."

Marical said that she adopted certain styles of clothing and accompanying jewellery to move away from perceived whiteness in her communities of colour. Dress both united and separated people from each other. Included in a repertoire of potentially oppositional strategies were the ways participants chose to dress or how they wore their hair. Particular costumes were used as an indicator of collective identification to publicly project a particular ethnic identity. As Marical explained,

> And you know, a lot of times when I was like younger, I used to wear an African medallion on my neck. Or I feel sometimes – I don't do this though, for other reasons – but you know I should wear like an Ashanti cloth or I should wear a specific signifier because I don't want to be mistaken for someone who's white. I don't want to be that invisible. I don't want to have to feel like I'm hiding something when I'm not, and the worst thing that always happens to me, and it just upsets me to no end, like I still haven't developed a thick enough skin, is I've had a lot of flack all my life from members of the black community. It's like, "I don't know who the hell she thinks she is, she thinks she's white." And you know, for at least the last decade, all my fucking life has been devoted to aspects of black culture, you know, and there's no way that anyone who had ever talked to me would get that idea. It's like just so preposterous. But just by looking at me, people are, well, "She thinks she's white." And it's like well, fuck, I can't do anything. You know what I mean? Except for stay out in the sun for longer. You know, and then I'm just going to get skin cancer. You know what I mean? Like I wish I was three shades darker but I'm not, you know, and it's such a ridiculous thing. But it comes down to something that basic. Like if this skin of mine were like a couple of shades darker, things would be different, you know, or at least a little bit different, a lot different, but they're not. It's not in my features, it's not the way I am, it's just that my packaging doesn't fit with my insides, you know, and that's really – that's like a difficult, difficult thing.

There are several threads of whiteness and blackness tangled in the above narrative. Earlier in the interview, Marical explained to me how she had often been positioned as "the token ethnic" by virtue of her phenotype. Here, however, she explored the ways that she had experienced hostility from members of the black community who raced her as white, her racial authenticity being continually challenged and contested by virtue of her light skin. Marical experienced the razor's edge of racialized categories. By insisting that her "packaging doesn't fit with my insides," she illustrated how her phenotype clashed with her politicized identification as a black woman. Marical also expressed frustration with her hair as a signifier of whiteness.

She had toyed with the idea of cutting it or changing it but had despaired that doing so would make her look more white:

> And my hair's all frizzy, you know. But see, everything is like so bloody political, I think, when you're mixed race. Everything, your whole body, is like, is a political terrain. I'm tired of my hair. My hair's driving me crazy, okay? I've got this like big bush of a head of hair. And I wanted to dye it something, you know, I thought, okay, I'm going to dye it blond. But I, you know, I'm really torn about that. I'm like, oh my God, well is it going to make me look like I'm more white or is, you know, and I don't want that. Or like everything, like the decision to grow my hair, my decision to cut my hair. What if I cut all the curl out, then people will think that I'm white. You know what I mean? Like it's like this major thing. I can't ever be – not, I can be comfortable in my skin, but I mean it's just like this weird thing 'cause it's all like appearance and identity and people's screwed-up notions.

The failure to acknowledge the space between whiteness and blackness hides the reality that many women with lighter than black skin colour may have the option of passing as white. Marical expressed deep discomfort with the idea of passing as white, as clearly indicated by her tentative contemplations about dyeing her hair blond. For Marical, passing as nonwhite depended on a series of visual markers – ranging from her Ashanti clothing to her jewellery and her hair. Marical wanted to move away from her ability to adopt this currency. Although she was often perceived as white in some situations, she deliberately attempted to dislodge this perception by adopting certain visual cues that granted her ethnic group membership, emphasizing her identification with particular cultural practices. Marical acknowledged that she could, at times, wear the "knapsack of white privilege" (McIntosh 1988, 10). However, she read this dubious carte blanche entitlement as a sign of remaining invisible. In this way, whiteness was dislodged as something desirable for Marical.

It was the recognition of particular physical features as white, and their cultural significance, that some women in this study rejected. This positioning indicated a movement among some mixed race women to distance themselves from the normative currency of whiteness and clearly illustrated how physical characteristics and other cues, like skin colour, jewellery, or one's name, had been conflated with racial authenticity.

Some women went so far as to change their name in order to appear less white. In cases where they were judged to be of European ancestry because of their phenotype, the invisibility of their nonwhite identity was doubled when hidden behind an Anglicized name. As Ang-Lygate (1997, 180) notes, "Eurocentric naming practices render us invisible to each other, robbing us of pre-immigration identities, thus limiting opportunities for mutual recognition, affirmation and validation of our diasporic identities." Some participants changed their name to identify with their particular state of noncultural neutrality. Rhiannon had changed her name during college:

> I made a conscious decision to use my mother's maiden name. I think it was largely because I wanted to, in some way, make it obvious that I was of Chinese descent from one side of my family. I think that it's been a common experience for me for people to assume that I'm white, you know, nothing but white, not mixed race at all. I was getting kind of tired of that. I wanted to at least have it in my name that by name I had Chinese ancestry, and so that's when I started using my mother's maiden name as my last name.

Rhiannon's light eyes and brown hair often concealed her Asian ancestry, and she was therefore positioned as white outside of her family. She re-inscribed her public self by changing her name. Thus a different public persona emerged, recoding the way that people positioned her. In this way, she was no longer seen as being culturally neutral. Instead, she chose to position herself as culturally distinct from her peers. Changing her name was Rhiannon's way of empowering herself. Marical expressed similar sentiments about having a name that was not traditionally associated with whiteness. For her, changing her name was a symbol of her move away from whiteness:

> My middle name is Jane. But like Marical is just not an Anglo name, and I really like that. I like the fact that, that I'm identified by my name as not being white.

By changing her name, Marical actively sought a verbal marker to render her entrance into a particular community of colour. Some participants displayed an ability to comprehend the very real links between whiteness and privilege. At the same time, they revealed that since their perceived whiteness was often a liability, they deliberately dislodged perceptions of themselves as white by adopting particular cultural cues. The decisions regarding these choices were always in flux because the women in this study were racialized in dramatically different ways depending upon a variety of factors.

Conclusion

The policing of whiteness and the construction of essentialized boundaries around racial identity had implications for mixed race women in this study. Their stories illustrate the impossibility of being fixed by a single label when one is doubly racially marked. There are particular ways that women who are mixed race articulate the multiple tensions surrounding their ancestry within this increasingly two-tiered discourse. Participants' identifications with whiteness shifted through different spaces depending on the tensions of race, gender, and class. Whiteness was embodied through a series of tangled knots and roots. The tensions pulling on these knots shifted and changed daily. The women's deliberation upon their own ethnic identity was a strategic response to a shifting sense of time and place. Mixed race women in this study revealed an ability to employ a wide range of individual and personal strategies in order to combat particular readings of their whiteness by showing how attributes normally associated with whiteness – namely, white skin and privilege – are constructed. I have attempted to show in this chapter how women of mixed race trouble the spaces of whiteness. Depending on particular social contexts, their personal and public affiliation with whiteness shifts. Participants opened up possibilities for self-definition and political engagement by recognizing how their membership in whiteness was assigned in particular sociological and economic contexts. I am reminded here of the interviews with Marical, Davy, and Naela, in particular, who each explained that in some communities their whiteness was read as a liability. In this chapter, I have been concerned with the ability of mixed race women to grasp the subtleties of these situations and to choose the most effective strategy in the moment for transcending these boundaries. Paying attention to these nuanced dynamics allows us to think in terms of allegiances and connections as opposed to fragmentation and dissent, aiding in the avoidance of potential essentialism through a complex exploration of how processes of racialization are always shifting. This chapter has attempted to make space for the coexistence of different meanings in a more precise exploration of the racialization process, where meanings associated with racialized categories, like privilege and power, fluctuate in different places and are constructed in various ways. This chapter has attempted to disclose the currency of whiteness while demonstrating the ways that some mixed race women attempt to refuse it.

To conclude, I want to ask about future points of departure. These women's stories offer up one way of imagining what Gillian Rose (1993) deems a "paradoxical space." By "paradoxical," Rose means that spaces would be charted differently on a two-dimensional map, where centre and margin, inside and outside, would be occupied simultaneously. They articulate specific arguments about power and identity. There are other axes of social identity between these spaces of whiteness and blackness that have not yet been fully contemplated, potential places of dialogue that go beyond the dominant discourses of identity. We can also ask how some mixed race women, in their zeal to move away from whiteness, might divest themselves of the material privileges that accompany their brand of racial difference. Their proximity to whiteness allows them an opportunity to resist it. The next chapter addresses Teresa Kay Williams's (1996) disquieting questions about inhabiting the shades of grey, discussed above, by further exploring Rose's ideas and examining how mixed race women in this study developed unusual allegiances across racialized divides by employing the term "mixed race" to describe themselves in everyday dialogue.

# 5
Mongrels, Interpreters, Ambassadors, and Bridges?
Mapping Liberal Affinities among Mixed Race Women

> How are we going to find an adequate symbolic language to account for the fractured and plural identities of those ... who participate in several cultures?
>
> — SIMON 1991, 23

In Chapter 1 I explained how the mixed race woman has been made intelligible through the prism of racialized hierarchies that have historically positioned her as out of place. Nonbelonging is the dominant framework for mixed race identity. The supposed desire for assimilation into her parents' ethnic groups is popularly read as the trademark of the individual's experience of mixed race. In this chapter, I engage with ideas in feminist theory and participants' narratives to develop some alternative ways of interpreting the experience of mixed race beyond these characterizations. This chapter addresses Simon's (1991) claim that we must develop a different kind of language to understand better the experiences of those who live and work in more than one culture.

Dalmage (2004, 6) notes that "the Multicultural Movement has expanded its racial language, at times allowing for a more sophisticated understanding of race and racism. Primarily, a language is being created that is challenging notions of authenticity and the lines that divide racial communities." This chapter hopes to add to this expanded racial language by chronicling a different way of looking at the multiracial subject that pays attention to the affinities and affections they develop. McNeil (2010, 67) states, "All one can do is add context and understanding by introducing names and ideas that are often ignored in the study of mixed-race identities." I explore how some mixed race women inhabit what I call "mobile paradoxical spaces." I draw from this spatial metaphor to demonstrate some of the more complicated and unconventional alliances that mixed race women forge outside of ties to their own ethnicities. In other words, rather than further objectifying mixed race women and reinscribing them as out of place, I want to think about how we might envision how some mixed race women position themselves within the centres of their own cartographies.

I have coined the term "mobile paradoxical spaces" based upon a consideration of the work of two theorists, Gillian Rose and Elspeth Probyn, both of whom have largely influenced my thinking in this chapter. I provide examples of the ways that my informants occupied these mobile paradoxical spaces by exploring their attachment to the identification of mixed race – a label they negotiated, challenged, and contested daily. I suggest that interviews provide an exemplary site for examining the "constitutive contradictions" (Kondo 1997, 55) of identifying as mixed race. I hint at how women in my study further occupied mobile paradoxical spaces by actively creating alliances with others, often transcending socially constructed lines of difference.

As I demonstrated in Chapter 1, the public imaginary of the mixed race individual is often marked by a relentless negativity. The popular discourse is made up of a series of myths that explicitly declare the mixed race individual to be "out of place" or to have "no place to call home" (Root 1992; Tizard and Phoenix 1993; Ifekwunigwe 1999; Olumide 2002; Dalmage 2004; DaCosta 2007), which fractionalizes the mixed race person's experience. Although the "out of place" metaphor is a tired one, it still fuels the dichotomous and divisive situation in critical mixed race theory. "Out of place" brings to mind images of isolation, fear, dread, terror, loneliness, or despair (Cresswell 1996). This tendency to focus upon mixed race individuals' problematic nature through the use of terms like "marginal," "groupless," and "outsider" reflects a pervasive psychopathology. Much of this discourse derives from ideas about people's attachment to their ethnic community. It presumes that people of shared ancestry necessarily share a common bond. However, obviously shared ethnicity does not mean interests are always aligned. We deny or devalue other social axes of difference when we reduce individuals to their ethnic identity. As Ifekwunigwe (1997a, 127) remarks, mixed race "experiences of multiple identities, which are necessarily contradictory, socioculturally constructed and essentialized, demand new paradigms for looking at belonging."

I respond to Simon's (1991) challenging question that opened this chapter by exploring a spatial metaphor to counter the dominant popular imaginary. There are other spatial metaphors associated with a mixed race identity. Root (1996b, xxi), for example, uses the metaphor of "border crossing" to highlight the shifting of foreground and background, a concept I explore in greater detail in Chapter 6. However, in this chapter, I focus upon the development of a new spatial metaphor in light of my informants' revelations. I want to offer sharper explorations of the mixed race experience by mapping out the rapidly shifting modalities of forces that shape everyday life. Thus I turn away from the inside-outside model of exclusion (Sibley 1995) as a guide for thinking about the complex patterns of social relations. This model necessitates rendering singular the object for inquiry. It does not allow for a vision of the interconnectedness between supposedly discrete entities, totalizing the diversity of social life by setting up an opposition between authentic and inauthentic social relations (I.M. Young 1986). I am much less interested in where informants felt out of place than in where they felt in place. I want to talk about the productive spaces that are created out of a desire to create connections. I embrace Probyn's (1996, 41) definition of desire as "a method of doing things, of getting places ... Desire here is the mode of connection and communication between things, inevitably giving way to the literalness of things." There are other varied and diverse senses of belonging that call for a more reflexive, spatialized vocabulary to weave together these colourful tapestries of identity.

As I commented in Chapter 1, to provide a more accurate account of how individuals move in the social world, I believe that we need to transcend those discourses of identity that seek to allocate belonging through a certain articulation of difference. I suggest a perspective that turns away from conflict, divisions, and difference and toward notions of alliances, affiliations, and unity. To do so, I propose the notion of mobile paradoxical spaces, which suggests how participants negotiated their experiences of being propelled into forms of living with others by creating and fashioning coalitions. I suggest that mobile paradoxical spaces were an inherent part of my informants' daily existence. These identifications served as a "marker of ... contemporary social fluidity and dispossession [and] a ... new stability, self-assurance and quietism" (R.J.C. Young 1995, 4). Through the interpretation of my informants' stories, I attempt to answer the following questions: What are mobile paradoxical spaces, and can they be mapped through interviews with mixed race women in this study? Are there ways of being that take pleasure in transcending traditional modes of identity formation? How can we demonstrate pluralities of belonging outside the familiar markers of race, class, and gender?

Defining Mobile Paradoxical Spaces

> Belonging cannot be housed simply within the material space of walls and roofs, of fenced topographies and well-drawn maps.
>
> — MUFTI AND SHOHAT 1997, 1

As noted above, my metaphor of mobile paradoxical spaces is inspired by the work of two feminist theorists: Gillian Rose and Elspeth Probyn. In particular, I combine Rose's (1993) "paradoxical space" and Probyn's (1996) exploration of "outside belongings," concepts examined in this section. First, however, I should explain briefly why I have coined a new spatial metaphor. I was initially reluctant to invent a new expression to describe the multitextured belongings forged by my participants for fear of creating another vacuous identity category. As I listened to their voices ringing with laughter on my tape recorder, I was reminded of Nandy's (1983) astute observation that instead of admitting the failure of our categories, social scientists prefer to clobber our empirical experiences until they fit those categories. Given that women in this study adamantly objected to being "boxed" within certain categories of identity, I was especially wary of creating a new one. The last thing I wanted to do was impose a new phrase on the experiences revealed in the interviews. Instead, the metaphor of mobile paradoxical spaces emerged through the long-term process of engaging with interviews, theorists, and my own experiences of mixed race. I hope that it hints at my discovery of the potential coalitions that can be forged among mixed race women.

Many cultural geographers have pointed out the limits of spatial interpretations for theoretical analysis (Smith and Katz 1993; McKittrick 2006). Keith (1991, 182) suggests that there is a "seductive danger of creating a false duality between the world of metaphors on one hand and a world of reality on the other." However, I deliberately use this metaphor to illuminate the social worlds of participants. Consequently, holding together the two different sites as proposed by Rose and Probyn may give us pause for more productive reflection upon the complex and contradictory relationships within the social. I hope the reader will discover some unexpected resonances between the real-life worlds of participants and the theoretical worlds of the academy. I wish to recognize my own complicit academic stance here as well. In mapping out mobile paradoxical spaces, I am very deliberately delineating borders and boundaries. It is imperative to acknowledge my own collusion as the cartographer who has developed her own legend in coining this metaphor, and I have employed it in particular ways to map out these spaces (for a cogent critique, see McKittrick 2006).

In developing the metaphor of mobile paradoxical spaces, I hope to resolve the inevitable impasse between metaphoric and real space, or between "the comfort of the abstract and the relevance of the empirical, the seduction of the ivory tower and the romance of the street" (Keith 1991, 182). I stand firmly by Pile's (1998) assertion that one way to contribute to the discipline is by "asking new questions and developing new metaphors." I do not read the coining of this new metaphor as an escape from reality. Rather, I envision it as the creation of a legend through which I may be able to map out some untravelled terrain. Through this prism, I hope that the day-to-day realities of participants can be brought to bear outside of previous misrepresentations. In short, I employ the metaphor because I believe it provides a way to illuminate the continually changing configurations of connections among participants.

I was perhaps predisposed to ponder paradox because it has been read as an inherently Canadian trait. For example, Moss (1998) has emphasized that "paradox as a way of coping with complexity is very Canadian." Indeed, many literary scholars in Canada have dissected notions of paradox. However, I focus primarily on the notion of paradox as developed by feminist geographer Gillian Rose, who has made a significant contribution in geography with her book *Feminism and Geography* (1993). In the final chapter of her book, Rose explores the possibility of a paradoxical space. This chapter resonated deeply with my own experiences as a mixed race woman, and after reading through my informants' interviews, I felt convinced that Rose's notion of "paradoxical space" was also very useful for describing the spaces forged by women of mixed race in my study.

First, a short synopsis of the book is useful for putting Rose's argument about paradoxical space into context. Rose's aim in *Feminism and Geography* is to question the enduring masculinism that has structured geographic inquiry. The majority of her book demonstrates how masculinity has shaped geographical epistemology as well as the theoretical contributions of the discipline. She develops this argument in the first half of the book through a series of essays in which she interrogates two kinds of masculinism within contemporary geography: social scientific masculinity and aesthetic masculinity. I was most inspired by the last half of the book, where Rose attempts to develop some possible feminist strategies to counter those sorts of powerful masculinisms inherent in the discipline.

Rose explores some descriptions of oppressive spaces as territories in which women are caught. She suggests that many women's difficulties in spaces might be understood through masculinist claims to know, reflected through claims to space and territory. Clearly, for many women, "being in space is not easy" (Rose 1993, 143), and Rose explains how women experience confinement in space – a recurring image in women's accounts of their lives.

To challenge these oppressive spaces, Rose (1993) explores how feminist writers imagine a space beyond this masculinist territorial logic. Citing Gloria Anzaldúa (1987), bell hooks (1990), and Donna Haraway (1991), among others, Rose assembles a cross-section of feminist work that challenges masculinisms. In her search for ways to overturn binary conceptions and construct a spatiality that makes room for the experiences of multiple "others" in nonhierarchical arrangements, Rose draws upon the work of feminists bell hooks (1990) and Minnie Bruce Pratt (1984) in particular. Both of these writers talk about occupying a doubled position, where one is located both inside and outside, neither here nor there, neither quite belonging nor completely excluded. These spaces, Rose argues, are inherently paradoxical.

Paradoxical space acknowledges multiple dimensions or ways of articulating "a sense of elsewhere beyond the territories of the master subject" (Rose 1993, 151). The key point is that women are envisioned as being located in several social spaces at the same time – within the centres and the margins – simultaneously. Rose (ibid., 152-53) examines the paradoxes of occupying these spaces at the same time, highlighting the subversive potential of this position: "The simultaneous occupation of centre and margin can critique the authority of masculinism ... help[ing] some feminists to think about both recognizing differences between women and continuing to struggle for change as women ... The spaces of separatism in these discussions, then, is also a space of interrelations – another paradox." Challenging insider-outsider positionings, paradoxical spaces "imply radically heterogeneous geometries" that are "lived, experienced and felt" (ibid., 140-41), creating "not so much a space of resistance as an entirely different geometry through which we can think power, knowledge, space and identity in critical and, hopefully, liberatory ways" (ibid., 159).

A politics of paradoxical space works toward an emancipatory geography that examines new relationships among power, knowledge, space, and social action. Exploring how the subject of feminism depends upon a paradoxical geography to acknowledge the power of hegemonic discourses while insisting on potential sites of resistance, Rose (1993, 155) invokes the metaphor of paradoxical space to articulate a geography that

> describes that subjectivity as that of both prisoner and exile; it allows the subject of feminism to occupy both the centre and the margin, the inside and the outside ... a geography structured by the dynamic tension between such poles ... a multidimensional geography structured by the simultaneous contradictory diversity of social relations ... a geography which is as multiple and contradictory and different as the subjectivity imagining it.

To summarize, paradoxical space is imagined as an intervention in masculinist claims of knowing. It evokes one possible geography that focuses upon women creating their own geographies of knowledge, where they are centred as subject, not marginalized as object. Rose explores a different kind of subjectivity, where women are neither victims nor perpetrators of the experiences of displacement. She imagines a reconceptualized territory where women are not positioned as "out of place" but as constitutive of their own spatialities, which do not replicate ancient exclusions in geography.

Paradoxical space gets at the mobility and simultaneity of particular subject positions. I find the idea particularly appealing because it suggests a way to theoretically map a geography that goes beyond dominant and dualistic discourses of identity. Feminist geographers have long identified the importance of moving beyond singular mappings of dualistic social power relations onto territorial spaces, like masculine and feminine onto public and private. Rose (1993) recognizes the malady and comes up with a potential cure by suggesting the possibility of a space beyond dualisms.

Rose (1993) admits that her argument about paradoxical space remains partial because it surfaces largely from her own rooted experience of everyday places. She is therefore tentative to offer paradoxical space as part of a new and improved feminist orthodoxy for thinking about space in geography. However, she ends *Feminism and Geography* (ibid., 160) by asking "for a geography that acknowledges that the grounds of its knowledge are unstable, shifting, uncertain, and above all, contested. Space itself [is] insecure, precarious, and fluctuating ... Other possibilities, other sorts of geographies, with different compulsions, desires and effects, complement and contest each other. This chapter has tried to describe just one of them. There are many more." With this cliffhanger, Rose firmly sets a radical agenda for the future of feminist geography. I initially expected that such a bold call would elicit myriad responses from feminist geographers. However, no one has yet attempted to map out the political terrain of Rose's paradoxical space (but see George 1996). I find this ironic, given that many scholars resoundingly concur that Rose's notion of paradoxical space "crackles with possibilities" (Katz 1997, 230). It seems many geographers identify with paradoxical space – indeed, celebrate it (see ibid.) – yet landscapes of paradoxical space have yet to be mapped. Untouched in this manner, paradoxical space sadly sits gathering dust on the shelf of feminist geography scholarship, a concept that is grounded only through theoretical examples in feminist studies.

In this chapter, I want to take paradoxical space off the shelf in order to explore some potentially exciting readings of mixed race. Although Rose may read her ideas as partial, her discussion is rich and tantalizing, pointing toward the possibilities of describing some new feminist geographies. In particular, many of her ideas about paradoxical space struck a chord with me as a mixed race woman. I see many parallels between Rose's idea of paradoxical space and the stories of women in this study, who explained to me that they were located in a variety of spaces at the same time – spaces that were, all at once, multidimensional, shifting, and contingent. The metaphor of paradoxical space helps to illuminate some of these experiences.

Many sections of the interview transcript immediately spring to mind. Marical explained that her experience of mixed race was rife with paradox:

> I'm a blond-haired, blue-eyed black girl, you know? That's a strange positioning to be ... I exist against all odds. You know, in a lot of ways? Unfortunately (laughter), my very existence stares all these basic theories about human existence right in their face. Like it challenges that. So your physicality, your whole body, totally, you know, challenges the idea that races shouldn't mix, that this is the way things are, that these

facts exist, that the truth exists in this way. Because if all this were true, then I wouldn't exist. And I exist – therefore, it cannot be true. You know it's like this total, it's ridiculous! It's like this existential nightmare! We are existential nightmares! (laughter)

Marical's mere existence trumpets a wake-up call to those who continue to falsely assume that racial categories exist as discrete entities. Yet the racialized hierarchy refuses to acknowledge her presence. Living in this space is not easy – it is, as Rose reminds us, precarious and fluctuating. But it is not completely hard, either. As I hope to show, Marical refused to locate herself solely within a marginal space. Instead, she adopted a productive stance structured by the diversity of social relations. Marical inhabited a paradoxical space that was as diverse as Marical herself.

This is only one example of the participants' occupation of paradoxical space. Like Rose says, there are many more. In response to Rose's call, I will provide more examples that ground paradoxical space in the lived world. I hope to contribute to an envisioning of space where women of mixed race do not see themselves as either "out of place" or part of a geography of exclusion. This is not an easy task. To take on this enterprise, I draw from Elspeth Probyn, whose *Outside Belongings* (1996) complements the work of Rose. Themes of mobility and paradox thread through both authors' explorations. In her "sociology of the skin" (Probyn 1996, 5), Probyn focuses upon notions of process and movement inherent in forging belongings. She asks how aspiration is played out among individuals, insisting upon the importance of mapping everyday manners of being. I find Probyn's work appealing for three reasons. First, she concerns herself with problematizing the particularities of identity. Second, she expresses a desire to spatialize identifications. Finally, she provides a compelling critique of belonging.

Similar to my concerns regarding fragmented and fluid identities, voiced in Chapter 1, Probyn (1996) longs for a term that captures more than "identity" can express. In her critique of identity politics – where one is stuck within the fixities of an identity category, such as "feminist," and feels compelled to act accordingly – Probyn proposes that we do not live out our lives as general categories. Instead, she hints that varied forms of existence offer alternative modes of belonging that spill over static identity boundaries. Insisting that identity classifications too often slide into modes of difference, where it becomes extremely difficult to talk at the same time about gender, nation, minority, majority, sexuality, and so on, she explains that she instead wishes to further ground the particularities of identity:

> That identity is problematic is hardly news within theoretical circles, where identity is, of course, fragmented, decentred, and all the rest. However, it seems to me that the discourse of identity as fragmented continues to be abstracted from the local ground in which one lives one's presumably decentred life ... I wonder why there is so little discussion of how these factors are embodied and how they play out in Peoria (or Bloomington or Burlington or Regina). (Ibid., 71)

Probyn seems almost exasperated by the intellectual hegemony of American scholarship, particularly in cultural studies, where the contemporary theoretical tone is one of "nowhereness and everywhereness" (ibid.). Against this disembodied tenor, Probyn encourages us to develop expressions outside of the general by looking at examples of specific local embodied practices in the everyday. She is concerned with how identity becomes altered and shaped along the rugged terrain of belonging. She insists that there is no fixed identity or final destination. Instead, she is fascinated with how people "get along," which leads her to ask how various forms of belonging are articulated:

> [I am concerned with developing] an ethical practice of belonging and a politics of singularity that must start from where one is – brutally and immediately from one's ... modes of being ... [so] that we may be able to catch the constructedness of alternative manners ... encourag[ing] the movement away from thinking and living difference and specificity as a negative ... to turn identity inside out so that instead of capturing us under its regime of difference as a negative measure, the desire of belonging becomes a force that proffers new modes of individuation. (Ibid., 23, 90-91)

Probyn calls for new ways of intervening in the social by "outsiding ourselves" (ibid., 152). She asks us to bring to the surface particular actions and feelings that are normally hidden even to ourselves. By doing so, Probyn imagines interconnectedness experienced between supposedly separate entities.

Lastly, I am inspired by Probyn's critique of the term "belonging" in light of my own work. Although I admit "belonging" can communicate ideas of home, security, and stability, it is not always a warmly persuasive term. Probyn (1996, 40) explains that "belonging" can convey notions of "longing to be" somewhere or the desire to be part of something, echoing Michel Foucault's concerns with "desire = lack." Foucault once told Gilles Deleuze (1994, 63), "With much kindness and affection ... I cannot stand the word desire; even if you use it differently, I can't help myself thinking or living desire = lack, or that desire says repression."

The implications of this idea for my own work struck me as invaluable. I documented in Chapter 1 how the mixed race individual has been positioned as "out of place" or "not belonging." This has exacerbated (mis)representations of the mixed race woman, who has been made intelligible in oppressive ways. In analyzing my interviews, I realized that participants did not dwell excessively upon passive or unfulfilled desires to belong. Instead, the interviews were rich with stories about active connections forged through movement across social cleavages. This focus reflects the kinds of questions I asked participants. Because questions remained open-ended, participants had the opportunity to talk about what mattered to them rather than about what mattered to me as a researcher. I suggest that participants in this study focused upon the ways that they got on and got by in a racialized world. I wondered whether there were other theoretical ways to talk about these processes of creating connections without using the term "belonging"? This question led me to Probyn's use of the term.

Probyn (1996) asks us to contemplate notions of belonging as movement rather than as static positionings. Probyn regards belonging neither as fixed nor as rooted in some deep authentic way but as being in constant movement. Modes of belonging are envisioned as "surface shifts" in an attempt to capture "the range of desiring identities that are displayed all around" (Probyn 1996, 19). Her exploration is not divorced from that of paradoxical space. Fundamental to her argument about belonging is the paradox that "any singularity of belonging must continually be freed and encouraged in its movement to constantly become other" (ibid., 153). Thus belonging can take on myriad forms. Probyn encourages the development of contradictory relations of belonging that may coexist, overlapping in paradoxical spheres.

By positioning the self as a point of departure as opposed to a site of authentic origin, Probyn provides a way to consider transcending traditional definitions of ethnicity. I doubt Probyn would disagree that the mixed race individual has been positioned as "out of place" in the social landscape. However, I think she would encourage me to move beyond simple inside-outside characterizations in order to ponder mixed race as a productive zone instead of a site of lack. My desire in this chapter is to talk about the productive spaces that difference makes. Probyn's work provides a springboard toward imagining creative alliances and coalitions in neither solely inclusionary nor solely exclusionary terms. Her inquiry offers critical insight into contemplating spaces where belonging is imagined as a form that is always in transit or on the move. The phrase "mobile paradoxical space" provides a fairly flexible and rich metaphoric range, and I emphasize its ambivalent, fluid, and contradictory nature. I believe the term conveys ideas about contradiction and movement, both of which were key themes that emerged from interviews among participants. Keeping this in mind, I ask how we might be able to map mobile paradoxical spaces in relation to participants' daily lives. What struck me while reading the interview transcript were the multiple ways that participants occupied mobile paradoxical spaces as they went about their daily living, whether performing the banal chore of grocery shopping in the Quickie-Mart, frantically finishing documentaries under tight time constraints, or frequenting smoky dance clubs on Friday nights. Participants actively moved away from thinking and living difference as a negative. Rather, they conveyed to me the importance of bridging dynamic tensions among groups. The interviews were sprinkled with stories about the day-to-day experience of making connections with individuals – about how strangers became friends (Probyn 1996). At the same time, however, I don't want to romanticize this process. As will become evident, the racialized circumstances under which these women believed coalitions were forged emerged in contexts where social capital played a role in the success of the encounter.

In the remainder of this chapter, I consider participants' acounts of occupying mobile paradoxical spaces. I argue that mobile paradoxical spaces are forged not only through interrelations with other individuals but also through participants' relationships with particular personal identifications. To elucidate this idea, I show how participants contemplated the "mixed race" label as a mobile paradoxical identification. This idea resonates with what Saldanha (2006, 19) deems a "machinic geography of bodies." Saldanha argues that a machinic geography of bodies would explore the connections that racialized bodies create with "things and places, how they work, travel, fight, write, love – how these bodies become viscous, slow down, get into certain habits, *into certain collectivities,* like city, social stratum, or racial formation" (ibid., my emphasis). The next section examines the ways that participants identified with, yet at the same time challenged, contested, and sometimes even discarded, the "mixed race" label.

Mapping out Mobile Paradoxical Spaces in Relation to the Identification of Mixed Race

> If it is generally true that selves are constituted in relation to communities that have been racially constructed, what happens when there are multiple, conflicting communities through which a self is constituted? What would a concept of the self look like that did not valorize purity and coherence?
>
> — ALCOFF 2006, 270

I draw upon a series of examples to explain what participants thought about the "mixed race" label. Although all the women who participated in the study had, at some point, identified as "mixed race," it became clear during the interviews that informants chose to emphasize the ways that they negotiated their use of the phrase in their day-to-day lives. I will look at the ways that participants paid attention to the historical, geographical, cultural, psychological, and imaginative boundaries that provided the ground for their political self-definition, enabling them to speak about specific modes of reading and knowing the dominant forces that shaped their lives. Most women shifted their emphasis in announcing their mixed race status depending upon the context. Their indvidual approaches were related to their age and development, as they found that certain needs were best met when they used a specific approach. Whether they designated themselves as mixed race depended upon a range of factors, indicating that people might change the ways that they identify themselves over their lifetime. I demonstrate both the potential productivity and the limitations of the "mixed race" label while considering the ways that it constructs individual, social, and political identities. I will begin to explore the potential of grounding my metaphor by looking at the ways that my informants contemplated, negotiated, and challenged the identification of mixed race. Themes of mobility and paradox animate the passages that follow. I propose that informants played with the "mixed race" label, envisioning it as a temporary linguistic home across racialized terrains, a kind of wayside station during a long trek, or perhaps a comfortable place to take shelter for longer periods of time. First, I demonstrate that participants enthused about the "mixed race" label because it provided a way to convey a sense of their identities outside of the binary racialized vocabulary. Second, I explore the ways that informants contested and challenged the constraints of the label.

At times, the "mixed race" label suggests a way to articulate a non-categorical identity outside the racialized discourse. It can interrogate the exclusionary operations by which racialized categories are constituted. My interview with Marical attests to this freedom. Marical was often caught up in the euphoria of mixed race possibilities during our interview. She sat on the edge of her chair and waved her hands excitedly as she described how the category of mixed race provided a way out of the oppositional racialized lexicon:

> We need so much to be able to declare ... "I'm not black and I'm not white and I don't give a fuck if those are the only two options on the page, okay?" I'm mixed race and I'm not going to fit into the categories that you've built for me. I think that's essential ... Being mixed just recognizes a multiplicity of identities. It recognizes that fluidity. It recognizes the fact that somebody might think I'm white, somebody might think I'm black, but you know that, that there is like a sort of, there's nothing definite about things... I get that all the time, "Are you white or are you black?" you know, and it took me a while to get there but I always [say now], "I'm not, I'm both, I'm not either. I'm mixed race."

Marical demonstrated how identifying as mixed race can call exclusionary procedures into question. For her, the term interpellated new kinds of political subjects and offered a more politically vigorous replacement for racist categories. By insisting that she was neither black nor white but both, Marical unveiled the subversive potential of a paradoxical position. Her simultaneous occupation of the centre and the margin (white and black, inside and outside) produced a paradoxical space, where her identity was imagined as located not only within various social spaces but also at the poles of each dimension. Her narrative reveals the potential for a space beyond the territories of a master subject. By identifying as mixed race, Marical refused to be pinned down by a static model of racial identification and seized an opportunity to trouble racialized categories of identity.

Marical further revealed how she used the identification in the context of teaching. Marical worked part-time in Toronto's inner-city district, teaching disadvantaged youth how to make documentaries with video cameras. When I asked how her students identified her, she said wryly, "They think I'm white, or half-breed," laughing at the word "half-breed." I asked her why she was laughing, and she replied, rolling her eyes,

> Because it's just such a ridiculous term! And I always laugh, you know why? Because fuck, the kids that I work with, okay I gotta stop swearing now, the youth that I work with, for the longest time, would say to me, "Are you a half-breed?" And I'm like (with a snarl and a monotone voice), "I'm like mixed race." I'd sit them down, and I'd be like (slowly and purposefully), "Half-breed ... doesn't belong ... in our vocabulary!" (laughter) It's mixed race. And yet it still comes up, over and over again. I mean they don't mean any harm, and it's no big deal. But, yeah.

Our conversation was filled with these sorts of stories. For Marical, identifying as mixed race was a transgressive move. It might seem like a politically peripheral act, but it exposed the practices of the dominant majority in ways that mainstream politics often cannot. By communicating this to her students, I believe Marical adopted an empowering educational stance. She refused to be objectified by the derogatory term "half-breed." Instead, she claimed her own space by flipping the situation around and explaining to the students why she chose to identify as mixed race. Marical hoped this act would disrupt her students' readings of racial categories.

By identifying as mixed race, Marical created her own political option in a social landscape where she was often threatened with racial effacement. In other words, the identification of mixed race offers a crossroads of identification. It redeploys the means through which racialized subjects have been constituted. The label can articulate alternative modes of experience that spill over the boundaries of racialized categories, providing a way for women like Marical to "write her face" (Kondo 1997, 240) and subsequently rewrite the social script of race.

Makeda spoke of encountering a language of powerlessness in attempting to identify herself. She chose to contest what she experienced as a stifling racialized vocabulary. By identifying as mixed race, she engaged in opposition that was not only reactive but also creative and affirmative:

> If there was any value in [identifying as] mixed race, it's that we can puncture the purisms that exist on either side, right? That we can start to show the fallacy of kinda hermetic racial constructs, that they, these things make sense, and that they are definitive and absolute, and that we kinda defy that? We say, "No (laughter), actually, they're not absolute, um, and that there have been transgressions" ... I think it's important to affirm people's experiences within the racist culture that might deny them the ability to affirm all of their identities.

Identifying as mixed race can provide a position from which to articulate and transform social experiences. The term deinstitutionalized the norm of racial categories for Makeda, creating a space within which she could validate her multiple identities. This effect of the term was identified by several participants who stressed the "limitless" aspects of the label, which further demonstrates the paradoxical leanings of the identification. As Makeda emphasized,

> Well, some days I feel like [the "mixed race" label is] limitless? I know that's a very strange thing to say, and it's also about subversion ... It just seems to be something that defies absolutes.

Makeda explored the potential of a place where her identity could not be pinned down by a stereotype. In identifying as mixed race, Makeda did not necessarily need to launch into a long history of explanation about her ethnic background. It was therefore an attractive identification to many informants because it offered a way out of identifying with static ethnic delineations in favour of practising what Kobayashi and Peake (1994) would call an "un-natural discourse." However, whereas some read the label as limitless, other informants stressed its limits.

Here, I address the ways that participants objected to the use of the "mixed race" label to identify themselves. I do so to highlight the paradoxical character of the term. Some informants subjected the label to scrutiny by challenging, contesting, and negotiating the category. Although all of the women in this study identified themselves to me as mixed race in order to take part in this study, I was often surprised at how clearly they articulated their distaste for the term. I do not want to suggest that some women identified with the term wholeheartedly and that others wholly discouraged its use. Rather, the very same women who were enthusiastic about the label were often, at other times during the interview, highly dismissive of its use. Participants told me that the "mixed race" label was constraining in three ways: it reified the notion of race, it subsumed differences among individuals, and it privileged the idea of race over and above other social identities.

First, some women did not want to use the term "mixed race" to identify themselves because the term "race" was problematic to them. During interviews, some informants pointed out the paradox of identifying as mixed race, as the term can reify social categories. More specifically, they feared that using the term "mixed race" in fact entrenched the notion of race, validating the socially constructed concept and perpetuating the notion of race as adding value. During a poignant moment with me, Makeda thoughtfully took a sip of her tea, gazed at me, and enunciated clearly,

> I don't really want another category for mixed race identity. I don't really necessarily want that identity to be codified, because I think whenever race is codified, whether it is considered pure or impure or mixed or whatever ... it just facilitates the management of races. We've become a new target group, for studies, and I don't think necessarily that is what exploring mixed race identity should be about ... It tends to support the idea that race is empirical? Like it's so empirical that in fact it's divisible, um, you can add two races and create a new one, and it becomes a science again. And I think we have to take race out of the category of science. I don't really see any point to creating a new category. I don't think that creating a new category actually answers the question. I think it postpones the question.

Makeda raised a very crucial question about the "mixed race" label: what does this category of identity actually do to challenge the fixity of racial categories? She suggested that asserting a mixed race identity may actually require belief in biological race. "Mixed-ness per se really challenges only the existing sets of categories, not the category of 'race' itself" (Garner 2010, 100). Makeda explained that she was concerned about the ways that mixed race people are being scrutinized, almost as though under a microscope, as a new group for social analysis – a group that can be predicated on reifying race as a biological category. As Kawash (1997, 129-30) states, "If we are to take seriously the idea that race is not a biological but a cultural fiction, then we must confront not only the fictionality of the biological way of understanding race but also the fictionality of the cultural way of seeing race." Makeda further suggested that unless the complicity of race is implicated in studies on mixed race individuals, mixed race studies can obscure, and may even prevent, potentially promising epistemological and pedagogical analyses of racialized experiences. She explained that use of the word "race" reinforces the myth that races actually do exist but does nothing to puncture the myth of racial purity. Makeda was skeptical about encouraging the development of yet another racial category and explored various political challenges concerning its usefulness. Sexton (2008, 5) has noted that it would be more useful for critical mixed race studies to "disassemble the architecture of multiracial discourse, itemizing the elementary binaries through which it establishes its operative terms and uncovering the relations of force it obscures in the process." As Makeda rightly suggested, creating a new category of mixed race may postpone, rather than address, questions about the paradox of race. It is interesting to note that earlier Makeda had discussed the potential of the term "mixed race" in a positive manner. It became obvious during the interviews that some women recognized the category's complicity in upholding the fixity of race.

Second, some women in this study defied and challenged any one meta-reading of a mixed race experience. During our interview, Davy expressed her concern with the ways that the term "mixed race" can create unwarranted generalizations about the individuals who adopt it. Davy suggested to me the importance of not homogenizing a mixed race experience:

> There's a common misunderstanding that anyone who calls themselves mixed race has had very similar life experiences. And it's not like that. We have some common threads, but you know, my experience as a racially mixed person ... who grew up in a country where white was the dominant race and culture, and I grew up totally outside of the black culture, my experience is very different from someone who is exactly the same genetic makeup as me, but with who both parents are black, and who grew up in, say, Mississippi. Or who grew up in Dominica. Or who grew up in Germany. You know, a totally different experience. And we can all look exactly the same, but our experiences are different depending on where we were located, geographically.

The specifities and particularities of the mixed race experience were emphasized by Davy. By talking about the experiences of someone who had lived in Dominica and Germany, Davy made a distinction between the processes of racialization in different places. Someone of identical "genetic makeup" would have a radically different experience in Germany, a country with a long and troubled history of ethnic conflict and tension, than in Dominica, which has a much larger mixed race population. In making this distinction, Davy emphasized that material realities shape what being mixed race means. Social conditions in the daily landscape are more complex than the term "mixed race" can encapsulate.

The experience of living in different places plays a role in how an individual experiences her ethnicities. Clearly, for Davy, location mattered (see Massey and Allen 1984)! She insisted that the experience of mixed race differs fundamentally depending upon location. Davy challenged the "mixed race" label because it projects the possibility of drawing all otherness into the whole it endorses. The label obscures the diversity of face-to-face interactions in very different social, economic, political, and cultural contexts. Therefore, an identification as mixed race can impose a unilateral homogeneity upon mixed race individuals when it is utilized as a unifying category, further fostering the myth of an "authentic" ethnicity and unveiling assumptions about the desirability of racial purity.

Third, many participants expressed concern with use of the "mixed race" label to define their racial identity because it tends to privilege race or descent over and above other social identities, illustrating a tendency to assume that such women do not engage in life on multiple and often conflicting levels (Ang-Lygate 1997). The literature on mixed race has assumed that race dictates identity (Thornton 1996). I do not dismiss the importance of racial components in determining both the development and the sorts of interactions that the mixed race person experiences. However, many women in this study felt that race and ethnicity comprised only a single aspect of their identity. My informants revealed how their experiences of being racialized represented only one dimension of their identity. As Emma and Katya pointed out,

> Overall, the issue of race in my life has been part of who I am, but it's only been part. (Emma)

> But for all intents and purposes, on a very very surface level, in the way that I can say that I am mixed, half-white and half-black, which to me does not go anywhere near to defining the reality of it. (Katya)

I suggest that Emma's and especially Katya's statements point out the limitations of using both race and ethnicity as concepts to define a person's identity. Theoretically, feminists still battle with these questions in regard to the complex interweave of race and gender. Many women told me that the "mixed race" label can prioritize race as its central analytical category, the primary social relation on which experiences are based and identities constructed. This can privilege race at the expense of other factors, like gender. Participants explained that racial identifications did not represent their entire sense of self. This point was hammered home by Faith and Julia, both of whom insisted on telling me that they saw themselves as "more than their race." In particular, both of these women pointed out the salience of gender during interviews with me.

Julia, a filmmaker, was actively engaged in trying to acquire funding for her latest project at the time of our interview. Given that the film was, understandably, the centre of her world at the time, many of her revelations around mixed race were framed through her readings of her current production. When I asked her how she read her mixed race status, she explained:

> Right now I think my primary thing is seeing myself first as a woman because even as a woman of mixed minority, of mixed race and being among men of various races, I still am subordinated to those men, and I think the fight as a woman to make it transcends all the racial boundaries. And to me, getting the story of women out there first is very much the priority. Like in dealing with [the characters in my film], I am fascinated first and foremost by the woman who is behind him who had his child and who deserted him.

Although Julia identified as mixed race in some arenas, she told me that in the context of "right now," she was more concerned with identifying as a woman and all the political struggles that might entail. These interviews showed me the impossibility of untangling race and gender distinctions as separate entities, reminding me of Gibson-Graham's (1996, 241) powerful insight that individuals are a "unique ensemble of contradictory and shifting subjectivities," where race and gender are undisputedly co-constructed (Ware 1992).

Faith echoed these sentiments. As we sat munching chocolate-chip cookies on a beautiful sunny day in Toronto, Faith joked on tape that when I next heard her voice, I would be transcribing her words in a small, damp room in rainy London. When we had almost reached the end of the interview, I stood up and brushed off the crumbs, saying almost as an afterthought, "I think that's pretty much it ... Well, wait, um, what's the biggest challenge facing you as a woman who is mixed?" Realizing how loaded that question was, I stammered, "Well, how do you see your mixed identity?" Before I could change the question, Faith looked at me oddly and shrugged, as if I had been missing the point throughout the entire interview:

> You know what, Minelle? Like I said, whether it's naive or not, I haven't really felt any challenges in being mixed. I tend to akin myself to the challenge of being a woman. Like I really do identify with that more.

There are a few points I would like to make here. First, Faith asserted, as she did throughout our interview, that she had experienced very little racism. This fascinated me because although she insisted that she had not experienced "out and out" racism, like being refused entry into exclusive places, she obviously had been called all sorts of racial slurs throughout her life. She did not, however, cite those experiences as racist. In telling me, "I really do identify with [being a woman] more," Faith asserted that the day-to-day challenges she faced were more clearly rooted in patriarchy than in racism.

    I wish to make a point regarding my role as an academic researcher in the production of this narrative. With the phrase "whether it's naive or not," Faith alluded to my more academic readings of race and gender. By practising what I call inoculation – denigrating herself as naive, or less academic – Faith could politely convey to me that she felt I was spending way too much time thinking about the academic issues of race and feminism. Indeed, she told me afterward that it seemed odd to her that I would study the kinds of dynamics she took for granted in her day-to-day life. These sorts of exchanges between the (academic) researcher and the (nonacademic) researched need to be more fully unravelled in relation to the kinds of information academics gather. I also want to flag my own anxiety as a young and inexperienced academic researcher. Over the course of my interview with Faith, I had obviously become so relaxed that I suddenly realized at the end that I had dropped my academic stance along the way. I then drastically overcompensated and stumbled over the phrasing of my question.

    Other women in the study explored the paradoxes of the "mixed race" label more abstractly, explaining that it can often encourage an essentialized identity that ignores the materiality of other key factors – like class, sexuality, temperament, and geography – which are continually being reinterpreted and negotiated in different spheres. Many mixed race creative writers have explored this theme. Explaining the ways that a friend would describe himself, Lisa Jones (1994, 64) insists that the term "biracial" "wouldn't have been fierce enough, specific enough, or ultimately progressive enough." As Renee Tajima (1996, 278) ironically says about her mixed race identity, "I was a Cubs fan long before I ever considered myself Asian American."

Darius explained that the "mixed race" label draws attention away from our potential sameness, furthering the divisive discourse on difference:

> Because of this concern that I have, like is it a good thing to just create a new barrier, another box, around ourselves as mixed race? Is it a good thing to call ourselves a community, because then we are basically just creating separation that sort of denies our commonalities as human beings, and I don't feel totally comfortable with that. At the same time I do recognize that we live in a racialized world, that we live in a world that separates us into different races, and makes boxes around us, so as long as there are boxes, then as long as, in exploring it, as long as there are boxes, then it's good for us to be able to find a definition for ourselves as individuals, and within a greater context. Especially if we can do that while also maintaining the awareness that it does change, and it does overlap, and it does, we have many different identities, within one identity. I certainly, the sum total of my experience of myself is not as a mixed race woman, usually. There are many many things that I identify with. And I would be concerned about that identity if that wasn't the case. You know, I wouldn't want myself to be put in such a box that that was my whole identity of myself. That's only my identity in the context of a conversation about race. In a different conversation, my identity is a totally different thing. Which is really related to a lot of other things we've talked about, in that how geography or situation or circumstance affects how one defines oneself.

Darius explained that the "mixed race" label is fraught with numerous paradoxes. When she agreed to do the interview, we initially talked on the phone for an hour, and she emphasized how pleased she was to discover that I was doing a study on mixed race women. Although she recognized the value of identifying as mixed race, she was also acutely aware that the label can generate new sorts of boundaries, borders, and exclusions. In acknowledging the "overlap" among the many different identities that made up her identity, Darius explained that she related to the term "mixed race" in a paradoxical way, depending upon her location and when race was a primary issue. Evidently, it was not a stable identification. Depending upon the conversation she was in or the place she found herself, Darius would identify herself differently. She emphasized that although her experience of mixed race had shaped her life in important and essential ways, she also had a wide array of other sorts of experiences. These aspects could be erased if she chose to identify only with the "mixed race" label as a description of herself. Darius's variable self was not just a matter of racial identity roles but also changed considerably, as she said, depending upon "geography or situation or circumstance," echoing Probyn's (1996) ideas about belonging being forged on the move.

Other informants who had not been as influenced by academic writing associated the "mixed race" label with a proliferation of political correctness, which they saw as "poisoning" the social landscape. Although they identified as mixed race in the initial request for participants, they revealed during their interview with me their concern that the "mixed race" identification may mean the development of another racial label void of any real political impetus.

I return to Faith's narrative here. Faith agreed wholeheartedly to do the interview but grimaced when I asked her whether she identified as a mixed race woman. She responded passionately: "I hate the word 'mixed,' I just hate it. I don't know why, it just seems like this hodgepodge, this mix." She frowned when discussing the label, suggesting that it discourages dialogue among groups and encourages dichotomies:

> I think [mixed race] is just another label. That is a label. It's just another social label ... If you're a strong, like, you feel strongly, and well developed, and understand who you are, as a person, especially as a mixed person, you have to realize that those races don't divide, define you. What about the whole Indian thing, like you know how you always say, like Indian people are taxi drivers, weird stupid things? You don't fit into any of those labels. You have to understand as a person that you are who you are. I am an ambitious person, or a kind person, or you're all those different things. That's what makes YOU, and if people accept themselves, and realize that, I mean, labels are going to

> be there, and they are important in the sense that yes, I am some Chinese. And I am some Polynesian. But not try and separate each other, by those things? Well why wouldn't you have a club for, well I guess they do, for philanthropists, people who are generous? Well they do. But then why would we have, why wouldn't we do clubs along those lines, different things on those lines, instead of by race? Yuck, it's annoying. It's getting out of hand, it's getting so political and ridiculous ... So yes, it's like another social label ... People should try and mix more!

Faith's frustration with the creation of another label was clearly visible in her statement that things were getting far too "political and ridiculous." Faith's thoughts reflected her lack of engagement in academe, which was where most of the women in this study had become aware of the term "mixed race" – in feminist theory courses, for example. The term has not yet become part of the common culture in Canada, and Faith's dismissal of it reflected that. Expressing her exasperation with the "mixed race" label, Faith insisted upon the importance of defining herself outside of racialized categories and instead focused upon her character traits (her kindness and ambition) as more accurately reflecting how she felt about her identity. Clearly, groupings on the basis of race undermined Faith's sense of her distinctiveness and subsumed her identity within an essentialized notion of self that she eschewed.

The paradox of this situation does not elude me. Although Faith prominently identified with the actual experience of being mixed race, she expressed her concerns about reading her life experiences through the "mixed race" label. By saying that "people should try and mix more," Faith suggested that the "mixed race" label obscures multiple truths about an individual's ability to affiliate with many groups. Faith was skeptical about the development of clubs celebrating mixed race:

> Well first of all I think it's ridiculous that they hold meetings. I think it's absolutely retarded. Maybe it can be useful, like I'm enjoying [doing this interview] thoroughly! Like I'm sure if there were three more of the women you interviewed here, we'd have a grand old time chatting. But I wouldn't start a club just so that we could do this once a week, or once a month. It's ridiculous! People need to get beyond those labels. You can't just start creating your own little clubs and weird things.

Faith subtly conveyed that although she felt a group of mixed race women would share some experiences in common, there may not be enough there to warrant the development of a friendship. Faith was loathe to separate herself into isolated compartments, so she rejected the "mixed race" label. I also add that Faith chose to claim the universal (over the particular) in this situation, which can be problematic in its denial of positionality. Denying the ways that particular groups have been oppressed can sometimes represent a denial of the strategic necessity of deploying those marked identities in shared political struggles (Kondo 1997). As Darius explained,

> I think there's got to be a way to include that possibility, that our being mixed has an impact upon everything else that we do, and on some level recognize that we're having this conversation for the purpose of exploring racial issues. Therefore, that is the language within which we're speaking. And, that is just one, that we agree to sort of suspend other things for the purpose of developing this one little area. And it's good to have, it's good to speak it. Because then you feel this certain sort of release of remembering that this isn't just yeah, my whole identity. Because then again, identity is such a complex thing. You know?

For Darius, it was important to develop further political consciousness around issues of mixed race – a priority clearly indicated by her contributions to, and pamphletting of, the *Mixed Messages* newsletter in Toronto, a biyearly compilation of news about mixed race individuals. Like Darius, some women in this study used the term "mixed race" politically, adopting it as an active political identification despite the risk of temporary essentialism. This finding is not dissimilar from that of DaCosta (2007, 138), whose own study of mixed race individuals showed that some mixed race people found meaning and solace through group conversations about the experience of multiraciality: "Telling these stories, often in group settings, produces ... a bonding kind of experience." Darius found a way to temporarily bridge the impasse between the paradoxes of the mixed race identification. I am reminded here of the work of Jackson (1991, 193), who has critiqued the social constructionist approach to race:

> In challenging the naturalness of categories like race ... we run the political danger of evacuating the very concepts around which people's struggles

against oppression are being organized ... we are searching for non-essentialist conceptions of race ... around which it is possible to mobilize politically, but we may have to face a dilemma in which we support one argument politically while rejecting its basis intellectually.

By discussing the importance of developing "this one little area" and "the language within which we're speaking," Darius emphasized her interest in encouraging a collective political consciousness for mixed race individuals while allowing for the freedom of individual actions among individuals who identify with the label. Although she asserted that the transgressive deconstruction of the mixed race category is important, she also emphasized that if the category of mixed race is dismantled, it becomes even more difficult to speak on behalf of other mixed race individuals. In her desire to read the label as a political rather than passive identification, she agreed to suspend judgment temporarily, illustrating a strategy of temporary essentialism.

Like Darius, other participants explained to me the specific times and places where they used the "mixed race" label as a political identification. This was often linked to significant crossroads in their lives – going to university, getting married, or having children. Rhiannon studied at a liberal arts college in the United States, where she participated in many "women of colour" events during her undergraduate years, and she even started up a mixed race discussion group in Toronto, since disbanded. Rhiannon explained that her university years had a profound impact upon her use of "mixed race" as an identification:

> Yeah, I'll use the term "mixed race" to define myself. I have used it. There was a time when I was in university which, when I really gravitated towards other mixed race women? And we were quite close. And we had some discussions, we would sit around and had discussions all the time. And for a time I think that was a very comfortable space for me? I'm sorta outside of that now.

By emphasizing that she still used the term, had used it, and was now outside of it, Rhiannon indicated some of the backwardness, forwardness, and unfixity of identity. During our interview, she explained that after university she had entered a very different stage in her personal life and that this change, in turn, had influenced her personal identifications as well. She no longer fixated upon her multiple heritages, and although she saw them as an important part of her total self, her mixed race was not the pressing issue that it may have been for her in college, as indicated by her statement that she was "outside of that now." Again, this echoes the work of DaCosta (2007), who found that story sharing among mixed race people created a valuable space where they could bond and feel connected to their group. A similar process occurs when I teach my course on multiraciality. This course tends to attract students who identify as mixed race, and students have in the past compared their sharing of stories (rightly or wrongly!) to their perception of an Alcoholics Anonymous meeting. They often jokingly preface a comment in class with, "My name is X, and I'm a mixed race person" – a tendency I explored briefly in the Introduction. However, this kind of bonding can present its own difficulties. DaCosta (ibid., 139) rightly notes that this "initial sense of euphoria is not enough to keep the group together [and] interest in the group tends to wane." Like Rhiannon, Darius explained how she had arrived at her use of the term "mixed race":

> I started using the term "Eurasian," and maybe I did say "mixed," of my own [volition], sometimes, if I didn't want to identify. When "Eurasian" started not really feeling comfortable, I would say, "I'm Japanese French Native Irish," like I would just list it off. And let people sort of piece it together how they want to. Or not. But now I say "mixed race." I use the word "mixed race" to identify myself, and that has definitely been a function of all these explorations I've been doing over the last two, three, four years around the issue, and speaking to people, and it's just been the one that has most comfortably fit me. So far.

Darius's reading of the "mixed race" label suggests to me that there is a "comfort zone" around use of the term, as indicated by her statement that "it's just been the one that has most comfortably fit me. So far." She did not deny that there could be a time when she "grew out" of the identification, but for now she read the label as a location for the creation of meaning. Like those who seize the term "black" as a political identification rather than a description of skin colour, some informants viewed mixed race as a place "where meaning is constructed rather than simply the place where meaning is discovered" (Alcoff 1988, 434).

To conclude this section, I reiterate that participants related to the "mixed race" label in a mobile and paradoxical way. At times they employed the identification, and at other times they voiced their concerns about the label. Thus their own relationship with the identification was always constructed in relation to wider cultural and sociological processes. Makalani (2001, 96) provides a critical reminder: "The decision by people of mixed parentage to assert a biracial identity is a personal choice, but such a choice is not made in a vacuum. It is made in a society where class exploitation, racism and sexism remain the most important fissures affecting the organization of society." Social, gendered, physical, professional, geographical, and racialized borders (and the rituals that define them) therefore become integral in the construction of the "mixed race" label. This label meant many different things to the many different mixed race women in this study and had a temporality for some of them. It was a product of struggle for some women, being inherently unstable, contextualized, and open to critical re-evaluation in light of shifting political priorities. Some of them saw the possibilities of using the term to challenge reified racialized categories, yet other participants explored the pitfalls of the term, insisting that it can often privilege race as the sole axis for analysis. I have used the work of Rose and Probyn to encourage a more nuanced exploration of these paradoxical relationships between various identities, one that allows questions of identity to be examined in radically different ways. In the next section, I explore how participants fashioned mobile paradoxical spaces in their relations with individuals. I show that they created productive sites of alliances and affinities, subverting readings of their mixed race as "out of place."

Mapping Out Mobile Paradoxical Spaces in Relation to Others

> [The answer to the question] who are you? ... [could be] how about you? Can we find common ground? Talk? Love? Create something together? What is there around us and between us that allows this?
>
> — IRIGARAY 1993, 178

In this section, I argue that the creation of connections between individuals across traditional social cleavages, such as race and gender, are an everyday reality and that the material engagements of those connections can be theorized more adequately. The discourse on difference acts as a vigilant gatekeeper, which hinders the free flow of dialogue about commonalities. To acknowledge and analyze the potential productivity and limitations of the contemporary discourse on difference, I consider how participants constructed alliances and affinities with others.

I have been inspired to explore the ways that mixed race people forge mobile paradoxical relationships with others in light of feminist geographer Geraldine Pratt's (1997) critique of Twine's (1996) study on mixed race girls in Berkeley, California. Urging feminist geographers to contemplate potential points of alliances across racial differences, Pratt (ibid., 362) wonders, "How do [women of mixed race] define themselves in terms of other communities?" This section of the chapter attempts to address this query. Instead of documenting my informants' hypothetical search for home, I want to examine "their appreciation of many homes" (Jones 1994, 3). Many of the women in this study explained that their ability to cross over the demarcations of racial divides made it seem easier for them to transcend other social cleavages. Instead of envisioning herself as being "out of place," for example, Makeda suggested that mixed race individuals have a range of allegiances and homes:

> Being mixed defies any sort of absolute characterization that you might have of community, or culture, because they can't really be applied to mixed race people? Because [we] have so many different allegiances, or affinities, or languages, or whatever.

Makeda insisted that she had forged several networks of connections, explaining that she had other ties, too, and that these multiple ties created experiences that connected her to others who might also have had multiple ties. Women of mixed race in this study continually demonstrated the fluidity of discursive relations between and within a variety of communities. Given their mixed race identity, they continually crossed racialized boundaries, and this experience led them to question other sorts of boundaries.

As Makeda suggested, having a wide range of cultural allegiances offered her a way to transcend any essentialized generalization of her identity. She explained that she actively searched for meeting places in her desire to create connections:

> Being mixed is a kinda very interesting place to be. I think it's been very important to make sure that I do attach myself to collectives, in some ways? Because I don't feel that just one speaks to me?

Makeda revealed that there were many collectives that she found appealing. Some mixed race writers have indicated how mixed race individuals can occupy these mobile paradoxical spaces. The filmmaker and creative writer Lisa Jones (1994, 65) provides a lesson for mixed race individuals, based upon her own experience of mixed race: "As you get older, chances are you will define yourself by your alliances with a multitude of communities. No one community will speak for you completely and no one community should be so static as to not let you share in others." Although these women were often positioned as racialized and gendered subjects, they had developed scattered mobile paradoxical spaces with a diverse range of collectives based on class, race, and gender dynamics. Madeleine, for example, narrated an episode where she deliberately forged a mobile paradoxical space outside of expected connections:

MADELEINE: I went to a coffee shop, and I walked in, and all the black kids were sitting over there, and there was a group of Chinese kids, and there were white kids over there, and I didn't know where to sit. I had no idea. I mean, and it wasn't like they were, like everybody was talking, it was like the black kids' little clique. I didn't know where to sit. I just wanted to. I just want a fucking coffee, you know. Anyway, so I got it [to take away], and then I walked around the corner, and there was this sort of big open area where kids were like sitting against the wall and stuff, and I just sat there and read my book and smoked cigarettes. I mean if I was there now, right, I think I would just pick the nicest place to sit, right. I would do two things, depending on how I felt. I would either just go okay, where's the best place to sit in here. Or secondly, I would go sit with the Chinese kids.

MINELLE: Really? And why do you think that is?

MADELEINE: Because people would just ... people would be expecting me to go to one or the other, that's why.

Madeleine narrated a classic adolescent experience, reminiscent of anxiety surrounding one's individual positioning in relation to the cliques in a crowded school cafeteria. Madeleine asserted that she would defy socially constructed expectations of where people expected her to sit. Although she decided to get the take-away coffee in order to avoid making a decision about where to sit, upon reflection she added that she would now sit with one of the groups outside of her own expected ethnic allegiances to subvert socially constructed stereotypes. In other words, she would exercise her own agency in a social situation to create her own mobile paradoxical space.

The mixed race woman can learn to establish her own sense of identity, which is not necessarily reflected back to her by her environments (Root 1997, 163). The mixed race writer Judy Scales-Trent (1995, 8) has described "what it is like to be both inside and outside the black community and the white community" and has written of being "able to find similarities between her life and the lives of others, thus finding a community I call 'home.'" Thornton (1996, 116) ehoes these words, claiming that as a "mixed race individual, I had to create my own community and sense of identity." Resonating with these writers' accounts, the narratives of the women in my study were similar. Some described their experience in terms of a series of transparencies, where their identities overlapped to create their own space. For example, Katya explained this idea in greater detail:

> I recognize that I occupy a space in both spheres. As well as something outside of that that is unique to people like me. This whole idea of membership between communities as well as a third, distinct, separate community.

There is no sense in the above narrative that Katya felt out of place. Instead, she suggested that she occupied a home in several spheres, as well as having a unique space to call her own. I propose that this "third, distinct, separate community" – where binary oppositions are upturned, marginality is seen as positive, and the potential for forging new alliances is augmented – was envisioned by some participants as a productive site of subversion. Again, DaCosta's (2007) research is illuminating here. Some multiracial participants in her study described their multiracial identity as a "third" space.

I want to end this section by returning to my interview with Marical. I have noted that Marical was excited about the mixed race identification. Much like my interview with Makeda, my discussion with Marical took on the form of a dialogue that found us swapping ideas, particularly academic ideas around mixed race. At one point in the interview, when I was enthusiastically extolling the virtues of Homi Bhabha, Marical pensively leaned back in her chair and sighed,

Yeah, I'm not so up on that theory, so I can't really, I'm not really sure about that Homi Bhabha stuff. But the hybridity stuff is fabulous, I really like that. But you see, it's so interesting because we've got to make a distinction between a politicized hybridity or a politicized third space and a real, like, it's like fucking neoliberal third space, you know? Like 'cause I don't buy this shit, "Oh we're all human beings." You know what I mean? I think it is very, very, very important to recognize racial dynamics or to recognize power dynamics in a society. And it does have to do with like race and gender and class and sexual orientation, that's so present. And I don't buy this idea where, "Oh, well, we're all members of the human race and we all should just get along." That is the stuff I think that was around in the '70s that fucked us up to begin with. There needs to [be a way to] go beyond our traditional definition of the space, I mean a race ... space.

I find Marical's reading particularly appealing because of the ways that she interacted with theory and her own personal life to make a statement about the ways that mixed race individuals have been seen through time. By asserting her desire for a new "race space," Marical insisted that there has got to be a way to move beyond images of mixed race individuals as solving the world's racial problems. These sorts of comments suggest that my informants were not dupes of the dominant discourse on mixed race identity, notwithstanding that they had obviously been influenced by academic writings on "third spaces" and on fluid and flexible identities. Nor were they postmodern champions of a cult that worships hybridity or spatial metaphors. Rather, I interpret their interviews to mean that there is a paradoxical space between these theoretical suppositions where these women lived out their lives, cultivating fine judgments about when to use which discourse. These interviews echo the theoretical ideas of Rose (1993). Women in this study occupied various paradoxical spaces. These spaces were "lived, experienced and felt" (ibid., 140-41). I suggest that participants recognized the need for alliances in struggle. "The space of separatism in these discussions, then, is also a space of interrelations – another paradox" (ibid., 153).

Interpreters, Ambassadors, and Translators

> We, the straddlers, transgressors, fence-sitters, disruptors, undefined and perhaps indefinable ... challenge classificatory schemes while at the same

time providing more of an imperative for racial categorization because of our contraventions.

— THOMPSON 2010, 263

Being biracial is sort of like being in a secret society ... Most people I know of that mix have a real ability to be in a room with anyone, black or white.

— HALLE BERRY, IN MAYNARD 2012

In this section, I want to consider more carefully the use of metaphors that interviewees invoked to describe their mixed race experience and at the same time problematize some of these descriptions, which are epitomized by Halle Berry's words above. Why did participants tend to see themselves as spies, interpreters, or translators – as unique and different because they identified as mixed race? Did they overly romanticize these ideas? Katya specifically employed the metaphors of interpreter, ambassador, and translator to describe how she felt about being mixed race:

> [I think I can look] at things from both sides. In acting like an ambassador. Which is something I recognized, I think, for many years, but didn't realize what it was that I was doing. And trying to explain one side to the other. I act as a translator. Interpreter. And I think that I do that, I feel that is one of my roles. Not necessarily something that I asked to take. But I felt some sort of duty that I did not want black people to be misunderstood. And I didn't want white people to be misunderstood. Or I didn't want black people to misunderstand white people. And [I am able] to move between, move across a spectrum, being able to be the ambassador, to present different sides, to represent the other in both circumstances. To come from an informed position on both sides. So a knowledge, a partnership. And I don't necessarily think that someone that was "here" or (points across) "here" would be able to give that much information.

One can read Katya's comment as a refusal to see her mixed race status as a problem: instead, she saw it as part of a potential solution in dealing with conflict. I think the mixing of the metaphors here – interpreter, ambassador, and translator – is important because of the mobility that is inherent within them. Katya explained that she could simultaneously act as an interpreter, translator, and ambassador between groups. Being an interpreter or translator is in tune with being an ambassador, a role that has been traditionally read as that of a negotiator. Katya saw herself as being able to interact with many groups, fostering communication and understanding. Stuart Hall (1992, 328-29) has alluded to this tendency, stating that "the future role of mixed people may be that of negotiators. Since they belong to many groups, they will be seen as insiders, with vested interests in making plans work for all sides."

Naela explained that she used the term "mongrel" as an empowering way to define herself in jest but added that her enthusiasm for the term was not shared by everyone:

> I was going out with this boy, I was sixteen, no wait maybe it was about two years ago, and we would write each other notes and stuff, and we would always call each other mongrels? So then I read this article, in some political journal, I realized that it was, it was something like *Maclean's*, the guy in the article was talking about the mongrelization? He said the mongrelization of the ... community or something, referring to people becoming all mixed up, and no culture or whatever. And I was just so grossed out by the term that I thought it was funny. And I just started calling myself a mongrel. And started calling him a mongrel, and we just called each other mongrel, mongoloid, whatever. Just sort of a pet name? But then, then I started going out with this other mixed guy. And I called him a mongrel. Right? And he was really really offended. He was like, that's really rude. Oh yeah and we used to call each other mutt. And he gave me this book on dogs. Like for my birthday ... We always used to play with it. Yeah I call myself mutt, mongrel. And mixed. Depending on who's asking.

It is obvious that for some people identity labels offer opportunities for connections and affinities, whereas for others the terms take on radically different meanings. Whereas using the "mongrel" label when jousting with one boyfriend was playful, with another it was offensive. Some mixed race women are able to negotiate this minefield of vocabulary, navigating people's perceptions of themselves and ducking and weaving through various spaces. As I discuss in Chapter 6, these processes are never stable and are often precarious. As Faith explained,

> I think I have a more interesting vantage point. Just because that whole thing that we're not one or the other, we can sometimes slide into both or other worlds, and check things out?

Marical echoed these sentiments. When I asked her whether she felt that her mixed race identity had affected the way she looked at race, she responded,

> Just because I always feel like I'm a fly on the wall, I feel kind of like I've been privy to certain ideas, and I seem to spend a lot of my life explaining things to black people, to white people, and white people to black people, just explaining. There's that, there's that book about psychotherapy and women of colour. There's a section on mixed race women. Are you familiar with it? And they say that a lot of mixed race women are really driven, as individuals. Because they're driven by the idea that they're different, or they're special, somehow. And I have to say that that rings true. Is that I have, because I've always felt that I was different. And deciding not to hate myself forever! (laughter) I've decided that I'm special. And I think that gives you a lot of freedom. I don't feel like I have a lot of things that contain me. Because I've broken most of the rules already, just by existing. So I feel like I have unlimited potential, to a large degree? You know? And I think that that's a really good thing.

Much like Katya, Marical explained that she could act as a translator across groups because, as a "fly on the wall," she played the role of observer. She demonstrated that at times the mixed race woman does experience alienation, clearly illustrated in the phrase "deciding not to hate myself forever." I do not want to dismiss the fact that at times the mixed race woman does in fact experience alienation as a result of society's rigid rules about racialization. However, alternative readings of the experience of marginalization are suggested by Marical. She had deliberately decided that she was "special," and although she recognized that she was seen as different in many ways, she also felt she had unlimited potential. Some women in this study suggested that occupying a space at the margin can provide a perspective from which to view the complexities of difference. These women's experiences of identity were not described as producing a sense of rootlessness or homelessness. Instead, they referred to notions of movement, to moving through categories, and to developing scattered senses of belonging to a diverse range of collectives.

Darius also acknowledged feelings of marginalization associated with her own multiraciality, yet she diffused dominant readings of marginalization as solely oppressive and alienating, interpreting it instead as a site of renewal:

> I kinda like the experience of being other. I grew up with the experience of being other. And I didn't grow up with it as, "You're other, you're different, therefore you're separate and you're ..." I actually feel that my experience of other, even though it sometimes made me feel alone, sometimes made me feel different, that it's really, really one of the biggest factors in what I see as my compassion in life? And that it, in a funny way, being other actually made me related to everybody, made me feel like I could relate to everyone in that they're other. Do you know what I mean? So I kinda felt like I didn't feel separate from anybody. Even though I felt a sort of individuality, I always felt a kind of connection to everybody because I could always see, I could always feel an empathy for where they felt separate. Or for where they felt different. Or if they were the underdog, or if they were someone that was, if someone experienced prejudice from someone else, or if they were so, so ironically the feeling of being other made me feel like related. So I like that about my experience. I think that's a good part of my experience. Because you know ultimately I think that we're in this world to know that we're connected. To each other, and to ourselves. And so I like the fact that I can be reminded sometimes that people can look for ways that they're related instead of where they're different all the time. There's so much of where we are different. There are so many boundaries, there are so many borders drawn around where we are different from one another.

Darius celebrated her experiences of marginal status rather than lamenting them. She wrote herself into a site of belonging rather than positioning herself outside of it. Darius insisted upon redrawing the lines of separation among individuals by focusing upon sites of similarity and the potential of forging coalitions through difference. She believed that we are all decentred, rendered minor, or oppressed in similar ways. The mobility of her positioning among others offered her the potential to explore the liberatory possibilities of mobile paradoxical spaces:

> I find that people usually experience me to be whatever they are. Okay that's a bit of an exaggeration. Like people who are like blond-haired and blue-eyed, and from Sweden, they don't necessarily ... but when I was living in LA, I definitely would get, I would blend into people's experiences with Mexican, [and they would speak to me in Spanish]. When I was in Thailand, a lot of the Thai people would say, "Are you Thai?" Even in Toronto, people will usually think that whatever they are, they will, they will also think that I am. They'll see me, and see themselves in me somehow. I find people usually speak to me in their own language. I kinda like it! You know, in a fun kind of way, it gives me a chance to interact with people. Or maybe it's more that I like the fact that I believe in this world that there is too much emphasis placed on where we're different, and actually it would be a much better world if people would find out where we are similar? And I like the experience of people looking for where they are related to each other. Rather than looking for ways they are different. So even though I'm you know, if someone's speaking to me in Spanish, and then I have to say, "Well I'm not Spanish," and I don't speak Spanish, I kinda like that they're looking to MEET somewhere. You know?

Instead of expressing anger at being continually asked about her identity, Darius interpreted the inquiry in a radically different fashion. Darius diverted a discourse on difference by focusing upon the potential for strategic sameness. She explained that she read being asked the question "Where are you from?" as a conduit for potential coalitions with others, despite differences.

So far, I have highlighted the metaphors that some participants employed to speak about their racialized identities. The terms "ambassador," "interpreter," and "spy" emerged at different times in the interviews. Rather than simply taking these terms at face value, it is necessary to interrogate them in more detail, as I do not want to glamorize their use (see also McNeil 2012). I am not the only scholar working in the arena of mixed race studies who has found that many mixed race people use these kinds of metaphors to describe their perceptions of multiraciality. In interviews, many have said that they see themselves as natural bridges between communities. Squires (2007, 187) notes that the "multiracial citizen is often described as a bridge, linking disparate racialized sections of the public." Romano (2003, 288) discusses the perception that "multiracial children ... not only will undermine racial categories, but ... also may have a unique ability to serve as racial ambassadors, shuttling back and forth between each of their racial homes in an effort to make peace." And Spencer (2011) devotes a chapter of his book to the false promise of racial bridging. It is imperative to think about these metaphors more suspiciously, as McNeil (2012) has persuasively argued. Revisiting Kawash's (1997) powerful idea about the ways that biological race are often veiled in cultural terms, it is absolutely crucial to remember that mixed race people are not, in and of themselves, natural bridges for racial reconciliation: "This is a biological argument dressed up in sociological attire" (Spencer 2011, 184).

Seeing Yourself in Others

I want to conclude this chapter by showing how some participants experienced a bond with others across racialized divides. Darius, for one, sought a form of identification with another. Although identifying as mixed race was an important aspect of her identity, what mattered more to her was not the unqualified fact of her lineage but her membership in a group of people who experienced themselves as, and were held by others to be, a mixed race community:

> I'd be on the bus, or the subway, or we'd be out somewhere, and one time I was seven or eight years old, and seeing other kids that were mixed. And not that they were the same or similar mixes as me, or they looked the same as me, but just that they were mixed. And they would be the one I would be focused on, across the room, you know? And [my father] would recognize that and say, "Ahhh, you've found your people, huh?!" (laughter) So in that kinda joking way, he was expressing to me, and acknowledging the fact that in some way, even though I'm very close to my family, in the experience of seeing myself reflected back, um, that I didn't have that experience of my family. I saw it more with strangers.

Darius connected across difference with a mere stranger based upon phenotype, imagining a belonging between herself and another through their shared trait of being mixed race. The difference between herself and her father was accentuated, whereas she imagined a special affinity with another because of their similar experience or way of life. She established a point of contact across a geography of division, creating a series of overlaps between herself and a stranger.

As a student, Rani had worked in Boston during the summers. She explained that, in her workplace, she had been able to move through a variety of contexts seamlessly, crossing borders not only in a racialized context but also in terms of socio-economic background and personality. Her comments, like those of Darius, suggest that we need to contemplate forms of belonging that are forged across gender, race, and class in order to include transitory configurations of factors such as personality and geography:

> You can assume certain identities, in different places, and people won't be threatened by you, because everybody can identify with at least part of what you are. You know? And that's definitely an asset. And in a place like [where I used to work], a lot of the work was highly politicized, I could sort of get in a group where the power structure was white, because they saw me as educated and could identify with my background. But you know, I could also find out what was going on on the ground level, with people who were, you know, were much more mixed in terms of racial composition. Because they felt that I belonged there. I would be welcomed. As a contributor. They saw me as part of that group. Right? I just find it really easy to slip in and out of different groups. There's just so many different ways to look at the ways in which people bond together. In terms of race, but also socio-economic background, and personality, and all of that.

Rani emphasized how individuals forged alliances with her, imagining that people identified with "at least part" of who she was. Rani explained that although her background as a student from an exclusive school allowed her access to the upper echelon of power structures, her identity as a person of colour allowed her to participate at the grassroots level. Rani bridged class and educational divides, suggesting an ability to hold, merge, and respect multiple perspectives simultaneously.

Experiencing a constantly challenged identity, women in this study occupied mobile paradoxical spaces to make themselves at home in an interminable discussion between traditional ethnic inheritances and the diverse present. They expressed their ability to form allegiances across difference and often attributed this ability to their mixed race heritage. Instead of lamenting feelings of grouplessness, or not fitting in, and using phrases that had negative connotations or conveyed anticommunity feelings, these women insisted upon discussing the ways that they occupied mobile paradoxical spaces and experienced fluid interaction among various groups. I have deliberately employed many of the ideas emerging from the work of Rose (1993) and Probyn (1996) to demonstrate the complex alliances that mixed race women in this study forged across racialized divides.

I have suggested some of the complex ways that participants inhabited mobile paradoxical spaces, both through their association with the "mixed race" label and through their relations with other individuals. The work of Rose and Probyn provides a useful framework for theoretically conceptualizing the contradictory and mobile nature of participants' affiliation with the "mixed race" label. Through a discussion of participants' diverse contemplations of this label as a temporary linguistic home, I have attempted to illustrate the challenge of using the identification of "mixed race" while pointing out its temporal contingencies, too. This interrogation of the label is my attempt to problematize, extend, disrupt, and rework the term. By thinking about how people get along and get by in a racialized world, I have suggested that relations of proximity between individuals can be more adequately theorized than presently envisioned. Consider what Katya said about how she saw herself:

> It wasn't until people started asking me (in a sad voice), "Oh you poor thing, how are you dealing with being mixed? You must be so confused!" And I would say, "Oh really?!" (laughter) "What am I supposed to be confused about?" And then they would say, "Oh you don't know who you are!" And I would say, "Oh sure I do. My name is Katya L'Engle Agarwal!" (laughter) As I got older, when I thought about what it meant to be biracial, or mixed, I had more articulate answers, like, "No, I'm not confused. I recognize that I occupy a space in both spheres. As well as something outside of that, that is unique to people like me."

Katya subverted the socially constructed myth about mixed race individuals being "out of place." She articulated a self-conscious defiance of the limitations of racialized language that imposed definitions upon her as a subject. To explicate the variety of ways she read her identity, she explained that she had moved through the use of various identifications over time. Participants explored the necessity of considering mixed race relations as co-constructed with other axes of domination and resistance, emphasizing that to be mixed race means to be internally and externally differentiated through intersections with other unfolding relationships. Many participants explained that in addition to their affiliation with multiple ethnic groups, they also maintained a healthy mixed race identity through membership with a group that identified as mixed race – evident in Rhiannon's mixed race discussion group, for example. I believe critical mixed race theory must be up to the task of rendering the social field vibrant by acknowledging these sorts of affiliations. I have grounded the theoretical ideas of both Rose (1993) and Probyn (1996) in the everyday by drawing from the metaphor of mobile paradoxical space to describe the experiences of mixed race women in this study. The metaphor gets at the simultaneous occupation of several contradictory subject positions. By showing how these ideas played out through participants' conflicted feelings about the "mixed race" label, I have tried to ground Probyn's (ibid.) claim that there is no fixed identity or final destination. The metaphor of mobile paradoxical space has acted as a guide in my travels through the multitextured stories of participants. I have chosen this approach to bridge the chasm between theoretical and empirical explorations. In the next chapter, I map out the carefully orchestrated strategies that informants employed in their negotiation of difference through various innovative racialized performances, thus illustrating their agency in both creating and destabilizing racialized categories.

6
Mixed Race Scanners
Performing Race

> Race is a complete illusion, make-believe. It's a costume. We all wear one ... That's the absurdity of the whole race game.
>
> — SENNA 1998, 391

As I demonstrated in Chapter 5, some mixed race women in this study were able to develop strategic sameness across racialized boundaries. In this chapter, I explore how some of the women enacted various innovative performances to negotiate difference – illustrating an ability to disrupt, and sometimes even to simultaneously create, racialized divides. I do so by engaging with excerpts from my own research diary, the voices of participants, and the work of Judith Butler (1990, 1993) to develop a more nuanced model of performativity. I suggest that some mixed race women act according to their perception of the racial encounter at the time. I read performances as "'presentations,' 'showings' and 'manifestations' of everyday life" (Thrift 1997, 127; see also Goffman 1959) and expand upon my definition further in this chapter. Performativity offers an effective means of uncovering the constructedness of the rigid rules of racialization. I insist that participants chose to act as scanners – explaining to me that they scanned and took in a situation to develop complex strategic responses and verbal replies to various racialized readings of their identities.

The experience of appearing racially ambiguous can sometimes offer a site for the performance of different racial identities. Other critical mixed race scholars have noted that there is a vital relationship between performativity and multiraciality (Ali 2003). Gary Lemons (2008, 30), a critical race feminist, has stated that "destabilizing ideas of white superiority, the idea (and reality) of 'black' people crossing the color line (*passing* as white) underscores the performativity of identity" (emphasis in original). Some mixed race women in this study demonstrated a desire to create new meanings out of imposed racial orders and took advantage of multiple, dynamic, and ambiguous spaces of politicized and racialized identities. Because some mixed race women can alter how they are perceived racially, they can often manipulate the kinds of subjective feedback and experiences to which they are exposed (Root 1997). Some mixed race women adopt identities that are, all at once, "strategic, tactical, mobile, multifaceted, blurred, awkward, ambivalent" (Pile 1997, 27). I hope to map out the situated practices through which mixed race women in this study not only contested but also produced and reworked their own localities.

First, I draw attention to Butler's notion of performativity. I argue that she displays a racial blindness in her model as explored in *Gender Trouble* (1990) and *Bodies That Matter* (1993). I use her ideas as a point of departure for exploring the parallels that can be drawn between the performative nature of gendered identities and that of racialized identities. It has been argued that a discussion of mixed race identities allows for the application of the concept of performance, where not only gender but also racial roles can be viewed as performances in varied contexts (Zack 1997). Unfortunately, this theoretical supposition has yet to be grounded. I show how some participants chose to perform "race trouble" through particular mobilizations of their mixed race identities, often causing "subversive confusion" (Butler 1990, 34). Second, I map out cartographies where racial performativity is imaginatively enacted, drawing on tales told by my informants. Finally, I ask what these varied performances tell us about the ways that mixed race women in this study contemplated their selves.

Performing Multiraciality

> We all skinwalk – change shapes, identities, from time to time, during the course of a day, during the course of our lives. I think about how we create these identities, how they are created for us, how they change, and how we reconcile these changes as we go along.
>
> — SCALES-TRENT 1995, 127

I turn first to a brief account of Butler's (1990, 1993) notion of performativity. Performance is now old hat in conversations about race and racial difference, often working to demonstrate how dichotomous social categories can be brought into question and sometimes even subverted through performances. Performativity, a concept that owes much to the seminal work of Erving Goffman (1959), begins to acknowledge the kinds of techniques and efforts enacted by mixed race people who stage crucial contextual identities. Butler's notion of performativity plays an important role in the development of my theoretical thinking in this chapter, and I begin by briefly exploring her contribution to critical studies in gender.

Butler is predominantly concerned with the question of what produces a stable core of gender. Her answer is that, performatively, acts and gestures do this work. Butler asserts that gender is produced through performance. She further suggests that some kinds of performances can, in fact, destabilize gender. Thus gender is read as a kind of cultural performance that results from the effect of an assortment of contested power relations. Relying upon a theory of the performative taken from speech-act theory and drawing upon ongoing actualizations of gender meanings in the present, Butler argues against the fixity of gender identity. Performativity is not read as a single or even deliberate act but "as the reiterative and citational practice by which discourse produces the effects that it names" (Butler 1993, 2). Gender is "performatively constituted" through "a stylized repetition of acts. The effect of gender is produced through the stylization of the body and, hence, must be understood as the mundane way in which bodily gestures, movements, and styles of various kinds constitute the illusion of an abiding gendered self" (Butler 1990, 140). Performativity for Butler (1993, 2) describes the relationship between language and the creation of the lived realities we inhabit – the "reiterative power of discourse to produce the phenomena that it regulates and constrains." Acts, gestures, and enactments are seen as performative in the sense that "the essence or identity that they otherwise purport to express are fabrications manufactured and sustained through corporeal signs and other discursive means. That the gendered body is performative suggests that it has no ... status apart from the various acts which constitute its reality" (Butler 1990, 136). By revealing how a parodic act like drag offers opportunities to destabilize and denaturalize gendered subject positions, Butler (ibid., 126-39) insists that we must come to grips with the fact that gender is merely an inscription of discursive imperatives – that is, an elaborate, socially constructed fabrication:

> If the inner truth of gender is a fabrication and if a true gender is a fantasy instituted and inscribed on the surface of bodies, then it seems that genders can be neither true nor false, but are only produced as the truth effects of a discourse of primary and stable identity ... The body is not a "being," but a variable boundary, a surface whose permeability is politically regulated, a signifying practice within a cultural field.

Gender is seen to be a significatory practice through which acts are to be understood as linguistic concepts, where gender subjectivities and identifications are produced discursively. Thus to recognize gender in this fashion is to read it in "the realm of cultural production" (Awkward 1995, 190) and contestation.

> Because gender is not a fact, the various acts of gender create the idea of gender, and without those acts, there would be no gender at all. Gender is, thus, a construction that regularly conceals its genesis; the tacit collective agreement to perform, produce, and sustain discrete and polar genders as cultural fictions is obscured by the credibility of those productions. (Butler 1990, 140)

There are some key reasons for my being drawn to Butler's theory of performativity. First, Butler insists that gender is produced through performance. Second, she claims that gendered performances are repeated through a series of stylized acts. By making these claims, she shifts gender from being substantively foundational to being socially temporal. I find Butler's work remarkably refreshing, as she reveals the very social constructedness of gender itself. The idea of gender as performative – an act, a style, a fabrication involved in a dramatic construction of meaning – is a crucial element of her argument and challenges traditional sociological thinking.

Butler's model of performativity is exciting, but I must admit that I have some misgivings about her theory. First, I find her work highly theoretical, and there is often a disturbingly metaphysical quality to her writing. Furthermore, her model demonstrates a racial blindness. Race is remarkably absent from discussions of performativity in both *Gender Trouble* (1990) and *Bodies That Matter* (1993).

Taking the theoretical issue first, like Bordo (1993, 111), I am concerned that Butler's ideas are "ingenious and exciting, and it sounds right – in theory." Her highly abstract argument hypnotizes readers with its dense and repetitive brilliance. However, beyond her discussion on drag, she provides little practical sense of what these new gendered configurations might look like in the lived world. I cannot help but think that one reason for this is because she chooses not to privilege space in her discussion of performativity. Butler seems reluctant to give concrete examples within the social. I want to bring energy to Butler's theoretical text by emphasizing the production of racialized meanings in the spatial. It is here that I turn to the dimension of race.

There is very little reference to race in Butler's argument. Her model of performativity has provided a much-needed attempt to theorize and affirm the value of gay and lesbian experiences that have long been carried out and hidden at the margins. But Butler does not move beyond gay and lesbian experiences to explore the interconnectedness of these identities with race. She investigates the dualisms inherent in heterosexual frames but does not intervene in the binaries of race. What about framings outside the patriarchal grid? Many feminist theorists have insisted that race and gender are co-constructed, but Butler chooses not to investigate these interconnections. Finally, what are the implications of performativity for those who are doubly racially marked?

In this chapter, I argue that much of Butler's argument can be developed and traced through the experiences of mixed race women. In Chapter 4 I explored the kinds of performances that women in this study employed to move away from their perceived whiteness in society – performances such as changing their names or donning particular outfits. Butler's argument relies upon bodies that are obviously gendered but evidently raceless. I am curious about the practices among participants who deliberately employed actions to deactivate the racialized readings of the surfaces of their bodies. Taking my cue from Butler (1990, 139), I want to play with the notion of performance and demonstrate through participants' experiences that racial categories, like gender categories, are "regulatory fictions" that can be produced through varied performances, if we take performance to suggest "a dramatic and contingent construction of meaning."

Let me explain some of the reasons for drawing this comparison between Butler's work and the stories of my informants. As I showed in Chapter 1, like gender, race is governed by culturally constructed rather than biological imperatives. However, it is essential to note that race is not a cultural construction in the same way that gender is. Although both are predicated on real or manufactured biological differences, race is a "science fiction," whereas sex (of which gender is a derivative) is not (for further analyses, see Stolcke 1993). Like gender, race is a permanently contested concept, and its "terms of cultural engagement, whether antagonistic or affiliative, are produced performatively" (Bhabha 1994, 2). This idea has not been neglected by researchers working in ethnic studies. Di Leonardo (1984), for example, has pointed out that culture and ethnicity can be things that individuals possess or lose, and Back (1996) has explored how youth inhabit and vacate particular ethnic identities. Building upon their research, I demonstrate that "parodic proliferations" (Butler 1990, 138) were enacted by my informants in an effort to deprive racist culture of its powerful essence. I show how participants actively performed and masqueraded race, rendering it indeterminate and unknown by subtly displacing and inverting categories. I compile the performative vocabularies that the women in my study employed to deliberately toy with others' interpretations of their ethnicities, hoping to uncover some of the complicated processes through which racialized identities are assigned. Unveiling the performances that my participants used to reinvent impressions of their ethnicities provides a practical illustration that racial categories are regulatory fictions. What better way is there to take the science out of race, as Makeda demanded in Chapter 5, than by moving the "science of race out of the laboratory into the real world" (Zack 1997, 12)?

So far, so good. But delve a little deeper, and new problems crop up almost immediately. It becomes clear that Butler's model cannot be relied upon completely to explore the complex affiliations forged among mixed race women. Butler depends upon a concept of self-identity that allows no escape from a logic of exclusion, where abject bodies are continually produced through the grids of patriarchal discourse that regulate their actions. Thus subversive actions are not really subversive but are only actions that skim the surface – as the repressed depths of identity can never be completely disrupted – often reinscribing the very trope they mean to contest.

This assumption may be challenged. In previous chapters I explained how the mixed race woman has been positioned as being "out of place" and can be denied admission to codes of racial intelligibility. This model fosters a divide between bodies that matter and other abjected bodies, developing yet another relentless dualism. I am concerned that Butler's emphasis on the discursive tends to obscure potentially promising explorations of subversion among identities that are seen as repressed. Any identity, according to Butler, is the system of a logic of power and language that generates identities as a function of a binary opposition between self and other, which seeks to conceal its own workings by making these identities appear natural.

Butler is not alone here. Nearly all literatures on performativity, especially Goffmanesque ones, tend to focus upon questions of the self-other dualism. In particular, they seem to be obsessed with questions about the authenticity of the self and about the sincerity of the performance, often articulated through a vocabulary that contrasts depth and surface. Given these tendencies, I was initially reluctant to develop a model of racialized performativity among participants for fear of perpetuating the myth of the mixed race woman as cunning or deceitful. The actor is often seen as a con artist (Bell and Valentine 1995). Upon reflection, however, I recognized the critical importance of documenting the various arenas of the "cultural game" being played on the street, where a sense of self becomes "not an essence, but a positioning" (S. Hall 1990, 226). I also feel that the theatre metaphor inherent in notions of performativity is somewhat misleading because the set design in situations cannot be staged in advance. The very aspect of a variably shifting place makes the spatial dimension chaotic, at best. These dynamics seem obscured in Butler's exploration of performativity.

I want to delineate the boundaries of my exploration of performativity here, as I acknowledge that it remains limited in an empirical sense. I am interested in the expressivity of performance, perceiving it less as a display than as a bodily practice that creates a self and space. The interviews provide examples from participants' experiences. I present their stories to ground the theoretical claims of de Lauretis (1986, 8), who insists that "the concept of multiple, shifting, and often self-contradictory identity, an identity that one decides to reclaim from a history of multiple assimilations, [requires that] one insists upon having a strategy." I show how participants employed identity strategically. Their tactics of intervention demonstrate the notion of critical positionality. Rather than focusing upon contestations on a microscale, I highlight the theory of performativity to contextualize its racialized properties, thus making it less fixed and more multiple, and to emphasize its social production and reproduction.

A second concern is that Butler's model of performativity does not leave much room for the exploration of the individual's capacity to exploit particular situations. According to Butler, all identity categories are expressions that are entrenched through language. In other words, any identity is the product of a system or logic of power/language that generates identities as functions of binary oppositions and seeks to conceal its own workings by making these identities appear natural. Butler's central argument, then, is that any identity is always a product of a logic of exclusion. This is a depressing line of argument. Butler paints a fairly dismal portrait where there is no escape from the logic of exclusion (for further detail, see Weir 1996). Her theory does not fully recognize the kinds of choices that participants made about how to represent themselves in a social world. Thus, in this chapter, I reflect more deeply upon informants' own participation in the ongoing process of the constitution of subjectivity. In Butler's more recent work, she has clarified what she means by a genuinely radical act, insisting that "we are never fully determined by the categories that construct us" because one can dissent from the norms of society by "occupying the very categories by which one is constituted and turning them in another direction or giving them a future they weren't supposed to have" (in Wallace 1998, 16). However, this is not to suggest that the mixed race women in this study had performed an escape from racist discourses or had successfully manipulated space outside of racialized representation. It would be naive and delusional, not to mention optimistic, to claim that these women were able to attain a complete freedom of creative racialized expression by virtue of their ability to contest and rework their identity. The ability to enact racial performativity did not mean that these women could avoid racial essentialism. Thus, although I emphasize their creative, imaginative, and critical stances, the constraints and conventions of their circumstances cannot be overlooked. These women were positioned as particular subjects by their framers and thus often experienced limited flexibility to subvert socially constructed framings of their identity. I trace the ways that these varied racialized performances contaminated dominant racial norms by subverting the values associated with racial categories. Disrupting the process of categorization does not mean that the categories are subsequently abandoned. Rather, it moves the focus from the categories as places of cultural value to the shifting process of cultural classification itself. It reveals these categories as false in their essentialist claims.

    I hasten to add that these women did not actively veil their ethnicities out of embarrassment about affiliating with what is most popularly seen to be a marginal group. Instead, I suggest that mixed race women divert and transform socially constructed representations of their racialized identities.

Katya explained that she chose to perform certain racialized roles in different situations:

> I have, you know, when necessary, when I need to, I [put on an] English accent. Which is again, white. And kinda dominating in a way. And people do here tend to pay more attention to you if you can speak in a manner that is reminiscent of an educated white man. Right? So I'll slow my sentences down, I'll speak really articulately, and I'll throw in a few complicated phrases. And big words. And people will shut up and listen. I do it on the phone too. I get a lot more respect (laughter). So you know. If I'm ever mad with the bank. That's exactly what I do. And I recognize that I do that. And not everybody can do that because they haven't had the privileges that I've had in terms of being, I mean I spent nine years in university. I recognize that I have a lot of advantages over a lot of black people. In that sense. Over a lot of white people, too.

Katya indicated that she participated in her own constitution through spontaneous acts in a constant attempt to make meanings of her own choosing. She even went so far as to account for these processes by explaining how her nine years in university had influenced her ability to "act educated," further making the point that an educated persona is envisioned as both white and "English." Katya's story led me to ponder whether there were ways theoretically to explore how mixed race women understand themselves, how others understand them, and how mixed race women express these divergent understandings to others, not least of all to an academic researcher like me. Butler (1993) insists that subversion is possible only when the law turns against itself and unexpected permutations emerge. I argue that Katya might have disagreed with this reading. Katya's body was racialized in various ways, yet she still found ways to liberate herself beyond readings of her culturally constructed body. Katya's narrative was rife with talk about interactions with others, including her own motivations for performing racialized identities.

In considering Katya's episode, I was reminded of a moment in my life when I deliberately enacted difference to denaturalize and resignify bodily categories:

> It's midnight on Sunday evening, and I've been in the office all day screening tapes. The team I'm working with has finally finished the piece which

airs tomorrow and I drag myself downstairs to catch a cab home. When I finally flag one down, I yawn loudly and climb in, grateful to sit down after being on my feet all day, absolutely exhausted. The cab driver takes one look at me in his rearview mirror and says brightly, "Atcha, you're Indian, aren't you?" He starts speaking quickly in Bengali. I sigh and shake my head tiredly. I've heard this one before, and know what's going to happen next. "No, I don't speak Bengali," I say. The taxi driver is shocked and raises his voice. "What? What kind of parents do you have, they don't teach you their native tongue? And what is a young girl like you doing out so late?" This is where I come back with a tight, "Well, actually, I'm part Scandinavian and Portuguese." He does a double-take, and apologizes, falling silent. I barely notice, as I'm half-asleep already. I sit back, kick off my heels, and dozily reflect over my day's work.

I made a choice within a particular moment to enact a performance in order to divert further questions about my ethnicity. I live out my own life through a series of separations and connections and all the spaces in between. Individuals are embodied, speaking subjects embedded within discursive structures. Thus, in this chapter, I want to focus on the diverse range of interactions where informants engaged in racialized performative acts. I argue that participants saw themselves as being located within specific social and historical contexts and as engaging in, dealing with, and moving through social meanings.

By drawing upon Butler's argument in the development of my own ideas about racialized performativity, I do not presume that informants necessarily manipulated the presentation of their outward racial self, like it was something picked out of the closet. Instead, it was something that their audiences, and subsequently themselves, viewed and responded to contextually. In fact, I suggest that racial performativity may have more to do with self-preservation than self-presentation, as I show later in this chapter when I unveil some of the covert identity strategies employed by mixed race women in this study.

In documenting some of these performances, I do not mean to suggest that there is an inevitable freedom to choose one's identity. Rather, performance is a matter of negotiating the racialized trap in which one can inevitably be caught. Before I consider the various racial performances enacted by participants, it is important to note that this fluidity was available to some more than others, as I explain below.

Racial Ambiguity

> For some reason, this week has been spectacular in regards to the number of times I've been asked about my ethnicity. I've been approached more than usual and I can't figure out why – haven't got my hair cut or changed anything about my appearance drastically. On Monday, I was too busy storming down a flight of stairs at college to notice a young man running after me. He grabbed my arm eagerly and started speaking Italian. "No, no, I'm not Italian," I stammered. On Wednesday, I was coming back from dinner at a friend's place in Tooting and I handed my travelcard to a woman who was about to purchase a ticket, knowing I wasn't going to need it for the rest of the night. She looked up at me, saying "thank you" in Spanish. I knew just enough Spanish to smile, and then went mute. When I didn't respond, she said, embarrassed, in fluent English, "Sorry, you just look so Spanish, you are Spanish, aren't you?" On Friday, I was wandering through Piccadilly Circus with some friends. I stopped to admire a sketching being done on the cobblestone sidewalks. The woman who was posing sat frozen and I smiled at her, saying, "Don't worry – the portrait of you is turning out great!" She relaxed for a moment, much to the chagrin of the artist, and gave me a big grin. Pretty soon, my friends and I were chatting with her and her companion, both of whom were tourists from Gibraltar. After a few minutes of chit-chat, she looked at me, scrutinizing my features, and stuttered, "I hope you won't mind me asking you this, but are you French?" I don't really mind being asked, but sometimes it just feels relentless!
>
> — EXCERPT FROM RESEARCH DIARY

The notion of racial performativity that I develop hinges upon perceptions of racial ambiguity, where the way a mixed race individual's racialized identity is read alters the "definition of the situation" (Goffman 1959, 17). I want to be clear that in addressing issues of racial ambiguity, I concur with Haritaworn (2009, 129), who reminds us of the value of denaturalizing "phenotypic ambiguity" to see it as a "product, rather than the cause, of racialization." Haritaworn states, "Ambiguity is never just a pre-social fact that can be objectively measured and read off particular bodies" (ibid.); rather, the notion of ambiguity must be situated within a particular set of practices and discourses. In extending a notion of racial performativity, two aspects are crucial. One is how informants are raced. The second is the choices that mixed race individuals make after they are racialized. Both aspects deal with interpretations – those of others and those of participants.

First, it must be acknowledged that the ability to perform particular racialized identities is often available only to some mixed race individuals who experience ambivalence from others regarding their racialized place in society. As I have discussed, the mixed race woman has been positioned as "out of place," and thus it follows that her body is often outside those that "matter." However, it is imperative to note that it is the mixed race woman's individual presence in particular places that renders her excluded. The same woman who is read as an outsider in one place may be read as an insider in another based upon others' readings of her phenotype. Although all individuals are raced in some form or fashion – "there are no unraced gendered persons, nor ungendered raced persons" (Bradford and Sartwell 1997, 191) – it became clear from my interviews that individuals had radically different experiences of racialization. Although Katya identified as a black woman, her racial identity was also read in various ways:

> So I've had an interesting experience in that I've been mistaken for coming from different parts of the world. And I think, what they assume, as related to their geographies and their experience, obviously. They try to categorize you, into something, so that they can define you within their own experience.

Katya's experience was not dissimilar from that of Darius, discussed in Chapter 5, who people thought was from everywhere. Even though Darius and Katya looked dramatically different, both women shared similar experiences regarding people's perceptions of their phenotype. I do think that mixed race women with light skin experience a greater fluidity in terms of their perceived racial ambiguity. However, the stories that follow were narrated by women whose appearance ranged from light-skinned to dark-skinned. Many informants experienced a wide array of racial labelling from others, even though some of them identified as black.

It is also crucial to note that this model of racial performativity does not perceive all mixed race women as actively disrupting and transgressing racial lines. Many mixed race women who do experience racial ambiguity choose not to identify as mixed race, or they pass as white, or they consciously decide to veil their ethnicities permanently because of the racism expressed in their home or workplace, among a host of other reasons, including upper-middle-class status in the case of most participants. To craft a critical oppositional politics with precision, we ought to consider how selves in the plural are interpreted and how these readings may be disrupted and complicated.

Haritaworn (2009, 129) reminds us of the dangers of assuming that mixed race people "abolish essentialist categories, let alone the entire project of race. However, in a context that constantly poke[s] and prod[s] at their physical and mental integrity, the pleasure, safety and unruly agency ... must be recognized as incidents of resistance and empowerment that are valid and important in themselves." The premature celebration of a coherent mixed race as implicated in new possibilities of a celebrated mixed race politics echoes the disturbing euphoria around cultural hybridity, an issue touched upon in Chapter 1. As I will dissect in greater detail, questions of context, author, and audience become significant. Being mixed race on its own is neither a political nor a transgressive act. It is those actions that follow processes of racialization that create possibilities for performances. Although some mixed race women may experience racial ambiguity, it is only through articulations of racial categories that racist dialogues and thoughts are disrupted. In other words, if all mixed race individuals were able to unsettle racism through their mere presence on the landscape, then by virtue of the many centuries of miscegenation, racism should have disappeared years ago.

Racial performativity relies upon an understanding that informants often actively respond to the ways that their racialized selves are perceived by others. I have explained how people glean supposed clues about a person's conduct from phenotypical traits that can form the foundation for racism. Many women in this study who experienced racial ambiguity explained that they felt hypervisible, constantly judged and evaluated, and weighed down by the pendular stresses of having to explain their ethnicity over and over again. This experience is heightened among mixed race women, who "are particularly vulnerable to society's reactions to their ambiguous features. These reactions echo the overvaluations placed on women's physical appearance ... [which turn her into] an object or a curiosity (Root 1997, 159). Because some mixed race women blur socially constructed racial boundaries, they do not fit neatly into the observer's schema of reality, provoking stares and scrutiny, a sort of racial voyeurism. Even mixed race researchers are not immune from this tendency. As Marin (1996, 113) admits,

> [Although] I discount any biologistic fact of pure race and therefore racial difference ... I find myself staring – to a degree that I have to consciously control it – at all persons of mixed-race heritage. In fact the way I determine that they are mixed-race is because I am staring, unable to stop looking until I can put ambiguity to rest, know what race is, call it something. And of course that's the problem. If race rests on the concept that racial difference is absolute, then to be mixed-race is not really possible. So I keep staring ... [knowing] that even as I look, I don't see them.

Some participants were conscious of the gaze of others and knew that they were continually being analyzed for clues to their racial background. Naela explained how she felt when she was being watched, reminiscent of having "an aggressive plastic lens pushing on her" (Rose 1993, 143):

> When I'm involved in political stuff, a seminar, or a march or a rally, like even International Women's Day, I feel like, I'm not, it's not me who's watching everyone else? I feel like my eyes reflect people's eyes watching me? Not my own eyes watching people?

Naela described the gaze that brings forth and accentuates a self-consciousness about being the object of the other. The situational context coloured what she saw in herself, what she saw in others, and how she perceived that others read her ethnic identity. She communicated a sense of being othered and objectified, which made her anxious. Naela was careful to point out that she experienced this unease when she was in certain sites – in this case, at political events, where her status as a "woman of colour" was scrutinized. Some political groups of colour have narrow criteria for group membership, and thus many mixed race individuals can experience feelings of exclusion because they don't look "coloured enough" (Root 1997, 161). Haritaworn (2009) pays close attention to this process of scrutiny in an analysis of mixed race identity, declaring it to be an intrusive reading practice of mixed race bodies. In identifying how interviewees of mixed race identity were subjected "to stares, remarks and sometimes public debates about their bodies," Haritaworn (ibid., 116) defines this process as a practice of symbolic violence in everyday encounters and sees these processes as "highly intrusive and violating of interviewees' personal boundaries."

Makeda expressed similar feelings of being scrutinized for clues as to her racial place in society. Although she was secure in her own sense of ethnic identity, she was aware of others' "slippery" perceptions of her racial background:

> I think it's a little bit that feels off to people, that's what they can't place, that is what allows for that slipperiness to occur? They feel like, "Well, she LOOKS something, but what is it?" Right? And it's that kind of category crisis. But it's not my crisis, it's theirs, usually. And they're going, "hmmm ..." And that is when I think that people always try to second-guess what a mixed race person is, perhaps more so, especially when their features or their physical appearance is kinda, in any way, slippery? You know? Or ill-defined or something? That people are anxious to define, I get that every day, or whatever. Any time I meet someone new.

By stating, "it's not my crisis, it's theirs," Makeda insisted that she knew who she was, whereas others floundered in their attempt to classify her racially. Within that moment of others' perception of ambiguity, spaces are created that are fraught with tension. For some mixed race women, particular places offer, due to their racially ambiguous appearance, sites where racial codes cannot be easily read.

Naela also hinted at the shifting nature of space in discussing how others interpreted her racially and, in turn, how she decided to interpret others' readings of her racialized identity:

> Like I said, it's always changing. I'm always getting certain reactions from people, and having to deal with different situations, sort of thing. Like work out in my head and the room and what the vibe is before I enter it.

The only stability in others' interpretations of Naela's ethnicity was the precariousness of each situation. Naela never knew how others would read her ethnicity, so she was continually negotiating hidden matrices of behaviour. She revealed that her perceptions of herself through the eyes of others were, in Bondi's (1993, 99) words, "informed by conceptions of space that recognize place, position, location, and so on as created, as produced." Hill (2001, 41) comments on the precarious nature of racial identity for those who identify as both black and white: "When you're black and white, negotiating racial identity is like going through a revolving door. You think you're surefooted and slipping through just fine until someone shoves the door and a big glass wall smacks you from behind and you stumble sheepishly into daylight, mumbling, 'What was *that* all about?'" (emphasis in original). Resistance to racist discourses enacted by participants' bodies in spaces was articulated in different ways in different places. I suggest that we "position ourselves in relation to others" (Rose 1993, 5) – as participants demonstrated through their ability to "size up the room" (I am reminded of Naela's narrative here) – which in turn has an effect upon how mixed race women define and re-define the possibilities of reworking the racialized self.

Choosing a performance in a particular space depends upon myriad conditions and is part of a complex exchange among a variety of actors for whom everyday interactions occur across racialized terrains. These exchanges are complex, partly because places cannot be seen as "inert, fixed backdrops" (Moore 1997, 87) where racialized meanings are inscribed, prescribed, and consistent. The grounds upon which strategies are performed are not permanent, fixed, or stable. Rather, they ought to be envisaged as continually shifting and changing. Spaces of interrelations where strategies are employed cannot be compared to multicoloured splatters of paint upon a blank canvas. Everyday spaces are rife with diverse social dynamics – rife with power and subjectivity.

In other words, racial performativity was one avenue open to women in this study because of their racial ambiguity. Some participants explained that they had a wide range of racialized identificatory options as a result of the "slippery" nature of the race categorization game. This chapter focuses on the ways that hegemonic representations of race reverberated for participants and on how they mobilized opportunities for the performance of contestory "wish-images" (Kondo 1997, 10) by assuming various racialized identities. At times, participants performed an array of identities in ways that reflected, and exposed, the unnaturalness and historical specificity of racial categories.

In the next section, I suggest that some women of mixed race in this study commanded a plurality of invented ethnic identities that accommodated various situations, which they adopted depending upon their reading of an encounter and their temperament at the time. I document the rich and creative strategies that participants deployed in their attempt to subvert the constraining forces of category reduction by assuming a range of identities.

Documenting Racial Performativity

> We are what we pretend to be, so we must be very careful who we pretend to be.
>
> — VONNEGUT 1961, V

I begin this section with two stories of racial performativity. In the first one, Naela put into play a performance to create alliances among others. In the other one, Katya deliberately dislodged particular stereotypes associated with her phenotype.

I have explored Naela's feeling of being continually under scrutiny by others because of her racialized identity. To develop my argument, I demonstrate that Naela did not simply challenge the gaze of others without assuming a stance to counteract their readings. The gaze demanded a response that enabled her to reconstitute herself as someone in control of how she viewed herself and how others looked at her:

> MINELLE: Did you ever find it easier to move within different ethnic circles because you were mixed?
>
> NAELA: Yeah. But I have to play different roles. Like I can't be exactly the same within, like in Chinese circles, like I have friends, like a group of Chinese friends, and they are all East Asian. And I have a group of, I started playing on this basketball team for East Asian women? With Chinese women, it's called Lady Dragons, and so it's an all-Chinese team. And first of all, there was a big thing about whether or not I could play. Because they weren't sure if the rules permitted it because I'm only half-Chinese. So it's okay, so I'm playing. So I went to the first practice, and I realized, like I consciously started trying to prove my Chineseness to them? And I make jokes a lot about myself? It's the only time I do really feel in a group like I have to prove myself, is when I'm with Chinese friends who all speak Cantonese. And who are all very proud of being Chinese. And so, yeah, it's still fun but I sorta play like the joker role? Among the women, especially. I just notice, I realized, it's strange. I try to prove myself by like showing how well I can write Chinese characters, and talking about Chinese food that others might not know about. Like it's really strange.

Naela relayed an experience where she felt she had to prove her ethnicity. In this situation, Naela enacted a performance to prove her ethnicity to others, especially the women, by exaggerating caricatures of racial stereotypes. She had mastered a series of "repetitive stylized acts" (Butler 1990, 140) around Chineseness that she hoped would be familiar to her Chinese peers and disrupt their readings of her perceived whiteness. Given the precariousness of her status in this situation, where her mere presence on the team was in fact debated, she felt required to prove her ethnic identifications to others.

Whereas Naela adopted particular forms of performativity to create and maintain alliances, Katya's performance was employed to subvert socially constructed ideas associated with racial categories. She explained that she deliberately moved away from stereotypes associated with the racialized categories of whiteness and blackness:

KATYA: I expend a lot of energy trying not to be what people thought I was. And being able to bring more information into the situation than they expected, or, in some cases, desire.

MINELLE: Can you give me some examples of that?

KATYA: Well growing up. High school, university. I was very acutely aware that people would look at me, and say, "Okay. A black woman, therefore she must be into reggae and funk. And she is a really good dancer. She's got rhythm, naturally!" Well the rhythm thing I couldn't hide! (laughter) I tried, but not for very long. I couldn't hide that. But I think that I was sparked, or spurred into appreciating, a music that was not particularly black music. And I did not delve into black music. I mean I was familiar with it. But I made some effort to, I was into punk and new wave, and all this kinda stuff. I mean this is what my friends were into. And sure, some of them were into reggae, and stuff like that. But I didn't know as much about reggae as they did. As some of my white friends.

MINELLE: Was that a conscious decision on your part?

KATYA: I'd say pretty close to conscious. I know I did certain things, I mean, if I just met you, and I got the impression that you would assume that I knew everything about funk and reggae, I would let you know that I had every Japan album that has ever been made, or I'm an AC-DC fan, which I'm not actually, but I'll just say that I'm a Led Zeppelin fan, or Jimmy Hendrix, actually he's kind of crossover in a way, he's black but he plays white people's music. So, yeah. I would let them know that, or if people would, I guess it was a desire to be unique in a way. I would let them know that my mother's white. "You think I'm just a plain black person? Well, it's a little bit more than that. It's not what you think. You THINK this. But this is not what you're thinking." So it was my little way, a strange, convoluted, demented way, of telling people, "Don't assume. Don't be so ignorant as to assume."

Katya's decision to tell others about her music preferences reflected her desire to enact a local intervention that could shift racist discourses, disrupting a smooth reproduction of dominant imaginaries of race. She pointed out the limitations of race as a concept for defining a person's identity. A preliminary reading of the narrative might suggest that Katya identified with other sorts of music to be seen as unique, articulating a politics of teen angst or dissent by refusing to conform, or that she practised internal racism by self-consciously positioning herself outside of reified notions of blackness. However, I suggest that Katya's decision to define herself outside of socially constructed stereotypes was a deliberate ploy to refuse conformity with reductionist or essentialist notions of race.

Katya employed a strategy of paradox, of serious play, exposing the constructedness of qualities associated with racial categories. In other words, she provided insight into the ways that public identities are manifested while attesting to the private choices she made in asserting agency by negotiating the tension created by the space between the public and the private. This space is eloquently described by Patricia Williams (1997, 72-73):

> The distance between the self, and the drama of one's stereotype ... Negotiating that distance is an ethical project of creating a livable space between the poles of other people's imagination and the nice calm centre of oneself where dignity resides. Creating and negotiating that space is the work of what I think of as the question at the centre of our resolution of racism ... Within that freedom [we may yet witness] the abandon of prejudgment, the willingness to see another viewpoint and be converted if only for a moment, to allow oneself to be held in a state of suspended knowing.

Williams's words resonate with many of my own experiences, and with those of some of my informants, because they hold the potential for a transformative future space, where readings around racialization are no longer simply passive or solely political but are productive sites laden with paradox. Katya shifted the question from "How do I look (appear to you)?" to "How do you look (see)?" She interrupted others' impressions of her that were based upon her phenotype.

Katya adopted the role of Anzaldúa's (1987) "new mestiza" to open up the possibility of crossing racial lines, developing new ways to understand herself and her relationship to others. The new mestiza provides a framework with which to deconstruct binary either-or identities and reconstruct a truly multiple self. The new mestiza is one who "copes by developing a tolerance for contradictions, a tolerance for ambiguity ... learns to juggle cultures ... [and] operates in a pluralistic mode" (ibid., 101). Katya explained that she was frustrated when others were unable to see through the external appearances of a collective "racialized" identity to the internal reality of her own individualized identity. In refusing to collude with insidious colour biases and categories, she contradicted the stereotype.

In the rest of this chapter, I explore more strategies employed by some mixed race women in this study who, like Katya, demonstrated ways of "doing difference." Often participants orchestrated arts of disguise. There were many reasons for these choices, although their intent was not always clear. Generally, the creation of the disguise depended on a firm grasp of the codes of meaning that were being manipulated by the person exercising the disguise. There were times when these women lied about their ethnicity to ward off questions about their racialized appearance. This strategy was employed to divert racist comments or to shock the person who had made the racist comment into silence. In discussing varied moments of racialized performativity, I unveil tales where informants pretended to be of a different ethnicity and adopted the role of "spy" or "trickster."

Pretending to Be a Different Ethnicity

> He asked me what my background was: "Maybe Indian or Mongolian or Persian?" and I said, "Yes, I'm maybe Indian Mongolian Persian." He gaped at me for a minute, then said, "What?" and I said, "Exactly."
>
> — MACLEAR 2012, 149

> Sometimes she's part Chinese and part black ... Sometimes she's part Ojibway, or else part Mayan, and one day she was even part Tibetan. She can be whatever she feels like, because who can tell?
>
> – ATWOOD 1993, 84

Two of the women I interviewed, Katya and Julia, were good friends in university. They both told me how they concocted a particular social script to deal with annoying inquiries about their ethnic background. Katya explained that she and Julia worked in tandem to stage their racialized performance:

> Julia and I used to [switch ethnic identities] all the time. I'd say I was half-Chinese, and half-German Canadian. And she'd say she was half-West Indian and half-Irish. And, people, you know, would go, "OH! Now, now that can't be right." You know? (laughter) And we'd just leave it there. Sometimes we would correct them, sometimes we wouldn't.

Katya and Julia joined forces to subvert socially constructed assumptions made about their phenotypes in particular situations. Their decision to switch ethnicities was based on their desire to force others to consider the limits of racial categories. Similarly, two participants in Haritaworn's (2009, 128) study of twenty-two people with mixed Thai and non-Thai parentage in Britain and Germany contested their racialization by pretending they were sisters; Haritaworn sees this as a "game ... a gendered and (hetero)-sexualized strategy that resisted not only multiculturalist assumptions of authentic and undiluted 'cultures' but also [the] 'best of both worlds' ideologies of multiraciality."

Darius explained how she camouflaged herself as Chinese to stun the racist, showing that agency may be mobilized in unusual forms. In what is admittedly my favourite anecdote among the stories I share here, she discussed her struggle to regulate racism's sprawling energy during an experience of simply cycling down the street to buy groceries:

> Recently, I was driving down the street on my bike, and somebody [in a car] cut me off and almost hit me, and I yelled out, "Jerk!" And this guy in a truck drove up beside me and said, "Fuckin' Chinese drivers, eh?" (laughter) And this is one time where I did say, "I'm Chinese, you

know." (laughter) So I pretended I was Chinese, because I wanted to see his reaction. And he was like (stutters), "Oh, um, well, ah, that's not what I meant!"

Darius could have easily agreed with him by nodding mutely or could have simply ignored his racist slur by jumping back on her bike and pedalling off without a second thought or glance back. However, within that split second, she deliberately decided that she was not going to obey the rules of the racist "game" being played by the truck driver. Morales (1996, 41) explains the rules of the racist game: "You say something bad about black people; I say something bad about black people; we pat each other on the back and go our separate ways, affirmed and fulfilled." The central strategy of authority is to force people to play its game and to make sure that the game is played by its rules. Darius refused to play the game by the truck driver's rules; instead, she played her own game and marked out her own rules. Her well-timed revelation, where she feigned being of a different ethnicity, provides an example of what might be called a "race-bender" (ibid., 48), as it disrupted the potential for the truck driver to engage in uninterrupted racist speech. Darius had the opportunity to partake in what the racist driver assumed would be a shared sense of outrage. However, she deliberately deflected this projected role by using the incident as a way to confuse the driver's socially constructed prism of a Chinese ethnicity and subsequently succeeded in reducing his level of comfort in this situation, as indicated by her reading of his reaction.

Darius appropriated the space in this encounter, employing her own devices to invoke "new political uses of the personal" (Bell and Valentine 1995, 154) through a self-conscious and provocative shock tactic. The performative choices available to those who blur racialized categories are limited by the regulatory regimes of race, which can curtail the range of performative possibilities. However, Darius attempted to mobilize the spaces within the oppressive racial grid by putting into action an ethnic performance that created an alternative to oppressive representations.

Like many participants, and certainly akin to my own experiences, Claudia had a low level of tolerance for people's curiosity when it felt as though prejudice, rather than ignorance, guided their inquisitiveness. Claudia often pretended to be from everywhere when people hounded her about her ethnicity. When she told them the truth and they ended up stating incredulously, "No, but you can't be!" she would baffle them by angrily barraging them with an entourage of identities:

> [Being asked "Where are you from?"] could really piss me off and sometimes I would, when people weren't satisfied with me saying that I was of Scottish-Irish-English background and Japanese, I would just start listing off like thousands and thousands of different places, just because they were annoying me. Or sometimes I would just make things up because they wouldn't believe me. I would sometimes say something really elaborate, I'd tell them that I was an Eskimo or a Native Canadian, or you know any of those things.

Frustrated by demands for self-classification, Claudia would spiel off a wide array of ethnicities, and the decision to do so took on varying importance in different times and places. The extent to which this "theatre of the absurd" is articulated reflects a refusal to comply with the arbitrary nature of racial classifications. Part of the pleasure in performing racialized identities is articulated in the act of bluffing, which is enacted in the "face of cultural configurations" (Butler 1990, 138) that are regularly assumed to be "natural." Claudia deliberately performed an "un-natural discourse" (Kobayashi and Peake 1994) by taking the inquirer on a rat-run through the labyrinth of ethnic options (Waters 1990). Both Claudia and Darius attempted to displace rules of rigid racial categorization and accompanying ethnic stereotypes by taking on a flurry of identities that suggested an openness to resignification and recontextualization (Butler 1990, 138).

These interviews revealed participants' encounters with constraints, their resistance, and the subsequent emergence of racialized meanings. Even something as simple as one's music preferences, a bike ride on a sunny day, or being introduced to someone at a party was laden with racialized meanings. These meanings and structures shifted and were reconfigured continually. The lengths to which participants would go to project themselves for different audiences depended upon the shifting forms of racist ideologies and discourses in different spaces. Whereas Naela explained that she had put into process a complex and lengthy series of acts to prove her ethnicity to the kids on the basketball team, Claudia's personal investment only involved reeling off a list of ethnicities, with the objective of halting further questions about her ethnicity.

The results of such choices by participants were indeterminate, contradictory, and sometimes even revolutionary. For example, it would be presumptuous to assume that as a result of Darius's intervention, the truck driver was rendered silent and consequently contemplated his own complicit positioning with racism – although Darius and I joked during the interview that we hoped this was indeed the case! I suggest that these forms of struggle are not always coherent – or progressive. Although Haritaworn (2009, 129), in his analysis of interviews with mixed race people, suggests that the "pleasure, safety and unruly agency" embedded in their stories "must be recognized as incidents of resistance and empowerment that are valid and important in themselves," not all methods of performance can be seen as acts of resistance. I suggest that in the presence of the powerful, individuals are often obliged to adopt strategic stances (Scott 1990). Often, doing so signifies exhaustion with the inquiry "Where are you from?" and offers a detraction from invasive or probing questions, as in Claudia's case. It can also provide an opportunity to shock or surprise people who make racist comments, silencing them from further questioning, as Darius demonstrated. However, strategies of covertness can also be employed, a necessary tactic at times due to vulnerability to racist attacks, which is often compounded by the variable of gender, a factor that rarely permits the luxury of direct confrontation. There were times when participants actively or passively veiled or concealed their ethnicity for safety's sake, where racial performativity was enacted primarily as a survival strategy. I want to illustrate some of these covert strategies by discussing how participants often presented anonymous stances in the face of oppressive situations or adopted the role of the "spy" or "trickster" to define their movement in particular places.

Some participants explained how they would adopt an anonymous stance to protect themselves from racist attacks, employing covertness by not saying anything about their ethnicity when it was assumed for them by others. Clearly, there are times – and spaces – when it is advantageous to conceal one's mixed race background. I hope the following example illustrates Probyn's (1990, 182) claim that "living with contradictions does not necessarily enable one to speak of them, and in fact for concrete reasons, it may be dangerous to do so." Rani described an incident where she obscured her ethnic identities to sidestep a potentially threatening situation, offering her an opportunity to escape likely persecution:

> I was in the subway [in New York City] stupidly at two a.m. in the morning with my friend Julie. And this guy was really harassing Julie about her ethnicity. She's black. To me, she's obviously black. But she's dyed her hair. Actually what he first said was, "You're black, aren't you?" And Julie said, "No," because she didn't want this guy to ... Well, it was just weird. And finally she said, "Yes, I'm black." And he said, "GOOD!" And then he flashes this gun. On the side of his hip (chuckle). And he goes, "Because us black people," and he looks at me, "and us Puerto Ricans, we gotta stick together." So I was thinking, "I'll happily be Puerto Rican for you today!" (laughter) No problem!

Rani's choice not to pipe up, "Well, no, actually, I am mixed," reflected her tentativeness to identify herself as mixed race in this arena (earlier in the interview, she had insisted that she defined herself as mixed race in most social spheres), where any open resistance might have resulted in instant retaliation. She explained that the situation was fraught with tension, such that any misspoken word could have meant disastrous consequences. Resistant political subjectivities are constituted through one's position in relation to authority, and this position can often leave people in awkward, contradictory, and dangerous places: "There are contexts in which downplaying one's assigned racial or sex identity might be a good thing to do and contexts in which playing it up may be good" (Shrage 1997, 188). Clearly, racism has an uncanny ability to adopt new stances in different times and places.

There were times when participants employed fugitive and covert strategies to move through spaces that might not have been accessible to them if they had proclaimed their ethnic allegiances aloud. They were often offered entry to spaces that were traditionally prohibited by virtue of their phenotype and were thus able to transgress certain racialized boundaries. For example, Julia explained that both Katya and she identified as "spies," subverting and revitalizing inversions of official discourses:

> We were talking about how we would both make great spies 'cause we don't look like we're people in the context that we're in when we're transplanted into that culture ... There's been instances where people have said things where I think they just don't realize what they're saying and I will correct them on it. And then they always do a double-take

and they look at me closer. I think if I had an affinity for languages, I would make a perfect spy because I can transcend those borders. I would be able to enter all those communities without them realizing that I'm nowhere near where those communities are.

By "passing" as white in everyday life, Julia suggested that she had the potential to shake the foundations of naturalized racial categories. At times, she chose to uncloak her ethnicity in order to shock people out of their stereotypes. Julia expressed a desire to destabilize racialized spaces by unsettling the link between racialized meanings and identities and thereby revealing the slipperiness of naturalized racial categories.

Envisioning oneself as a spy was a common thread throughout many interviews. At the end of our interview, Naela abruptly stopped me and told me there was something she had forgotten to talk about. Unprompted by a question, she said,

> Oh actually there's one more thing I wanted to say, and it's not exactly about people questioning my race, [it's more about me feeling] like a spy? There's this one memory I have, basically in Grade 7, the first dance I was at, at school. And I was talking to two girls, and they were talking about which boys they wanted to dance with. And these are girls that I had just met, like I had just got to that junior high school. And they were discussing, they were both discussing. And then they said, "Well what are you going to do if a Chinese boy asks you?" And they were like, "I don't want to dance if a Chinese boy asks me, they're too short." And they said this like, like, I mean, I was so shocked that they were saying this in front of me? Like because I can't believe that they're saying this, they, then I realized that they didn't realize that I was Chinese as well? They were saying such offensive things, right when I was RIGHT THERE. There were the three of us. And that was a big shocker. And I just said to her, I just said, "I'm half-Chinese. Why don't you want to dance with a Chinese boy?" I mean, they were just talking about Chinese people with such disdain! You know? And then I sorta realized, and we just changed the subject, or whatever. But that was just like, first I thought they were doing it just to get me going. To get me, to get some sort of response from me. To isolate me, to show me that they didn't like me. But then I realized that they didn't even know? And then I just felt, like I felt like I was, like that part of me was invisible?

Sort of? And that I had all these powers, so I made up this fantasy in my mind, like of being able to infiltrate all these racist groups, of people, and then go, "HA!" or whatever.

There are several tangled threads in the above narrative that I wish to tease out, some of which are reminiscent of my earlier comments about whiteness in Chapter 4. First, a preliminary reading indicates that Naela initially read the girls' decision to speak disparagingly about the Chinese boys as a slight against Naela herself, indicated by her statement that she thought they had done it "to isolate me, to show me that they didn't like me." She was surprised to discover that the girls had not identified her as being Chinese at all. When she discovered this, Naela chose to expose the girls' racist practices. With me, she expressed glee and amusement at her potential to undermine ethnic stereotypes in the future by infiltrating and destabilizing racist spaces. Other critical mixed race scholars have also highlighted the way that the term "spy" is employed by those involved in the mixed race movement, showing that some white mothers of mixed race children think about themselves as spies. Dalmage (2004, 214) cites "Donna," an Irish American mother of two interracial children:

> I'm allowed in [at a table of all whites] like I am one of them. I can listen in and use that information against them as well. I feel like a spy, they really don't know what I am. I may look white, but I'm not. It's like I'm not really white, you know? I'm white, but I'm not really one of them.

I caught glimpses of similarity between these interviewees and women engaged in managing lesbian identities in everyday spaces, as discussed by Bell and Valentine (1995, 148), who show that in different environments, gay women may adopt a short-term or strategic approach by "waiting to see how the land lies before 'coming out.'" Naela and Julia both focused upon the process of "coming out" – albeit in a way that differs drastically from the exploration in Bell and Valentine's account – by "playing the race card." This was envisaged as a strategy to attack and expose racism. Confronted by those around her who had made a racial remark, Naela chose to declare her ethnicity. She said that she looked forward to such encounters since they could become a source of discomfort and cause a momentary crisis of racial meaning, allowing her to pose a threat to boundaries and hierarchies by creating cultural anxiety.

By no means am I suggesting that the moment at the dance was not fraught with feelings of exclusion or unhappiness. However, in her telling of the story, Naela chose to focus upon her later reading of the incident as an opportunity for agency. This was not an uncommon tendency among the women I interviewed. The choice to emphasize the positive aspects of one's mixed race identity was a tacit thread woven through most interviews. However, it is crucial to note that this choice was not always made.

Chantal revealed some painful memories related to her experience of mixed race and said that she felt pity whenever she saw a black baby in a stroller being pushed by a white woman. As we were packing up after the interview, Chantal noted grimly that her insights might disrupt readings of the mixed race experience I had garnered from other participants – and that I might want to drop her interview from my case study. I feel this comment should not be overlooked. Chantal pointed out the very real paradox of mixed race, emphasizing that not all mixed race people share similar experiences of either absolute oppression or complete freedom. Instead, she stressed how appearance is a strong factor in the equation of these dimensions.

Julia introduced the notion of the trickster as a way to describe herself in the midst of a discussion about her latest film project, which followed the story of an animal trickster in northern Ontario. The notion of the "trickster" has been subjected to heightened scrutiny in cultural studies (Haraway and Harvey 1995; R.J.C. Young 1995; Landay 1998) and in literature (Beer 1998). Indeed, appearing on the academic horizon is now something called "trickster studies" (Landay 1998, 27). Geographers have also alluded to the trickster in relation to the development of an "un-naturalized discourse" where "practices that would in the past [have] ... been designated as ... witchcraft or voodoo ... [might] be seen as a means of bringing about social change" (Kobayashi and Peake 1994, 238). However, although academics have paid attention to the term "trickster," it is not employed widely in the vernacular. Hence I was astonished to hear one of my participants liken her identity to that of a trickster:

JULIA: I love being a trickster.

MINELLE: A what?

JULIA: A trickster. I really like the whole notion of the trickster pretending. In the traditional trickster fashion, the trickster always being someone who's defined by difference ... And I see myself as a trickster.

> So what I'm doing right now is masquerading as white but that's just so I can get off the ground ... I'm putting on the guise of a white human whenever I want. So that I can push my own ends and help save the animal community, which is the people who aren't in the privileged group. And I think I see that as what my role is. Turning things up, a little upside down, changing people's expectations, surprising them. I think being mixed heritage works to my benefit in that I find myself in situations like this where I can protect the interests of Asian people in situations where people are not anticipating me to be Asian.

Julia revealed the potential of the managed self to destabilize racist spaces by infiltrating them unnoticed. She readily admitted that by operating through spaces where she was read as white, while also being the other against whiteness, she could "masquerade" as white, which allowed her the opportunity to enjoy the privileges attending white skin. At the same time, however, Julia insisted that she had the ability to challenge how spaces and identities were constructed and encoded by occupying both spaces simultaneously and thus saw herself as being able to perform acts of resistance in a veiled fashion.

By deeming herself a trickster, Julia enacted "a skill [of] ceaselessly re-creating opacities and ambiguities – spaces of darkness and trickery – in the universe of technocratic transparency, a skill that disappears into them and reappears again, taking no responsibility for the administration of a totality" (de Certeau 1985, 18). Julia acknowledgeed her privilege in being able to masquerade as a "white person" and demonstrated how this privilege was doubled by her ability to move in and out of particular spaces in order to "speak up" for marginalized groups.

A brief review of the literature on the trickster shows some interesting results. The trickster is often explored as an ambiguous and equivocal mediator of contradiction, and I suggest that use of the trickster as a metaphor tells a story about racial hierarchies. The trickster earns his success not by physical prowess or strength but by his wit and cunning. He snakes through treacherous spaces wherein reside enemies who seek to defeat him, yet in principle he is unable to win any direct confrontation since he is smaller and weaker than his antagonists. Only by knowing the habits of his enemies does the trickster manage to escape their clutches and subsequently win victories (Scott 1990). In comic narratives the trickster has been considered a trope, a creative production, and an imaginative liberation: "the trickster is postmodern" (Vizenor 1989, 9). Ifekwunigwe (1997a, 147) uses the term "metis(se)" to describe individuals who have "British or European mothers and continental African or African Caribbean fathers," and I juxtapose this meaning against the definition of "metis" provided by the ancient Greeks:

> ["Metis" means to combine] flair, wisdom, forethought, subtlety of mind, deception, resourcefulness, vigilance, opportunism, various skills and experience acquired over the years. It is applied to situations which are transient, shifting, disconcerting, and ambiguous, situations which do not lend themselves to precise measurement, exact calculation, or rigorous logic. (Detienne and Vernant 1978, 3-4)

Clearly, this was the case for Julia, who read her own mixed race as allowing her to employ these strategies in order to achieve her own ends. Instead of being sighted and re-sited, an experience that mixed race people constantly reassign and reinterpret on various terrains, Julia asserted her ability to site her audience – to manipulate those who had so often manipulated and positioned her own identity.

Gender is a neglected yet important aspect of trickster studies (Landay 1998, 27). Female tricksters can "articulate the paradox of femininity and autonomy ... by transgressing the cultural delimiters of 'women's sphere' ... Female tricksters violate [gendered] boundaries" (ibid., 26). In the genre of the "passing" novel, mixed race women are often characterized by what is deemed the "trickster" tactic of deception and boundary crossing. On the whole, these experiences of being a trickster tend to be tragic ones (ibid., 19). However, Julia told a different story, as she clearly drew strength from imagining herself as a trickster. Ideas around female trickery in particular can underscore "the issue of women's exercise of covert power" (ibid., 29), challenging the ideals of femininity against which female tricksters rebel. It might be said that participants were "double tricksters" since they regularly contested both gendered and racialized representations.

To summarize, I have unveiled some stories that participants told me about actively performing a variety of ethnicities. At times, their strategies disrupted the rules of rigid racial categorization, unsettling accompanying ethnic stereotypes. Participants described several momentary configurations of attitudes and choices that were formed during interactions with others and that encapsulated a multiplicity of shifting definitions and interpretations. The interaction between such multiple affiliations is complex. It represents an engagement with invention and play in a continual process of becoming. In citing these stories, I have attempted to unfold a series of maps that show where participants drew new cartographies of identity, describing a politics of location that challenged traditional race readings by fragmenting and reconstituting the elements that made up their racial categories.

My broad purpose in this chapter has been to demonstrate how we might more fully read, interpret, and understand the various racialized performances employed by some mixed race women. I have tried to set into motion a critical process that explores the conditions of possibility for separate invocations of mixed race identity. Mixed race women in this study heeded Probyn's (1993, 172) insistence that "we need to keep moving and to keep speaking our selves in ways that will encourage other movements, that will recreate alternative positions." I wonder, however, as I close this final empirical chapter, whether there is in fact a method in all of this movement. I am curious about what all these racialized performances say about conceptions of race, ethnicity, resistance, the research process, and the self. I now engage with each of these elements in turn.

My initial point of departure was Butler's (1990, 139) assertion that gender is a "regulatory fiction," and in juxtaposing her findings with my own work, I further asserted that race is also a regulatory fiction. This phrase resonates with me because of its paradoxical nature. On the one hand, race is utterly fictional, a story, an untruth that is sometimes associated with a freedom from boundaries. But the very real limits of racial performativity are unveiled by the term "regulatory," which signals that performances take place in constrained places, the vigilant border guards constantly on patrol. Such performances rely upon how those enacting them have been rendered as particular subjects within the oppressive framework of racialized meanings. There was nothing inevitable, or natural, about the ways that participants in this study were raced.

I have suggested that some mixed race women rework their identities and disrupt social values associated with perceptions of race. More specifically, I think that particular meanings associated with racial representations are challenged and contested by some of these performances. Performances can trouble racialized lines by creating an "emotional/psychic earthquake with emotional reverberations" (Root 1996a, 9). Participants provided glimpses of multidimensional subject positions. "Lodged in the terrain of the social, they rearticulate a geography of possibility" (Probyn 1993, 172) by playing with racialized impressions of themselves, demonstrating the fabrication of race as a "fantasy instituted and inscribed on the surface of bodies" (Butler 1990, 136). I have tried to demonstrate how participants actively redrew their own racialized constitution in order to drain racial categories of their powerful essences. I feel that doing race differently holds the potential to employ racial performances as "sites of critical agency" (Butler 1993, x).

Although it might well seem that "the limits of what we are and what we can be may have been already mapped out by somebody else" (Rose 1993, 147), I suggest that participants rewrote themselves into the picture, becoming the authors of their own ethnicity. Participants challenged and interpreted ethnicity differently within particular socio-spatial contexts. The descriptive sociology in which participants engaged on the ground was powerfully freighted with the notion that ethnicity could betray traditionally defined senses of origin. For participants, ethnicity was more than something that was passed on through tradition, linked solely to birth and biology. Their interviews told another tale.

Some of the women in this study explored a variety of ethnic ties that were at times the same as those of their parents and at other times completely different. I suggest that appearance plays only one of many roles in potential ethnic identifications and does not preclude other possibilities. Some participants discussed their enthusiastic explorations of a variety of ethnic options. For example, Madeleine had recently been to Japan and explained that she felt a closer affinity to Japanese culture than to either one of her more traditionally defined ethnicities. It is equally important to note that parents do not necessarily exert the only influence upon their children's choices of ethnic identification, as my interview with Bella attested. Bella stressed her own allegiance to Judaism, which became the focus of our interview, as she explained how she held *Seders* and celebrated various holidays and events associated with Judaism, a religious affiliation that emerged over time and did not reflect her own parents' religious beliefs. I suggest that these women provide us with a way to rethink traditional definitions of ethnicity. By pursuing several ethnic options, participants produced new cartographies of varied ethnic allegiances.

There is no way of knowing whether these women's choices were enacted – or read – as strategies of resistance. Although participants' performances may have manifested a conceptual slippage between notions of the natural and the socially constructed, I am left asking whether these performances were in fact consistently indicative of participants' desire to make political or progressive statements? To consider this question, I draw from my interview with Naela. When I asked her why she chose to enact various performances, she responded with a laugh,

> I try all different sorts of ethnicities ... I'll just tell people I'm certain things, just to see what they say ... I can't remember an illustration, but sometimes, they'll be like, "Oh let me guess, you're Filipino, right?" And I'll go "yeah" and but then I'll tell them the truth, I kinda make fun of them to their face. Which is fun ... Sometimes I like to make up whatever, just for the hell of it, or because I'm bored! (laughter)

Naela explained that she had many reasons, ranging from boredom to anger, for employing racial performativity. She played with others' perceptions to suit her own mood. As Shotter (1993, 47) maintains, "there are many ... human activities in which – though we may loathe to admit it – we all remain deeply ignorant as to what we are doing, or why we are doing it."

I think it is misleading to describe an act of resistance as an encounter between the powerful and the weak. This notion locks resistance into a binary characterization that is hardly productive. A return to the experience of Darius with the truck driver may offer insight. Did Darius occupy a solely marginalized position? Or did she adopt an oppressive stance by putting the truck driver ill at ease? Who was the powerful one in this situation? Interventions made on one level can be compromised by reinscriptions of power on another level (Kondo 1997). It may be helpful to ask how various positionalities highlight the necessity of carefully attending to the kinds of power relations that were understood and explored by participants during encounters in particular sites. Notably, some of the women's identity strategies cited here actually reinvested racist ideals by reidealizing them and reconsolidating their hegemonic status – far from what antiracist practitioners would see as a progressive move. Performances can in fact reinforce a binary and oppositional mode of racial identification. Some seemingly subversive actions taken by informants may have been constituted out of, and actively maintained, racialized boundaries; indeed, the term "subversive" itself can imply that transcendent liberation from power relations is not always possible. As Kondo (ibid., 13) indicates, "some degree of complicity with the dominant is inevitable."

The intentions and meanings of identity strategies are clearly not straightforward. The consequences of negotiating various racialized positions are not open to simple or transparent readings. Participants acknowledged that they were not able to alter systematic racism through racial performativity; rather, at stake was the hope that their interventions, in some small way, would sometimes generate subversions that did matter. The articulation of an "un-natural discourse" (Kobayashi and Peake 1994) may generate unpredictable dissonances. But we can never be certain that this will be the inevitable result. The effects of these strategies are incalculable. The interviews provide a unique lens through which to view the possibilities not for pristine resistance or opposition, as though such a thing were possible, but for a power-sensitive analysis that examines the construction of complex and shifting *selves,* in the plural, in all their cultural and situational specificity.

Conclusion: What Do These Readings Tell Us about the Mixed Race Self?

> I always think of mixed race people as sort of human Rorschach tests. That the world looks at you if you're racially ambiguous and their reaction to that ambiguity and what they read in it tells you a lot more about them than it does about you.
>
> — DANZY SENNA, ON NATIONAL PUBLIC RADIO 2011

I have explored examples of racial performativity because I feel it is worthwhile to examine the ways that many participants actively recombined conventionally racialized elements into new and often unexpected syntheses that disrupted racial binaries. Many of these strategies shook things up a little, unveiling new possibilities of identity configuration. Participants sometimes radically recontextualized stereotypes in ways that constituted a rethinking of racial categories. As Greg Carter (2013, 228) suggests, "political mixed race can challenge acquaintances' preconceptions about race. This can happen by ... calling out someone who has assumed you do not identify a certain way." I argue that these strategies are employed as a way of getting on and getting by in a racialized world. My concern lies more with the moment of the performance, which, "like a landscape, is only a small part of a mysterious narrative" (Michaels 1996, 107). I am interested in the "performative context," which "is crucial in thinking about the subversive possibilities. It locates the significance of the masquerade not with the masquerader's intentions, but with their relation to their audience, which is to say the discursive context of the performance of masquerade" (Rose 1996, 73). Participants' performances reflected their acute understanding of the audience for whom the performances were staged. How their specific audience would read the performance was gauged beforehand.

I was curious about why some women chose to narrate these examples of racialized performativity to me as a researcher. At times, these stories were told to me after the interview was over. Although mixed race women have often been read as a marginal group, I have attempted to demonstrate that during the interviews, participants challenged any fixed reading of themselves as marginal, often with anger and indignation. They refused rehearsed social scripts, defying racialized interpretations of their selves based upon stereotypes about mixed race women, who are apparently "unable to deal with their biculturality ... [and are subsequently] torn and confused" (Nakashima 1992, 171). However, the interview itself is also a site of performance. It is possible that participants projected various identities throughout the interview process to contest the systematic dominant representations of themselves as weak or in positions of relative powerlessness. By telling me stories that they knew I was planning to present to the general public (or at the very least to the halls of academe), participants blurred the lines between resistance and power, further challenging the socially constructed myths about mixed race individuals.

Finally, I am curious about what these examples of racial performativity tell us about the self. As I mentioned earlier in the chapter, there is always the concern that in discussions of performativity, the "real" self is disguised by several masks in the performance of various others (see Radhakrishnan 1996). In the interviews, these issues were not necessarily articulated through a vocabulary that contrasted the dualism of depth and surface. Rather, the interviews suggest that informants participated actively in their own composition – their performance constituting "the very subject it is said to express" (Butler 1990, 24) – through particular spontaneous acts and reactive responses to others' interpretations of their racialized selves. They stressed to me, as the researcher, their understanding of the development of their own capacity to deliberate upon others' interpretations of themselves. In emphasizing this point, I can hear Makeda's voice insisting, "It's not my crisis, it's theirs."

An emphasis upon context provides a way of moving the dialogue away from focusing upon the individual's performance of a racialized identity and toward imagining identities as "being produced in relation to other people at specific times and places" (Walker 1995, 71). By focusing upon the particular temporal contingency of these performances, I have attempted to show that "while the self is not contained in any one moment or place, it can be made to appear at certain intersections" (Probyn 1993, 167). Novelist Jeanette Winterson (1989, 80) reads the self as "not contained in any moment of any place, but it is only in the intersection of moment and place that the self might, for a moment, be seen vanishing through a door, which disappears at once." Participants opened up the possibility of the self as process, where the "self is not simply put forward, but rather is reworked in its enunciation" (Probyn 1993, 2). Unveiling the performative strategies among participants reveals their understanding of racialized processes – and that they acknowledged their ability to intervene and disrupt racialized social scripts. By enacting racial performativity, participants showed a recognition of their complex role in a sea of social meanings, where they grasped and took control of racialized readings of their selves.

Finally, it is crucial to note that women of mixed race in this study actually shared very little apart from living in Toronto. I agree with Thornton (1996), who insists that mixed race people do not necessarily share a common experience that validates a particular group designation. Their phenotypes are radically dissimilar. Their jobs vary widely. Some are mothers, some are culture vultures, and their friends, family, and hobbies are very different. However, they do share similar experiences around racial classifications, where perceptions of their phenotypes are alike. They told me about the shifting ways that their identities were read in a variety of spheres, about their disenchantment with particular identity classifications, and about the subsequent development of strategies to thwart those stifling categories. Agency among mixed race women in this study emerged as a continual negotiation of the regulatory fictions of race.

7
Present Tense
The Future of Critical Mixed Race Studies

> The trajectory of multiracial research desperately needs to be self-critical, to be willing to adopt new lenses with which to view the phenomena at hand; in sum, the field of multiracial identity is at a place where those investigating such processes must begin to answer the classic question, so what?
>
> — BRUNSMA 2006, 5

I have shared stories told to me by some women who identified as mixed race, explaining that some stories were influenced by the romanticization of racial mixing that occurred in the 1990s. Whereas some may read this romanticization as a step forward, I argue that we should be more wary. The love affair with mixing has allowed for a depoliticization of mixed race as an anticolonial category of identity. As Greg Carter (2013, 228) states, "Mixed race can disrupt the status quo, but not on its own."

In this final chapter, I address what multiracial studies might look like if we seriously considered Brunsma's "so what?" question above. I argue that the current state of critical mixed race studies is mired in what I call the *present tense*. I use this term to draw attention to the present-day temporality that is the foundational focus of much work in this subdiscipline.

The emphasis on documenting the contemporary experiences of mixed race people requires and, in turn, regulates a certain epistemological framework. This focus on the present has resulted in part from a reliance on qualitative, open-ended interviews with mixed race subjects who understandably tend to emphasize their own present-day experience of mixed race. Makalani (2001, 84) explains, "The scholarship [in critical mixed race theory] ... exhibits a near singular focus on personal experience ... blur[ring] the line between group historical experience and personal experience ... and mak[ing] the structural character of racism an ancillary concern." Such analyses do not necessarily do much to illuminate both the coercive and the consensual historical and geographical conditions under which multiracial identity becomes possible. The geopolitical histories that inform those shifting conditions become occluded. Our job as critical mixed race scholars should be to make these conditions more visible, ensuring that we do not romanticize the colonial histories that produce hybrid subjects. As Ibrahim (2012, xxxi) reflects, "The question that remains is what potentials are lost when we dream our antagonisms to both public and personal logics away, rather than *attending to what exactly produced them*" (my emphasis).

Future research would benefit from considering in more detail how aspirational readings of the mixed race experience limit the emancipatory potential of critical mixed race studies. Optimism permeates the discourse but to no politicized end. To be sure, it has been important for critical mixed race studies to counter the prevailing psychopathology surrounding the multiracial subject as torn and confused about his or her racial identity (Ifekwunigwe 2004). However, the vacant euphoria over the mixed race subject as articulated on different scales can dangerously infer the multiracial subject's supposed racial superiority over his or her monoracial counterparts, keeping white supremacy and racial reification firmly in place. As Spencer (2011, 227) reminds us, "Multiracial ideology is far more complicit ... than it is subversive of current deployments of race in the United States."

If critical mixed race studies hopes to retain its critical status, it will have to take a long, cold, and hard look at the ways that the multiracial movement and the ongoing discussion about multiraciality in the academic context have upheld ongoing racial inequalities (see Makalani 2001; DaCosta 2007; and Ibrahim 2012), particularly among different racial groups, including blacks, Indigenous peoples, and individuals who identify as mixed race but are not of white descent.

As scholars engaging in mixed race studies, we need to stop congratulating ourselves for consistently pointing out the socially constructed nature of race and the malleability of the racial experience for some (but of course, not all) self-identified mixed race people whose appearance is ambiguous. Makalani (2001, 85) emphasizes that "the current intellectual fashion is to argue that races are social constructions ... [This] stresses their social character, but does not differentiate them from other social constructions such as family or community." A focus on an individual's personal experience of race on a day-to-day level can actually work to obscure structural racism. It remains a singular and individualized story. Of course, I am not denying the value of sharing stories about our experiences. But there is a limit to what these stories can do by themselves if they are disconnected from collective common struggles. We need to examine how the capitalist mode of production has informed the emergence and implementation of the mixed race category of identification and how neoliberalism infuses and props up racial capitalism (see McNeil 2012). We also should pay closer attention to the way that social capital informs mixed race Canadians' experiences. Canadian mixed race scholar Rachel Gorman (2011, 11) offers poignant words in a piece that speaks to her personal experience:

> An analysis of race that conceptualizes in/equality through reference to bourgeois "passing" cannot produce anti-racist politics, only neoliberal politics. This kind of an analysis continues to highlight the transnational elite – those who, in the Obama era, we might hazard to recognize as the global bourgeoisie – while obscuring global apartheid. My father was an anti-colonial, anti-fascist, socialist organizer. Ideologues of race in a liberal world do not see my father as a symbol of racial unity, healing the wounds of Portuguese imperialism and slavery in Africa – in fact, they do not see him at all.

Gorman is particularly persuasive in pointing out that a focus on personal experiences may both capitalize upon and reinforce neoliberal individualism and, in turn, feed racial capitalism (see also McNeil 2012). This is the tension that requires unravelling in critical mixed race theory – hence my suggestion that we are caught in a present tense. Gorman starkly reminds us that we must be attentive to the ongoing depoliticization and erasure of the economic dimensions of race in studies of multiraciality.

Too few studies have attended to the cultural capital that is strategically deployed by some mixed race women. Several empirical mixed race studies, and I include my own among them, have involved tabulating the experiences of mixed race people of upper- and middle-class status. Class privilege permeates those stories that have been heard and has implications for the trajectory of research in this area.

McNeil (2010, 121) wryly states that "it has become de rigueur for monographs on 'mixed-race' published in the twenty-first century to remind the reader that 'mixed-race' does not just mean black/white or non-white/white mixing." I have to admit to some uneasiness regarding McNeil's claim, as I feel he somewhat undermines the contributions of those scholars who have been tabulating the stories of those who are not of a black-white mix, as indicated by his patronizing use of the term "de rigueur." However, McNeil makes a good point. There must be a place for analyses of different mixes, to be sure. But we need to pay closer attention to the politics of methodological practice in detailing those differences and their corresponding political implications. How do studies of the experiences of people who are differently mixed beyond black and white further embed biological understandings of race? Are we up to the task of speaking more carefully about the significant *difference of experience* among people of different mixes? As Ibrahim (2012, 31) reminds us, "If multiracialism … emerge[s] as a new social identity, then this suggests that multiracial subjects – those whose identities are comprised of multiple racial and ethnic heritages – make up a coherent categorical group."

We have somewhat disingenuously assumed that all people who identify as mixed share similar experiences, as though there were a unified pan-multiraciality. *There is not.* Although people of different racialized backgrounds may choose to identify as mixed race, the historical freight associated with these backgrounds is not the same. Within the category of mixed race identity lie distinct racial subjectivities that cannot be easily united under a single banner. Ibrahim (2007, 165) surmises that *all* "racial communities are already fraught with multiple disjunctions of experience." We require more analyses of the experiences of those who define themselves as mixed but who are not part white or part black in order to understand their relationship to both whiteness and blackness (see also Bettez 2012). I am not saying that we just need more studies that explore the mixed race relationship to whiteness and blackness – although, of course, that would shed light in this subdiscipline, too. Instead, I am insisting that we need to explore in more detail the relationship between whiteness and blackness for people who do not identify as either black or white. I believe this omission demonstrates a pernicious kind of racial epistemological violence, where whiteness as an epistemological space remains privileged. The black-white binary that has structured so much of the thinking in critical mixed race analysis has opened up spaces for some to speak about their mixed race experience, but it has also foreclosed other spaces. We would do well to open up these spaces if we are to understand how a multiplicity of interracial intimacies beyond the white-other binary creates shifting matrices of racial dynamics that may help to prevent us from chafing in our present theoretical straitjackets. The conceptual tools we have at our disposal are not sufficient for speaking to the global racial formations that confront us, including neoliberal policy changes and global immigration patterns. Mapping how different racial logics emerge and are sustained in the historical moment as influenced by state-sponsored and -sanctioned policies will help us to understand the permanence and flexible global networks of coloniality and how they intersect to affect the currency of multiraciality.

Beliefs about race and racial difference play a fundamental role in constituting how, when, and where the mixed race body materializes and emerges in public discourse. Ideas about a unified category of mixed race identity and about who is included under the "mixed race" label have centred on the concerns of those of partially white heritage, who tend to be economically advantaged. In turn, this focus has justified particular forms of racism within the multiracial movement. The category of mixed race is marked by internal differences rather than by any kind of universal sameness.

Moving beyond a focus on the present tense and toward historical specificity and an anticolonial engagement requires attending to at least two key issues. First, in countries such as Canada, the United States, New Zealand, and Australia, certain prior racial formations, including white-black, white-Indigenous, and white-nonwhite have deeply structured, sutured, and informed the racial contexts where mixed race people identify themselves. Second, this means that mixed race people may participate in inextricably intertwined racial formations where they experience racial privilege in relation to groups of people who are counted as black or Indigenous (including those who might be considered mixed but are instead seen as black). In Chapter 1, I insisted that future conversations about multiraciality must come to terms with its complex and complicit relationship not only with blackness but also in particular with Indigeneity. Some mixed race people seek refuge in the spaces that are defined as neither black nor Indigenous. Mixed race theorists have not integrated an understanding of Canada as a colonial state into their frameworks. I have only hinted at the possibilities here. Room must be made for more.

Like critical race scholars who have been writing about the relationship between anticolonialism, antiracism, and the white-settler state (see Lawrence and Dua 2005; Sharma and Wright 2009; Augustus 2010; Razack, Smith, and Thobani 2010; Morgensen 2011; and A. Smith 2012), critical mixed race scholars need to more cogently reflect upon their relationship with coloniality. If multiraciality is to mean anything in a politically progressive sense, it must come to terms not only with its relationship to whiteness but also with how it has allowed a particular ongoing form of white supremacy to thrive. A much deeper engagement with issues of empire, imperialism, and colonialism may allow this kind of conversation to emerge.

There remains a paucity of literature in the Canadian context that squarely positions an analysis of the multiracial subject within the confines and territoriality of colonialism and empire (but see Mawani 2009). As I suggested in Chapter 2, far too much mixed race research in a contemporary context is governed by a methodological approach that relies on current-day interviews, so most participants tend to speak in the present, about their day-to-day lives in the here and now, and do not address their histories – or more important, how they see themselves implicated in history more broadly. In my study, this focus on the *present tense* did not necessarily allow participants to explore the historical tensions surrounding race, empire, and imperialism that shaped and clouded their experiences of race in mid-1990s Canada.

I am not the first to point out the weaknesses of the interview approach in examinations of multiraciality – Rockquemore, Brunsma, and Delgado (2009) show that most of the research in this field is informed through qualitative, open-ended interviews. There is no doubt that interviews can yield productive information and that they shaped much mixed race agency in the mid-1990s, when critical multiracial studies was, arguably, still in its relative infancy. However, the predominant patterns that have emerged in the interviews conducted with self-identified mixed race people should encourage us to consider new ways of approaching this topic – or at least to explore the similarities and differences more clearly.

As I have pointed out, other critical scholars working in the field of mixed race research have shown that the themes that emerge in interviews are often similar – many mixed race people proudly consider themselves to be racial ambassadors, or bridges (Spencer 2011; McNeil 2012). What we have yet to explore is why these are the stories that are told with regularity to researchers. Perhaps it is because the mixed race identification of so many critical scholars working on mixed race issues compels some participants to develop a point of alliance or sameness with the researcher based on mixed race, or perhaps it is because participants often parrot back the message track around multiraciality that tends to be communicated in popular culture, given the cultural commodification of multiraciality. The similarity of themes across interviews may also reflect, at least in part, the relatively privileged class status of the subjects – and maybe also of the interviewers – as shaped by post-1960s immigration policies in Canada. Whatever the reasons for the frequency of some stories, it will be important for the field to consider means of gathering information about the experience of multiraciality that go beyond asking similar questions through the qualitative, open-ended interview (see Rockquemore, Brunsma, and Delgado 2009).

Ibrahim (2012, 3) notes that "the multiracial movement expanded a mode of temporality that reconstituted racial embodiment and the truth of race – a mode that, in advancing new forms of human embodiment, seemed to reinvent personhood." Ibrahim's focus on embodiment is instructive. There are limitations to an individualized, embodied epistemological approach – one that is often framed through the interview process. When we emphasize what the individual mixed race body can or cannot do by highlighting the micro-politics of mixed race people's agency and acts of resistance without embedding their bodily practices within systemic patterns of structural racism and, in particular, within *colonial* practices in the Canadian context, the result is an almost exclusive focus on the micro-practices of the singular body. This focus may advance colonial epistemological violence by shying away from the complex and underresearched relationship between mixed race immigrant identities and Indigenous identities while allowing us to avoid harder questions about the structural character of racism and about the relationship between mixed race people's group historical experience and personal experience (Makalani 2001).

Makalani (2001, 84) is right when he states that "an uncritical acceptance of reported experiences, with an individual identity being emphasized irrespective of social context or history ... conflate[s] ... [identity] with race." We might instead ask about the epistemological and ontological consequences of a continued focus on individual bodily practices in critical mixed race studies. Elam (2011, 135) hints at the implications, suggesting in a different context that "biracial features do not chronicle the real story, the racial injustices that lurk beneath [one's] skin and beneath the surface of official history." Returning to the words of Ibrahim (2012, 7-8, 13) helps to elucidate my point:

> The recognition that our behaviour as private individuals is inextricably linked to relations of power was a significant precondition for the emergence of the multiracial movement of the 1990s ... To some degree, efforts to raise awareness through personal, lived experience did the work of developing a knowledge project that bore political implications ... It provide[d] the starting point for critical analyses of how some individuals are denied agency ... [However,] by avoiding racial politics ... multiracial organizations seemed to be at a loss for how to account for its own place in history or for its own temporal movement.

This book provides only a glimpse of how we might begin to reconcile these approaches. Although I briefly touched upon issues of anticolonialism in Chapter 1, this book does not develop a fuller anticolonial framework for the study of multiraciality. This will have to be explored in other texts. I simply raise the issue that the epistemological explorations of critical mixed race studies in Canada have not fully articulated what would constitute transparent anticolonialist resistance. Gorman (2011, 1) invites us to explore this terrain: "Mixed race subjects also emerge variously as a threat or an opportunity to settler colonial nation-building projects which have relied on a range of strategies to differentiate Indigenous, African-descended, immigrant, and white as discrete categories." Studies about, for, and by mixed race people in Canada have ostensibly made race the ontological pivot for our analyses, yet the development of an anticolonial approach to multiraciality remains buried, particularly one that pays attention to issues of Indigenous agency. Bonita Lawrence rightly states that "there is a need for people who are racialized to really get to know Indigenous peoples and their concerns ... people of colour *could* be allies not just settlers" (in S. Rutherford 2010, 13, emphasis in original). Mixed race Canadians can contribute to this conversation through a more careful engagement with the intersection of white-settler colonialism, white supremacy, and multiraciality. The architecture of colonial discourse has always been locked into a language of binaries, not dissimilar from the architecture of mixed race discourse. The language with which we choose to narrate stories about our past, present, and future needs to be rearranged and disrupted, splintering the complacent dominant imaginary. The myth that the mixed race body represents an embodiment of inclusion derives from a colonial logic that remains stubbornly persistent.

A Cautionary Tale: Saul's Celebration of Mixing in *A Fair Country*

In this penultimate section, I want to raise what I see as an intellectual red flag for Canadian critical mixed race studies by drawing attention to a particular excavation of mixing as a neoliberal good (see McNeil 2012), illustrated through a critique of the work of Canadian public intellectual John Ralston Saul. I think such an analysis helps us to understand how an ontological focus on mixing can actually evacuate a politicized understanding of issues of race and colonialism in the Canadian context. It actively works to dilute, rather than distil, the politicization of race. Reading mixing as positive ensures that white supremacy is kept in place. I discussed this issue briefly in Chapter 1, and here I pay attention to Saul's bestselling book *A Fair Country* (2008) to demonstrate the dangers of popularizing miscegenation through a facile interpretation of mixing.

In 2008 John Ralston Saul, one of Canada's foremost public intellectuals and political thinkers, as well as the author of several books about the Canadian political imagination, penned *A Fair Country: Telling Truths about Canada*. The book is a call to arms to all Canadians, encouraging them to consider that Canadians have blocked their own progress by not considering the ways that Canada is, in his words, a "Metis nation." Saul makes the case with unabashed optimism and enthusiasm that Canadians are fundamentally shaped by Aboriginal peoples – and that Canadians owe more to Aboriginal influences than to European ones. Insisting that many of the tenets that Canadians hold dear – including ethnoracial diversity, fairness, a commitment to peaceful negotiation, and social solidarity – have their roots in Aboriginality, Saul argues that Canadians must come to grips with the Aboriginal aspects of their past in order to embrace a politically progressive future.

Although the book was met with acclaim when it was published, I read it warily. The political scientist Daniel Salee (2010, 325) has cleverly critiqued Saul's book, claiming that Saul takes "enormous liberties with reality [, depicting] Canada as an inclusive, non-racial, social-democratic dreamland thanks to Aboriginal influences." He insists that Saul infantilizes and essentializes the diversity of Aboriginal communities. Salee (ibid., 324) summarizes Saul's main argument: "Canadians have lost touch with their fundamental essence as a Metis nation. They fail to recognize that many of the tenets by which they identify and characterize themselves, such as ethnocultural diversity, egalitarianism, pacifism and social solidarity, have their roots in Aboriginal notions." Saul (2008, 54-55) says that Canadians owe the following to Aboriginal influences: "Our obsession with egalitarianism. Our desire to maintain a balance between individuals and groups. The delight we take in playing with our non-monolithic idea of society – a delight in complexity ... Our preference for consensus – again an expression of society as a balance of complexity, a sort of equilibrium." Saul encourages his readers to embrace Canada's nature, which he sees as inextricably informed by "Metis" values and culture. However, he never really defines what he means by "Metis." Saul provides a convenient way out of the collective guilt that white Canadians face in light of the horrors exposed by the Indian Residential Schools Truth and Reconciliation Commission, established in 2008. Saul (ibid., 27) does admit that Canadians "don't know what to do with the least palatable part of the settler story. We wanted the land. It belonged to someone else. We took it." But he speeds by this point and marches on to propose a thesis mired in relentless optimism. The book seems to be particularly seductive to those susceptible to the neoliberal siren call.

So what does Saul's celebration of mixing have to do with this study of multiraciality? I am less interested in criticizing Saul for the blatant assumption that the relationship between Aboriginals and Europeans can be characterized as one of equal give and take, when of course, the stark reality is that Europeans established European hegemony through genocide in Canada. Nor am I keen to analyze how he presumes a constitutive, essentialized Indigeneity. I am more interested in how he appropriates the notion of "Metis" as a euphemism for integration to further his argument. Being "Metis," of course, is not the same as being integrated. The conflation is instructive. It is useful to consider how Saul's employment of a particular rhetorical device has implications for people who identify as mixed race in Canada, as well as Aboriginal peoples.

Saul encourages us to leave the past behind. He wants to celebrate the ways that Aboriginal people have contributed to the Canadian polity rather than fully acknowledging that it was never a fair incorporation. Thus he refuses to interrogate the colonial mythologies upon which his argument flourishes.

Andrea Smith (2012) speaks powerfully about the relationship between white supremacy and the logic of genocide. She reminds us that for non-Indigenous people to rightfully inherit all that is Indigenous, including land as well as Indigenous spirituality and culture, Indigenous peoples must disappear. This disappearance is made possible through miscegenation. Smith (ibid., 69) says, "It is acceptable to singularly possess land that is the home of indigenous peoples, because indigenous peoples have disappeared." Saul is able to claim that "Canadians have lost touch with their fundamental essence as a Metis nation" (Salee 2010, 324) because of the ongoing disappearance of Indigenous peoples. What better way to ensure that the process of disappearing continues than by diluting Indigenous peoples through miscegenation? Saul can then claim an alliance to "Metis" culture by using the pronoun "we" as though he is part of that "Metis nation" he so proudly speaks about.

There are resonances here for studying a potential anticolonial multiraciality as articulated by racialized immigrant groups. In taking an "interpretative licence with history," Saul attempts to "right a moral wrong committed by the near total historical erasure of Indigenous peoples and cultures" (Salee 2010, 327). It is convenient to gloss over history through this "race to innocence" (Fellows and Razack 1998), but Saul's celebration of mixing remains a wolf in sheep's clothing. His argument offers up a humanistic sense of inclusiveness through an upbeat and superficial acceptance of racial difference, refusing to acknowledge that the relationship between Aboriginal people and white settlers has always been inegalitarian. A happy-go-lucky list celebrating all the *good* Saul feels that Aboriginal people have brought to the white Anglo-Canadian way of life merely reinforces the white-settler state as benevolent through the process of mixing and masks ongoing power differentials that have persistently worked against Indigenous peoples.

Saul's text may serve as an important cautionary tale for mixed race people in Canada. I have provided numerous examples to show that many mixed race people prize their multiracial status and that some of them celebrate or even flaunt the way that they see themselves as moving across difference. They see two as "better than one." This rhetoric has damaging implications if it is confined to the Anglo-Canadian, white-settler comfort zone. Exclamations by mixed race people about their affection for their multiracial status do nothing to unsettle coloniality. *In fact, such celebration may work to further embed it.* Mixed race Canadians, as I suggested in Chapter 3, can demonstrate a kind of racial impotency, acting as colourful beacons for Canadian multiculturalism and sketching the framework for a cheerful reassertion and reconfiguration of Canada's national mythology. The mixed race Canadian subject can be celebrated and employed as a model for a benevolent and egalitarian project of what it means to be Canadian – the very model of the "Metis" that Saul is committed to projecting for his readers. Ongoing enthusiasm, euphoria, and celebration over multiraciality in Canada might be seen as a teetering racial barometer that measures Canadians' apprehension over race relations. The model multiracial who is envisioned as forward-thinking and as a symbol of racial egalitarianism is reassuring for white Canadians, serving to perpetuate a historically inaccurate vision of Canada that only helps Canadians to feel better about historical injustices. In other words, speaking of mixing in and of itself cannot be seen as positive or progressive. Employing it as a way of speaking optimistically about racial harmony is problematic. It can distract us from analyzing more precise forms of racial oppression, particularly among members of the most marginalized racialized groups. Salee (2010, 327) takes Saul to task for perpetuating the idea that Canadians can "finally be the great nation they have long aspired to be," and such a critique is prescient for a critical exploration of multiracial identities.

It remains an open question how blackness and Indigeneity correspond with each other. Although Chapter 1 has focused on the ways that the "mixed race" label incorporates white nationalist frameworks and erases Indigeneity, it is worthwhile remembering that we need to not only decolonize mixed race but also denationalize mixed race. Coloniality is about Indigeneity, but it also involves interracial encounters among many differently located groups of people. To challenge the pervasive whiteness of mixed race studies, we must attend to this issue. White supremacist logics have dramatically shaped the way we understand mixed race ontologies.

Multiracial Amnesia

> Mixed racialism is in resounding want of a history – and a redress to injury – at the beginning of the twenty-first century.
>
> — IBRAHIM 2007, 157

I have suggested that in identifying as mixed race, a certain kind of strategic forgetting about racialized histories must take place. Ibrahim (2007, 156) contends that "the mixed racial figure now represents post-integration discourses." In speaking about Danzy Senna's novel *Caucasia,* Ibrahim (ibid.) insists that "historical narratives of racism and ahistorical imaginings become melded into a social memory that need not pay attention to the terms of structural change to be socially attentive." As I proposed in Chapter 1 through an analysis of a *Toronto Star* article, the tendency to see multiraciality as something new and different obscures histories. For some, it may be simply far more convenient to discard these histories, and Canadian multiculturalism as a policy and practice certainly supports the strategic forgetting I describe. We must be careful to ensure that mixed race people do not become an insipid voice for racial tolerance and acceptance. Instead, *we must come to grips with the opportunities, privilege, and power that accompany the experience of being mixed race and of being seen as mixed race. How do we unconsciously facilitate a forgetfulness about the original struggles and conflicts that our ancestors faced without compromising our authenticity when telling our stories about our complex experiences of race? How will we choose to remember our pasts?*

McKittrick (2011, 4) suggests that the "geographies of our past leak into the geographies of our future ... The stories we tell are tethered to human acts that preserve, *obscure, and erase our histories in the name of what lies ahead"* (my emphasis). I am not sure how we can begin this process of narrating the human acts of our ancestors – a process of remembering and naming, rather than forgetting, the complex colonial pasts that inform our multiracial present and future. But this process of recalling and carefully tracing these histories will allow, I hope, for a different kind of storytelling, one whose narratives are not only materially palpable and marked in particular geographies but are also able to unveil the legacy of past and present racial injustices. The act of unearthing buried stories may help us to see that the past traumas of colonization have ongoing resonances for us that inextricably shape our present as well as our future. As Ralina Joseph (2013, xv) urges us to consider, "What happens after the missing story is told, or the incorrect story is righted?"

But I have a few caveats. It is important not to relegate our telling of multiracial histories to individualized, romanticized tales of the interracial intimacies of our parents, with a nostalgic focus on their personal affection for each other, as though they managed to overcome the racial struggles of their time – and, therefore, of our times as well. These stories do not take us anywhere *new*. They do not contribute to fighting social-justice struggles in a colonized and racist world. When we focus on "multiracial" as a category of identity that is understood as individualized, contemporary, and current, as a way of imagining an optimistic postracial future, discourses on multiraciality can "retain something of the magical, a smoke-screen that obscures the shadows of racial history and racism's relation to concrete conditions" (Ibrahim 2007, 170).

We should also be very careful not to simply dig up new stories about old forms of racism by excavating and tabulating the experiences of racism among our ancestors. Such a response may inadvertently lead us to hijack these stories in the service of telling redemptive tales of our present and future (Stoler 1997), furthering projects that may have more to do with preserving stories about culture and identity than with carefully locating these stories within grids of nuanced antiracist and anticolonial politics that influence our future. Stories about forms of racism in the past can easily be harnessed to sustain a racist present.

The question is not whether individuals who identify as mixed race are willing to challenge their portrayal as anthropological bio-curiosities. We know the answer to this question through the research findings of scholars who investigated mixed race issues during the 1990s. The agency offered through the mobilization of particular forms of cultural capital has allowed some mixed race people opportunities to mount myriad forms of challenge to stereotypes of their identities, as evidenced through their romanticization in the post-1990s era. The question is whether we are willing to be more honest about the ways that we may be complicit in contributing to the oppression of other racialized groups in the process of resisting these stereotypes and whether we can do so without becoming paralyzed by guilt. It has been argued elsewhere that the "mixed race" label offers opportunities for mixed race people to distance themselves from blackness (Sexton 2008). Intellectually and materially, it has also offered opportunities for mixed race people to distance themselves from Indigeneity. We should be more vigilant in our efforts to understand the tactical and strategic qualities of the popular multiracial discourse that maintains white supremacy, particularly where this discourse seizes upon both the dramatic and elemental, or extraordinary and ordinary, elements of earlier racial discourses, which are then mobilized to benefit mixed race people. I encourage us to come up with different methodological approaches and analyses rather than idly embracing the privileges that arise from these perceptions. It is up to us to develop more nuanced politicized subject positions that address how various forms of political economy and the commodification of various identities produce racialized social systems that correspondingly inform and shift the contours of racial categories.

A Final Word: From Present Tense to Multiracial Futures

> i don't consider myself mixed raced
> but of *misplaced biography*
> i cannot uproot my grandmother's stories
> not because she passed away
> but because she's too busy
> to pass on herstory
> forgetting her past unlocks my future's mystery.
>
> — MORRIS 2010, 41, MY EMPHASIS

What would unlocking our futures' mysteries look like? How can we tell a deeper story about colonial racial encounters in the past, present, and future while ensuring that when we tell intellectual tales about these stories, we make the political and economic histories of these encounters visible? Is there a way of remembering and engaging with multiracial histories that recognizes the violent materiality that often accompanies interracial intimacies while also acknowledging these intimacies as sites of continuing and ongoing racisms, not just as sites of intercultural exchange? What would a recontextualization of these histories mean to our understanding of the present? We might begin by "unthinking our present geographical organization" in order to move toward documenting a multiracial sense of place that is "virtually impossible under Eurocentric geographic arrangements" (McKittrick 2007, 101, 103). Such a revisioning calls for a drastic shift in imagination beyond seeing mixed race people as confined and constrained or limitless and unstoppable.

In recommending that we detail the specifics of our complex diasporic racialized histories, I want to end by sharing Makeda's story. She was one of the few women in this study who chose to speak about her family's complex familial lines. She suggested that her own mixed race status offered her an opportunity to consider the mutability of racial categories, and she addressed the specifics of diasporic experiences between generations:

> One of the things I really like is that feeling that I have ancestors from completely different parts of the world. You know, who have lived for hundreds, thousands of years, without probably imagining that descendants of theirs would end up having a child with someone from a totally other continent. And to think that I have these ancestors who have lived for generation after generation in totally different parts of the world, who came from totally different cultures, spoke different languages, you know, never, whose paths I can only assume, never crossed each other. And yet all these ancestors have, in a sense, have been brought together in me? That's something that, that gives me ah, a sense of awe, almost. A sense of wonder? I also think I have come to value over the years the learning that I've gained from that sort of dance of identity. I think that it's been tricky. But it's been very valuable. And I wouldn't have learned what I have learned or in the way I've learned it if I hadn't been mixed race.

Throughout the process of writing this book, I have tried to keep in mind Makeda's notion of a sense of wonder. She demonstrated "active attentiveness to a racial past" (Ibrahim 2007, 171) by articulating what she had learned through identifying as multiracial. The stories of mixed race women chronicled here provide examples of splintered racialized knowledges, glimpses of the possibilities of mapping the mixed race experience that are not necessarily founded on hapless optimism about a future raceless society or stuck in dehumanizing and objectifying representations of the past. Some interviews hint at something else, something beyond our current ways of knowing, being resplendent with anecdotes that allow us to contemplate the experiences of multiraciality beyond their previously intellectualized confines. This is just one attempt at a map. I look forward to seeing more.

References

Afsheen, S. 2011. *Under Five Flags: Life Like a Turbulent River Flows*. Bloomington, IN:Xlibris.
Ahmed, S. 2008. Multiculturalism and the Promise of Happiness. *New Formations* 63: 121-37.
–. 2012. *On Being Included: Racism and Diversity in Institutional Life*. Durham, NC, and London: Duke University Press.
Alcoff, L. 1988. Cultural Feminism versus Poststructuralism: The Identity Crisis in Feminist Theory. *Signs* 13 (3): 405-36.
–. 2006. *Visible Identities: Race, Gender and the Self.* New York: Oxford University Press.
–. 2009. Latinos beyond the Binary. *Southern Journal of Philosophy* 47 (S1): 112-28.
Alfred, T., and J. Corntassel. 2005. Being Indigenous: Resurgences against Contemporary Colonialism. *Government and Opposition* 40 (4): 597-614.
Ali, S. 2003. *Mixed-Race, Post-Race: Gender, New Ethnicities and Cultural Practices*. Oxford: Berg.
–. 2006. Racialising Research: Managing Power and Politics? *Ethnic and Racial Studies* 29 (3): 471-86.
Allman, K. 1996. (Un)natural Boundaries: Mixed Race, Gender and Sexuality. In *The Multiracial Experience: Racial Borders as the New Frontier*, ed. M.P.P. Root, 277-91. London: Sage.
Andersen, C. 2014. *"Métis": Race, Recognition, and the Struggle for Indigenous Peoplehood*. Vancouver: UBC Press.
Anderson, K. 1996. Engendering Race Research: Unsettling the Self-Other Dichotomy. In *BodySpace: Destabilizing Geographies of Gender and Sexuality*, ed. N. Duncan, 197-212. London: Routledge.
Ang-Lygate, M. 1997. Charting the Spaces of (Un)location: On Theorizing Diaspora. In *Black British Feminism: A Reader*, ed. H. Mirza, 168-87. London: Routledge.
Anzaldúa, G. 1987. *Borderlands/La Frontera: The New Mestiza*. San Francisco, CA: Spinsters of San Francisco/Aunt Lute Books.
Appiah, A. 1997. "But Would That Still Be Me?" Notes on "Gender," Race and Ethnicity as Sources of "Identity." In *Race/Sex: Their Sameness, Difference, and Interplay*, ed. N. Zack, 75-83. London: Routledge.

Arat-Koç, S. 2010. New Whiteness(es), Beyond the Colour Line? Assessing the Contradictions and Complexities of "Whiteness" in the (Geo)Political Economy of Capitalist Globalism. In *States of Race: Critical Race Feminism for the 21st Century*, ed. S. Razack, M. Smith, and S. Thobani, 147-68. Toronto: Between the Lines.

Atwood, M. 1993. *The Robber Bride*. Toronto: McClelland and Stewart.

Augustus, C. 2010. Mixed Race, Legal Space: A Comparative History of Indigenous Mixed-Blood Identity in Law (Canada, the United States, Australia). Seminar presented at the University of Wollongong, Australia, 21 April.

Awkward, M. 1995. *Negotiating Difference: Race, Gender and the Politics of Positionality*. Chicago, IL: University of Chicago Press.

Azoulay, K.G. 1997. *Black, Jewish and Interracial: It's Not the Color of Your Skin, but the Race of Your Kin, and Other Myths of Identity*. Durham, NC, and London: Duke University Press.

Back, L. 1996. *New Ethnicities and Urban Culture*. London: UCL Press.

Barrett, S. 1992. *Is God a Racist? The Right Wing in Canada*. Toronto: Mercury.

Barzun, J. 1938. *Race: A Study in Modern Superstition*. London: Methuen.

Baumann, G. 1996. *Contesting Culture: Discourses of Identity in Multi-Ethnic London*. Cambridge, UK: Cambridge University Press.

Baureiss, G. 1974. The Chinese Community in Calgary. *Alberta Historical Review* 22 (2): 1-8.

–. 1985. Discrimination and Response: The Chinese in Canada. In *Ethnicity and Ethnic Relations in Canada: A Book of Readings,* ed. R. Bienvenue and J. Goldstein, 241-63. Toronto: Butterworths.

Beer, J. 1998. Doing It with Mirrors: History and Cultural Identity from *The Diviners* to *The Robber Bride*. Paper presented at the British Association for Canadian Studies Conference, Staffordshire, United Kingdom, 6 April.

Bell, D., and G. Valentine. 1995. The Sexed Self: Strategies of Performance, Sites of Resistance. In *Mapping the Subject: Geographies of Cultural Transformation,* ed. S. Pile and N. Thrift, 143-58. London: Routledge.

Beltrán, M., and C. Fojas, eds. 2008. *Mixed Race Hollywood*. New York: New York University Press.

Berzon, J.R. 1978. *Neither White nor Black: The Mulatto Character in American Fiction*. New York: New York University Press.

Bettez, S.C. 2012. *But Don't Call Me White: Mixed Race Women Exposing Nuances of Privilege and Oppression Politics*. Rotterdam, Netherlands: Sense.

Bhabha, H. 1990. Interview with Homi Bhabha. In *Identity: Community, Culture, Difference,* ed. J. Rutherford, 207-22. London: Lawrence and Wishart.

–. 1994. *The Location of Culture*. New York and London: Routledge.

Bienvenue, R., and J. Goldstein, eds. 1985. *Ethnicity and Ethnic Relations in Canada: A Book of Readings*. Toronto: Butterworths.

Bissoondath, N. 1994. *Selling Illusions: The Cult of Multiculturalism in Canada*. Toronto: Penguin.

Blaagaard, B. 2011. Workings of Whiteness: An Interview with Vron Ware. *Social Identities* 17 (1): 153-61.

Blunt, A. 2003. Geographies of Diaspora and Mixed Descent: Anglo-Indians in India and Britain. *International Journal of Population Geography* 9 (4): 281-94.

Bombay, S.S. 2010. The Land Knows. In *Other Tongues: Mixed-Race Women Speak Out,* ed. A. DeRango-Adem and A. Thompson, 255-59. Toronto: Inanna.

Bondi, L. 1993. Locating Identity Politics. In *Place and the Politics of Identity,* ed. M. Keith and S. Pile, 84-102. London: Routledge.

Bonnett, A. 1997. Geography, "Race" and Whiteness: Invisible Traditions and Current Challenges. *Area* 29 (3): 193-99.
Bordo, S. 1993. *Unbearable Weight: Feminism, Western Culture, and the Body*. Berkeley: University of California Press.
Boudreau, J.A, R. Keil, and D. Young. 2009. *Changing Toronto: Governing Urban Neoliberalism*. Toronto: University of Toronto Press.
Bradford, J., and C. Sartwell. 1997. Voiced Bodies/Embodied Voices. In *Race/Sex: Their Sameness, Difference, and Interplay*, ed. N. Zack, 191-205. London: Routledge.
Brown, W. 2006. *Regulating Aversion: Tolerance in the Age of Identity and Empire*. Princeton, NJ: Princeton University Press.
Brunsma, D.L., ed. 2006. *Mixed Messages: Multiracial Identities in the "Color-Blind" Era*. Boulder, CO: Lynne Rienner.
Bulkin, E., M. Pratt, and B. Smith. 1984. *Yours in Struggle: Three Feminist Perspectives on Anti-Semitism and Racism*. Ithaca, NY: Firebrand Books.
Butler, J. 1990. *Gender Trouble: Feminism and the Subversion of Identity*. London: Routledge.
–. 1993. *Bodies That Matter: On the Discursive Limits of "Sex."* London: Routledge.
Camper, C., ed. 1994. *Miscegenation Blues: Voices of Mixed Race Women*. Toronto: Sister Vision.
Canada, House of Commons. 1980-93. *Debates*. Ottawa: Queen's Printer.
–. 1984. *Report of Special Committee on Participation of Visible Minorities in Canadian Society (Equality Now!)*. Ottawa: Queen's Printer.
Canada, Royal Commission on Bilingualism and Biculturalism. 1962. *Report of the Royal Commission on Bilingualism and Biculturalism: The Cultural Contribution of the Other Ethnic Groups*. Ottawa: Queen's Printer.
Canada, Standing Committee on Multiculturalism. 1987. *Multiculturalism: Building the Canadian Mosaic*. Ottawa: Queen's Printer.
Carter, G. 2013. *The United States of the United Races: A Utopian History of Racial Mixing*. New York: New York University Press.
Carter, R.T. 1995. *The Influence of Race and Racial Identity in Psychotherapy: Toward a Racially Inclusive Model*. New York: John Wiley and Sons.
Castle, W.E. 1926. Biological and Social Consequences of Race Crossing. *American Journal of Physical Anthropology* 9 (2): 145-56.
Catungal, J.P., and D. Leslie. 2009. Contesting the Creative City: Race, Nation, Multiculturalism. *Geoforum* 40 (5): 701-4.
Chambers, I. 1994. *Migrancy, Culture and Identity*. London: Routledge.
Chouinard, V., and A. Grant. 1996. On Being Not Even Anywhere Near the Project: Ways of Putting Ourselves in the Picture. In *BodySpace: Destabilizing Geographies of Gender and Sexuality*, ed. N. Duncan, 169-91. London: Routledge.
Christian, M. 2000. *Multiracial Identity: An International Perspective*. New York: St. Martin's Press.
Chung, A. 2006. Are We All Going to Become Latte? *Toronto Star*, 9 July.
Clarke, G.E. 2011. "For a Multicultural, Multi-faith, Multiracial Canada: A Manifesto." In *Home and Native Land: Unsettling Multiculturalism in Canada*, ed. M. Chazan, L. Helps, A. Stanley, and S. Thakkar, 51-57. Toronto: Between the Lines.
Clifford, J. 1986. Introduction: Partial Truths. In *Writing Culture: The Poetics and Politics of Ethnography*, ed. J. Clifford and G. Marcus, 1-26. Berkeley: University of California Press.
Collins, P.H. 1990. *Black Feminist Thought: Knowledge, Consciousness and the Politics of Empowerment*. London: Routledge.
Comas-Diaz, L. 1996. LatiNegra: Mental Health Issues of African Latinas. In *The Multiracial Experience: Racial Borders as the New Frontier*, ed. M.P.P. Root, 167-91. London: Sage.

Compton, Wayde. 2004. "Declaration of the Halfrican Nation." In *Performance Bond*, 15-16. Vancouver: Arsenal Pulp.

Cresswell, T. 1996. *In Place/Out of Place: Geography, Ideology, and Transgression*. Minneapolis: University of Minnesota Press.

Cryderman, B., C. O'Toole, and A. Fleras, eds. 1992. *Police, Race and Ethnicity: A Guide for Police Services*. Toronto: Butterworths.

Culjak, T. 2001. Searching for Place in Between: The Autobiographies of Three Canadian Métis Women. *American Review of Canadian Studies* 31 (1-2): 137-59.

DaCosta, K.M. 2007. *Making Multiracials: State, Family, and Market in the Redrawing of the Color Line*. Stanford, CA: Stanford University Press.

Dalmage, H.M. 2004. *The Politics of Multiracialism: Challenging Racial Thinking*. Albany, NY: SUNY Press.

Daniel, G.R. 2002. *More Than Black? Multiracial Identity and the New Racial Order*. Philadelphia, PA: Temple University Press.

Davenport, C.B. 1917. The Effects of Race Intermingling. *Proceedings of the American Philosophical Society* 56 (4): 364-68.

Davis, J. 1991. *Who Is Black? One Nation's Definition*. University Park, PA: Pennsylvania State University Press.

Dawkins, M.A. 2012. *Clearly Visible: Racial Passing and the Color of Cultural Identity*. Waco, TX: Baylor University Press.

de Certeau, M. 1985. *The Practice of Everyday Life*. Berkeley: University of California Press.

de Lauretis, T. 1986. Feminist Studies/Critical Studies. In *Feminist Studies/Critical Studies*, ed. T. de Lauretis, 1-19. London: MacMillan.

Dei, G.J. 2007. Speaking Race: Silence, Salience, and the Politics of Anti-racist Scholarship. In *Race and Racism in 21st-Century Canada: Continuity, Complexity, and Change*, ed. S.P. Hier and B.S. Bolaria, 53-66. Peterborough, ON: Broadview.

Deleuze, G. 1994. Désir et plaisir. *Le Magazine Littéraire* 325 (October): 59-65.

Delgado, R., and J. Stefancic, eds. 1997. *Critical White Studies: Looking behind the Mirror*. Philadelphia, PA: Temple University Press.

–, eds. 2001. *Critical Race Theory: An Introduction*. New York: New York University Press.

DeRango-Adem, A., and A. Thompson, eds. 2010. *Other Tongues: Mixed-Race Women Speak Out*. Toronto: Inanna.

Detienne, M., and J.P. Vernant. 1978. *Cunning Intelligence in Greek Culture and Society*. Trans. J. Lloyd. Atlantic Highlands, NJ: Humanities.

DeVries, L. 2011. *Conflict in Caledonia: Aboriginal Land Rights and the Rule of Law*. Vancouver: UBC Press.

di Leonardo, M. 1984. *The Varieties of Ethnic Experience*. Ithaca, NY: Cornell University Press.

Dickason, O.P. 1992. *Canada's First Nations: A History of Founding Peoples from Earliest Times*. Toronto: McClelland and Stewart.

Dover, C. 1937. *Half-Caste*. London: Secker and Warburg.

Du Bois, W.E.B. 1989. *Souls of Black Folk*. 1903. Reprint, New York: Penguin.

Durrow, H. 2010. *The Girl Who Fell from the Sky*. Chapel Hill, NC: Algonquin Books.

Edwards, R., S. Ali, C. Caballero, and M. Song, eds. 2012. *International Perspectives on Racial and Ethnic Mixedness and Mixing*. London: Routledge.

Eisenstein, Z. 1996. *Hatreds: Racialized and Sexualized Conflicts in the 21st Century*. London: Routledge.

Elam, M. 2011. *The Souls of Mixed Folk: Race, Politics, and Aesthetics in the New Millennium*. Stanford, CA: Stanford University Press.

Elliott, J.L., and A. Fleras. 1990. Immigration and the Canadian Ethnic Mosaic. In *Race and Ethnic Relations in Canada,* ed. P. Li, 54-71. Oxford: Oxford University Press.

Erikson, E.H. 1959. Identity and the Life Cycle. *Psychological Issues* 1 (1): 18-164.

Fellows, M.L., and S. Razack. 1998. The Race to Innocence: Confronting Hierarchical Relations among Women. *Journal of Race, Gender and Justice* 1 (2): 335-53.

Ferber, A.L., ed. 2004. *Home-Grown Hate: Gender and Organized Racism.* New York: Routledge.

Fine, M. 1997. Witnessing Whiteness. In *Off White: Readings on Race, Power and Society,* ed. M. Fine, L. Weis, L.C. Powell, and L.M. Wong, 57-66. London: Routledge.

Fine, M., L. Weis, L.C. Powell, and L.M. Wong, eds. 1997. *Off White: Readings on Race, Power and Society.* London: Routledge.

Fleras, A., and J.L. Elliott, eds. 1992. *Multiculturalism in Canada: The Challenge of Diversity.* Scarborough, ON: Nelson Canada.

Florida, R. 2002. *The Rise of the Creative Class.* New York: Basic Books.

Foster, J.E. 1985. Some Questions and Perspectives on the Problem of Métis Roots. In *The New Peoples: Being and Becoming Métis in North America,* ed. J. Peterson and J.S.H. Brown, 73-91. Winnipeg: University of Manitoba Press.

Francis, M. 2011. *Creative Subversions: Whiteness, Indigeneity, and the National Imaginary.* Vancouver: UBC Press.

Frankenberg, R. 1993. *White Women, Race Matters: The Social Construction of Whiteness.* Minneapolis: University of Minnesota Press.

–, ed. 1997. *Destabilizing Whiteness: Essays in Social and Cultural Criticism.* Durham, NC, and London: Duke University Press.

Funderburg, L. 1994. *Black, White, Other: Biracial Americans Talk about Race and Identity.* New York: Morrow.

Furedi, F. 1998. *The Silent War: Imperialism and the Changing Perception of Race.* New Brunswick, NJ: Rutgers University Press.

Garner, S. 2010. *Racisms: An Introduction.* London: Sage.

George, R.M. 1996. *The Politics of Home.* Cambridge, UK: Cambridge University Press.

Gibbs, J., and G. Hines. 1992. Negotiating Ethnic Identity: Issues for Black-White Biracial Adolescents. In *Racially Mixed People in America,* ed. M.P.P. Root, 223-39. Newbury Park, CA: Sage.

Gibbs, J., and Huang and Associates, eds. 1989. *Children of Color: Psychological Interventions with Minority Youth.* San Francisco, CA: Jossey-Bass.

Gibson-Graham, J.K. 1996. Reflections on Postmodern Feminist Social Research. In *BodySpace: Destabilizing Geographies of Gender and Sexuality,* ed. N. Duncan, 234-45. London: Routledge.

Gilbert, M.R. 1994. The Politics of Location: Doing Feminist Research at "Home." *Professional Geographer* 46 (1): 90-96.

Gilroy, P. 2000. *Against Race: Imagining Political Culture beyond the Color Line.* Cambridge, MA: Harvard University Press.

Goffman, E. 1959. *The Presentation of Self in Everyday Life.* New York: Doubleday Anchor.

Goldberg, D.T., ed. 1993. *Racist Culture: Philosophy and the Politics of Meaning.* Cambridge, MA: Blackwell.

–. 1995. Made in the USA. In *American Mixed Race: The Culture of Microdiversity,* ed. N. Zack, 237-55. London: Rowman and Littlefield.

–. 2008. Presidential Race. 27 October. http://threatofrace.org/2008/10/blog/presidential-race-by-david-theo-goldberg/#content.

Gordon, L.R. 1997. *Her Majesty's Other Children: Sketches of Racism from a Neocolonial Age.* Lanham, MD: Rowman and Littlefield.

Gorman, R. 2011. "Obama's My Dad": Mixed Race Suspects, Political Anxiety and the New Imperialism. *Thirdspace: A Journal of Feminist Theory and Culture* 10 (1): 1-14. http://journals.sfu.ca/thirdspace/index.php/journal/article/view/gorman/444.

Gwyn, R.J. 1996. *Nationalism without Walls: The Unbearable Lightness of Being Canadian.* Toronto: McClelland and Stewart.

Hall, C.I. 1996. 2001: A Race Odyssey. In *The Multiracial Experience: Racial Borders as the New Frontier,* ed. M.P.P. Root, 395-411. London: Sage.

Hall, S. 1988. New Ethnicities. In *Black Film, British Cinema,* ed. K. Mercer, 26-31. London: Institute of Contemporary Arts.

–. 1990. Cultural Identity and Diaspora. In *Identity: Community, Culture, Difference,* ed. J. Rutherford, 222-38. London: Lawrence and Wishart.

–. 1992. Cultural Studies and Its Theoretical Legacies. In *Cultural Studies,* ed. L. Grossberg, C. Nelson, and P.A. Treichler, 328-45. New York: Routledge.

–. 1997. The Local and the Global: Globalization and Ethnicity. In *Dangerous Liaisons: Gender, Nation and Postcolonial Perspectives,* ed. A. McClintock, A. Mufti, and E. Shohat, 173-87. Minneapolis: University of Minnesota Press.

–. 1998. Subjects in History: Making Diasporic Identities. In *The House that Race Built,* ed. Wahmeena Lubiano, 289-300. New York: Vintage.

Haraway, D. 1991. *Simians, Cyborgs and Women: The Reinvention of Nature.* London: Free Association Press.

Haraway, D., and D. Harvey. 1995. Nature, Politics and Possibilities: A Debate and Discussion with David Harvey and Donna Haraway. *Environment and Planning D: Society and Space* 13 (5): 507-27.

Haritaworn, J. 2009. Hybrid Border Crossers? Towards a Radical Socialisation of "Mixed Race." *Journal of Ethnic and Migration Studies* 35 (1): 115-32.

Henry, F., and C. Tator. 1985. Racism in Canada: Social Myths and Strategies for Change. In *Ethnicity and Ethnic Relations in Canada: A Book of Readings,* ed. R. Bienvenue and J. Goldstein, 321-35. Toronto: Butterworths.

Hill, L. 2001. *Black Berry, Sweet Juice: On Being Black and White in Canada.* Toronto: HarperCollins Canada.

hooks, bell. 1989. *Talking Back: Thinking Feminist, Thinking Black.* Boston, MA: South End.

–. 1990. *Yearning: Race, Gender and Cultural Politics.* Boston, MA: South End.

Howard, Cori. 2008. Mixed Emotions. *Chatelaine,* November, 255-60.

Hudson, M. 1987. Multiculturalism, Government Policy and Constitutional Enshrinement – A Comparative Study. In *Multiculturalism and the Charter: A Legal Perspective,* ed. Canadian Human Rights Foundation, 59-123. Toronto: Carswell.

Ibrahim, Habiba. 2007. Canary in a Coal Mine: Performing Biracial Difference in *Caucasia. Lit: Literature Interpretation Theory* 18 (2): 155-72.

–. 2012. *Troubling the Family: The Promise of Personhood and the Rise of Multiracialism.* Minneapolis: University of Minnesota Press.

Ifekwunigwe, J.O. 1997a. Diaspora's Daughters, Africa's Orphans? On Lineage, Authenticity and "Mixed Race" Identity. In *Black British Feminism: A Reader,* ed. H. Mirza, 127-53. London: Routledge.

–. 1997b. Lecture notes from Rules of Metissage. Course taught by J.O. Ifekwunigwe, University of East London, Fall 1997.

–. 1998. Personal correspondence. 15 January.

–. 1999. *Scattered Be-Longings: Cultural Paradoxes of Race, Culture and Nation.* London: Routledge.

–. 2004. *"Mixed Race" Studies: A Reader.* London: Routledge.

Ignatiev, N. 1995. *How the Irish Became White.* New York: Routledge.

Ignatiev, N., and J. Garvey, eds. 1996. *Race Traitor*. London: Routledge.

Iijima-Hall, C.C. 1992. Please Choose One: Ethnic Identity Choices for Biracial Individuals. In *Racially Mixed People in America,* ed. M.P.P. Root, 250-65. Newbury Park, CA: Sage.

Irigaray, L. 1993. *Sexes and Genealogies*. Trans. G.C. Gill. New York: Columbia University Press.

Jackson, P. 1991. The Racialization of Labour in Post-war Bradford. *Journal of Historical Geography* 18 (2): 190-209.

Johnson, L.C. 1994. What Future for Feminist Geography? *Gender, Place and Culture* 1 (1): 103-13.

Jones, L. 1994. *Bulletproof Diva: Tales of Race, Sex, and Hair*. New York: Doubleday.

Jordan, J. 1992. *Technical Difficulties*. London: Virago.

Joseph, C. 1995. On Your Mark! Get Set! Go Multi-Culti! *This Magazine,* December-January, 24-32.

Joseph, R. 2013. *Transcending Blackness: From the New Millennium Mulatta to the Exceptional Multiracial*. Durham, NC: Duke University Press.

Kalbach, W. 1992. A Demographic Review of Racial and Ethnic Groups in Canada. In *Multiculturalism in Canada: The Challenge of Diversity,* ed. A. Fleras and J.L. Elliott, 18-47. Scarborough, ON: Nelson Canada.

Katz, C. 1997. Review of *Feminism and Geography: The Limits of Geographical Knowledge,* by G. Rose. *Ecumene* 4 (2): 227-30.

Kawash, S. 1997. *Dislocating the Color Line: Identity, Hybridity and Singularity in African-American Narrative*. Stanford, CA: Stanford University Press.

Keil, Roger. 2002. "Common Sense" Neoliberalism: Progressive Conservative Urbanism in Toronto, Canada. *Antipode* 34 (3): 578-601.

Keith, M. 1989. Riots as a Social Problem in British Cities. In *Social Problems and the City: New Perspectives,* ed. D. Herbert and D. Smith, 289-307. Oxford: Oxford University Press.

–. 1991. Knowing Your Place: The Imagined Geographies of Racial Subordination. In *New Words, New Worlds: Reconceptualizing Social and Cultural Geography,* ed. C. Philo, 178-93. Lampeter, UK: Social and Cultural Geography Study Group, Institute of British Geographers.

Kienlen, A. 2010. "why i don't say i'm white." In *Other Tongues: Mixed-Race Women Speak Out,* ed. A. DeRango-Adem and A. Thompson, 43. Toronto: Inanna.

King, R.C., and K.M. DaCosta. 1996. Changing Face, Changing Race: The Remaking of Race in the Japanese American and African American Communities. In *The Multiracial Experience: Racial Borders as the New Frontier,* ed. M.P.P. Root, 227-45. London: Sage.

King-O'Riain, R.C., S. Small, M. Mahtani, M. Song, and P. Spickard, eds. 2014. *Global Mixed Race*. New York: NYU Press.

Kobayashi, A. 1993. Multiculturalism: Representing a Canadian Institution. In *Place/Culture/Representation,* ed. J.S. Duncan and D. Ley, 205-31. London: Routledge.

–. 1994. Coloring the Field: Gender, Race, and the Politics of Fieldwork. *Professional Geographer* 46 (1): 73-80.

–. 2003. GPC Ten Years On: Is Self-Reflexivity Enough? *Gender, Place and Culture* 10 (4): 345-49.

Kobayashi, A., and L. Peake. 1994. Un-natural Discourse: Race and Gender in Geography. *Gender, Place and Culture* 1 (3): 225-43.

Kondo, D.K. 1997. *About Face: Performing Race in Fashion and Theater*. London: Routledge.

Krauss, W.W. 1941. Race Crossing in Hawaii. *Journal of Heredity* 32 (11): 371-78.

Kwan, S., and K. Speirs, eds. 2004. *Mixing It Up: Multiracial Subjects*. Austin: University of Texas Press.

Lafond, D. 2009. Multiracial Men in Toronto: Identities, Masculinities and Multiculturalism. MA thesis, Ontario Institute for Studies in Education, University of Toronto.

Lahiri, J. 1999. *Interpreter of Maladies: Stories.* Boston, MA: Houghton Mifflin.
Landay, L. 1998. *Madcaps, Screwballs and Con Women: The Female Trickster in American Culture.* Philadelphia: University of Pennsylvania Press.
Langer, S.K. 1942. *Philosophy in a New Key: A Study in the Symbolism of Reason, Rite, and Art.* Cambridge, MA: Harvard University Press.
Lavie, S., and T. Swedenburg. 1996. Introduction: Displacement, Diaspora, and Geographies of Identity. In *Displacement, Diaspora, and Geographies of Identity,* ed. S. Lavie and T. Swedenburg, 1-25. Durham, NC, and London: Duke University Press.
Lawrence, B. 2003. Gender, Race, and the Regulation of Native Identity in Canada and the United States: An Overview. *Hypatia: A Journal of Feminist Philosophy* 18 (2): 3-31.
–. 2004. "Real" Indians and Others: Mixed-Blood Urban Native Peoples and Indigenous Nationhood. Vancouver: UBC Press.
Lawrence, B., and E. Dua. 2005. Decolonizing Anti-Racism. *Social Justice: A Journal of Crime, Conflict and World Order* 32 (4): 120-43.
Lazarre, J. 1996. *Beyond the Whiteness of Whiteness: Memoir of a White Mother of Black Sons.* Durham, NC: Duke University Press.
Lemons, G.L. 2008. *Black Male Outsider: Teaching as a Pro-feminist Man: A Memoir.* Albany, NY: SUNY Press.
Ley, D. 1984. Pluralism and the Canadian State. In *Geography and Ethnic Pluralism,* ed. C. Clarke, D. Ley, and C. Peach, 87-110. London: Allen and Unwin.
Lischke, U., and D.T. McNab, eds. 2007. *The Long Journey of a Forgotten People: Studies in Métis Identities and Family Histories.* Waterloo, ON: Wilfrid Laurier University Press.
Mackey, E. 2002. *The House of Difference: Cultural Politics and National Identity in Canada.* Toronto: University of Toronto Press.
MacKinnon, C. 1997. From Practice to Theory, or What Is a White Woman Anyway? In *Critical White Studies: Looking behind the Mirror,* ed. R. Delgado and J. Stefancic, 300-5. Philadelphia PA: Temple University Press.
Maclear, K. 2012. *Stray Love.* Toronto: HarperCollins Canada.
Mahoney, J., and C. Alphonso. 2005. How the Lines between Races Are Blurring. *Globe and Mail,* 24 March.
Mahtani, M., and A. Moreno. 2001. Same Difference? Towards a More Unified Discourse in "Mixed Race" Theory. In *Rethinking "Mixed Race,"* ed. D. Parker and M. Song, 65-76. London: Pluto.
Makalani, M. 2001. A Biracial Identity or a New Race? The Historical Limitations and Political Implications of a Biracial Identity. *Souls: A Critical Journal of Black Politics, Culture and Society* 3 (4): 83-112.
Malarek, V. 1987. *Heaven's Gate: Canada's Immigration Fiasco.* Toronto: MacMillan.
Malik, K. 1996. *The Meaning of Race: Race, History and Culture in Western Society.* London: MacMillan.
Marin, L. 1996. Bringing It on Home: Teaching/Mothering Antiracism. In *Everyday Acts against Racism: Raising Children in a Multiracial World,* ed. M. Reddy, 110-32. Seattle, WA: Seal.
Massey, D., and J. Allen, eds. 1984. *Geography Matters!* Cambridge, UK: Cambridge University Press.
Mathabane, M., and G. Mathabane. 1992. *Love in Black and White: The Triumph of Love over Prejudice and Taboo.* New York: HarperCollins.
Maugham, S. 1944. *The Razor's Edge.* London: Reprint Society.
Mawani, R. 2009. *Colonial Proximities: Crossracial Encounters and Juridical Truths in British Columbia, 1871-1921.* Vancouver: UBC Press.

–. 2012. Specters of Indigeneity in British Indian Migration, 1914. *Law and Society Review* 46 (2): 369-403.
Maynard, J. 2012. Roles of a Lifetime. *T: The New York Times Style Magazine,* Winter. http://tmagazine.blogs.nytimes.com/2012/10/18/roles-of-a-lifetime-halle-berry/?_php=true&_type=blogs&_php=true&_type=blogs&_r=1.
McIntosh, P. 1988. White Privilege and Male Privilege: A Personal Account of Coming to See Correspondences through Work in Women's Studies. Working Paper No. 189. Center for Research on Women, Wellesley College, Massachusetts. http://files.eric.ed.gov/fulltext/ED335262.pdf.
–. 1989. White Privilege: Unpacking the Invisible Knapsack. *Peace and Freedom,* July-August, 10-12.
McKittrick, K. 2006. *Demonic Grounds: Black Women and the Cartographies of Struggle.* Minneapolis: University of Minnesota Press.
–. 2007. Freedom Is a Secret: The Future Usability of the Underground. In *Black Geographies and the Politics of Place,* ed. K. McKittrick and C. Woods, 97-114. Toronto/Boston, MA: Between the Lines/South End.
–. 2011. Wait Canada Anticipate Black. Paper presented at the Association for Canadian Studies Conference, Ottawa, Ontario. Also forthcoming in *CLR James Journal.*
McKittrick, K., and C. Woods, eds. 2007. *Black Geographies and the Politics of Place.* Toronto/Boston, MA: Between the Lines/South End.
McLeod, K.A. 1981. Multiculturalism and Multicultural Education: Policy and Practice. In *Education and Canadian Multiculturalism: Some Problems and Some Solutions,* ed. D. Dorotich, 1-23. Saskatoon: Canadian Society for the Study of Education/University of Saskatchewan Press.
McNeil, D. 2010. *Sex and Race in the Black Atlantic: Mulatto Devils and Multiracial Messiahs.* New York: Routledge.
–. 2012. "Mixture Is a Neoliberal Good": Mixed-Race Metaphors and Post-Racial Masks. *Darkmatter* 9 (1). http://www.darkmatter101.org/site/2012/07/02/mixture-is-a-neoliberal-good-mixed-race-metaphors-and-post-racial-masks.
Michaels, A. 1996. *Fugitive Pieces.* Toronto: McClelland and Stewart.
Minh-ha, T.T. 1989. *Woman, Native, Other: Writing Postcoloniality and Feminism.* Bloomington: Indiana University Press.
Mirza, H. 1997. Introduction: Mapping a Genealogy of Black British Feminism. In *Black British Feminism: A Reader,* ed. H. Mirza, 1-31. London: Routledge.
Mitchell, K. 1997. Different Diasporas and the Hype of Hybridity. *Environment and Planning D: Society and Space* 15 (5): 533-53.
Montagu, A. 1952. *Man's Most Dangerous Myth: The Fallacy of Race.* New York: Harper and Brothers.
Moore, D. 1997. Remapping Resistance. In *Geographies of Resistance,* ed. S. Pile and M. Keith, 87-107. London: Routledge.
Morales, J. 1996. Unpacking the White Privilege Diaper Bag. In *Everyday Acts against Racism: Raising Children in a Multiracial World,* ed. M. Reddy, 40-50. Seattle, WA: Seal.
Morgensen, S. 2011. *Spaces between Us: Queer Settler Colonialism and Indigenous Decolonization.* Minneapolis: University of Minnesota Press.
Morris, N. 2010. Conversations of Confrontation. In *Other Tongues: Mixed-Race Women Speak Out,* ed. A. DeRango-Adem and A. Thompson, 39-42. Toronto: Inanna.
Morton, S.G. 1848. Account of a Craniological Collection with Remarks on the Classification of Some Families of the Human Race. *Transactions of the American Ethnological Society* 2: 215-22.

Moss, J. 1998. Meta Incognita. Paper presented at the British Association of Canadian Studies, Staffordshire, United Kingdom, 6 April.

Mufti, A., and E. Shohat. 1997. Introduction. In *Dangerous Liaisons: Gender, Nation and Postcolonial Perspectives,* ed. A. McClintock, A. Mufti, and E. Shohat, 1-15. Minneapolis: University of Minnesota Press.

Mukherjee, A. 1994. *Oppositional Aesthetics: Readings from a Hyphenated Space.* Toronto: TSAR.

Mullings, B. 1999. Insider or Outsider, Both or Neither: Some Dilemmas of Interviewing in a Cross-Cultural Setting. *Geoforum* 30 (4): 337-50.

Nakashima, C. 1992. An Invisible Monster: The Creation and Denial of Mixed-Race People in America. In *Racially Mixed People in America,* ed. M.P.P. Root, 162-81. Newbury Park, CA: Sage.

Nandy, A. 1983. *The Intimate Enemy, Loss and Recovery of Self under Colonialism.* New Delhi, India: Oxford University Press.

Nast, H. 1994. Opening Remarks on "Women in the Field": Feminist Methodologies. *Professional Geographer* 46 (1): 54-66.

National Public Radio. 2011. A Mixed Race Take on What It Means to Be "Free." Interview with Danzy Senna. 24 June. http://m.npr.org/story/137395343.

Nyong'o, T. 2009. *The Amalgamation Waltz: Race, Performance, and the Ruses of Memory.* Minneapolis: University of Minnesota Press.

Oakley, A. 1981. Interviewing Women: A Contradiction in Terms. In *Doing Feminist Research,* ed. H. Roberts, 30-61. London: RKP Press.

–. 1986. *From Here to Maternity: Becoming a Mother.* Harmondsworth, UK: Penguin.

Obama, Barack. 2004. *Dreams from My Father: A Story of Race and Inheritance.* New York: Random House.

Olumide, J. 2002. *Raiding the Gene Pool: The Social Construction of Mixed Race.* London: Pluto.

Omi, M., and H. Winant. 1994. *Racial Formation in the United States.* London: Routledge.

–. 2012. Racial Formation Rules: Continuity, Instability and Change. In *Racial Formation in the Twenty-First Century,* ed. D. Martinez HoSang, O. LaBennett, and L. Pulido, 302-31. Berkeley: University of California Press.

Palmer, H. 1975. *Immigration and the Rise of Multiculturalism.* Toronto: Copp Clark.

Park, R.E. 1931. Mentality of Racial Hybrids. *American Journal of Sociology* 36 (4): 534-51.

Parker, D., and M. Song, eds. 2001. *Rethinking "Mixed Race."* London: Pluto.

Pellegrini, G.M. 2005. Multiracial Identity in the Post–Civil Rights Era. *Social Identities: Journal for the Study of Race, Nation and Culture* 11 (5): 531-49.

Peter, K. 1981. The Myth of Multiculturalism and Other Political Fables. In *Ethnicity, Power and Politics in Canada,* ed. J. Dahlie and T. Fernando, 67-91. Toronto: Methuen.

Peterson, J. 1985. Many Roads to Red River: Métis Genesis in the Great Lakes Region, 1680-1815. In *The New Peoples: Being and Becoming Métis in North America,* ed. J. Peterson and J.S.H. Brown, 37-71. Winnipeg: University of Manitoba Press.

Philip, M.N. 1992. *Frontiers: Selected Essays and Writings on Racism and Culture, 1984-1992.* Stratford, ON: Mercury.

Pile, S. 1997. Introduction: Opposition, Political Identities and Spaces of Resistance. In *Geographies of Resistance,* ed. S. Pile and M. Keith, 1-32. London: Routledge.

–. 1998. Personal correspondence. 15 January.

Plummer, K. 1995. *Telling Sexual Stories: Power, Change, and Social Worlds.* London: Routledge.

Pratt, G. 1997. Re-placing Race: Reactions to "Brown Skinned White Girls." *Gender, Place and Culture* 4 (3): 361-63.

Pratt, M.B. 1984. Identity: Skin Blood Heart. In *Yours in Struggle: Three Feminist Perspectives on Anti-Semitism and Racism,* ed. E. Bulkin, M.B. Pratt, and B. Smith, 9-65. Brooklyn, NY: Long Haul.

Probyn, E. 1990. Travels in the Postmodern: Making Sense of the Local. In *Feminism/Postmodernism*, ed. L. Nicholson, 176-90. London: Routledge.

–. 1993. *Sexing the Self: Gendered Positions in Cultural Studies*. London: Routledge.

–. 1996. *Outside Belongings*. London: Routledge.

Racette, S.F. 2001. Métis Man or Canadian Icon: Who Owns Louis Riel? In *Rielisms*, 42-53. Catalogue of an exhibition held at the Winnipeg Art Gallery, 13 January to 18 March. Winnipeg: Winnipeg Art Gallery.

–. 2004. Sewing Ourselves Together: Clothing, Decorative Arts and the Expression of Métis and Half Breed Identity. PhD diss., University of Manitoba.

Radhakrishnan, R. 1996. *Diasporic Mediations: Between Home and Location*. Minneapolis: University of Minnesota Press.

Razack, S., ed. 2002. *Race, Space, and the Law: Unmapping a White Settler Society*. Toronto: Between the Lines.

–. 2005. Sherene Razack, Editor of *Race, Space, and the Law: Unmapping a White Settler Society*, in Conversation with Zoë Druick. http://www.btlbooks.com/Links/razack_interview.htm (now offline).

Razack, S., M. Smith, and S. Thobani, eds. 2010. *States of Race: Critical Race Feminism for the 21st Century*. Toronto: Between the Lines.

Reddy, M. 1994. *Crossing the Color Line: Race, Parenting and Culture*. New Brunswick, NJ: Rutgers University Press.

Reed, A. 1997. Yackety-Yak about Race. *The Progressive* 61 (12): 45-51.

Rex, J. 1996. *Ethnic Minorities in the Modern Nation State: Working Papers in the Theory of Multiculturalism and Political Integration*. New York: St. Martin's Press.

Roberts, D., and M. Mahtani. 2010. Neoliberalizing Race, Racing Neoliberalism: Placing "Race" in Neoliberal Discourses. *Antipode* 42 (2): 248-57.

Rockquemore, K.A., D.L. Brunsma, and R. Delgado. 2009. Racing to Theory, or Re-theorizing Race: Understanding the Struggle to Build Valid Multiracial Identity Theories. *Journal of Social Issues* 65 (1): 13-34.

Roediger, D. 1991. *The Wages of Whiteness: Race and the Making of the American Working Class*. London: Verso.

Romano, R.C. 2003. *Race Mixing: Black-White Marriage in Postwar America*. Cambridge, MA: Harvard University Press.

Root, M.P.P. 1990. Resolving "Other" Status: Identity Development of Biracial Individuals. In *Diversity and Complexity in Feminist Therapy*, ed. S. Brown and M.P.P. Root, 185-205. New York: Haworth.

–, ed. 1992. *Racially Mixed People in America*. Newbury Park, CA: Sage.

–. 1994. Mixed Race Women. In *Women of Color and Mental Health: The Healing Tapestry*, ed. L. Comas Diaz and B. Green. New York: Guilford.

–. 1996a. A Bill of Rights for Racially Mixed People. In *The Multiracial Experience: Racial Borders as the New Frontier*, ed. M.P.P. Root, 3-14. London: Sage.

–. 1996b. The Multiracial Experience: Racial Borders as a Significant Frontier in Race Relations. In *The Multiracial Experience: Racial Borders as the New Frontier*, ed. M.P.P. Root, xiii-xxviii. London: Sage.

–, ed. 1996c. *The Multiracial Experience: Racial Borders as the New Frontier*. London: Sage.

–. 1997. Mixed-Race Women. In *Race/Sex: Their Sameness, Difference, and Interplay*, ed. N. Zack, 157-75. London: Routledge.

Rose, G. 1993. *Feminism and Geography: The Limits of Geographical Knowledge*. Minneapolis: University of Minnesota Press.

–. 1996. As If the Mirrors Had Bled: Masculine Dwelling, Masculinist Theory and Feminist Masquerade. In *BodySpace: Destabilizing Geographies of Gender and Sexuality*, ed. N. Duncan, 56-74. London: Routledge.

–. 1997. Situating Knowledges: Positionality, Reflexivities and Other Tactics. *Progress in Human Geography* 21 (3): 305-20.

Rowe, C.A. 2008. *Power Lines: On the Subject of Feminist Alliances*. Durham, NC: Duke University Press.

Roy, P. 1981. Citizens without Votes: East Asians in British Columbia, 1872-1947. In *Ethnicity, Power and Politics in Canada*, ed. J. Dahlie and T. Fernando, 151-71. Toronto: Methuen.

Rutherford, J., ed. 1990. *Identity: Community, Culture, Difference*. London: Lawrence and Wishart.

Rutherford, S. 2010. Colonialism and the Indigenous Present: An Interview with Bonita Lawrence. *Race and Class* 52 (1): 9-18.

Said, E. 1991. What Is Patriotism? *The Nation*, 15 July, 116.

Saldanha, A.P. 2006. Re-ontologising Race: The Machinic Geography of Phenotype. *Environment and Planning D: Society and Space* 24 (1): 9-24.

Salee, D. 2010. Indigenous Peoples and Settler Angst in Canada: A Review Essay. *International Journal of Canadian Studies* 41 (1): 315-33.

Saul, J.R. 2008. *A Fair Country: Telling Truths about Canada*. Toronto: Viking Canada.

Scales-Trent, J. 1995. *Notes of a White Black Woman: Race, Color, Community*. University Park, PA: Pennsylvania State University Press.

Scott, J.C. 1990. *Domination and the Arts of Resistance: Hidden Transcripts*. New Haven, CT: Yale University Press.

Senna, D. 1998. *Caucasia*. London: Riverhead Books.

–. 2003. *Symptomatic*. New York: Riverhead Books.

–. 2011. *You Are Free*. New York: Riverhead Books.

Sexton, J. 2008. *Amalgamation Schemes: Antiblackness and the Critique of Multiracialism*. Minneapolis: University of Minnesota Press.

–. 2010. *Racial Theories in Context*. San Diego, CA: Cognella.

Sharma, N., and C. Wright. 2009. Decolonizing Resistance, Challenging Colonial States. *Social Justice* 35 (3): 120-38.

Shotter, J. 1993. *Cultural Politics of Everyday Life*. Milton Keynes, UK: Open University Press.

Shrage, L. 1997. Passing beyond the Other Race or Sex. In *Race/Sex: Their Sameness, Difference, and Interplay*, ed. N. Zack, 183-91. London: Routledge.

Sibley, D. 1995. *Geographies of Exclusion: Society and Difference in the West*. London: Routledge.

Simon, S. 1991. Notes from La Rue Jeanne-Mance. *Matrix* 35: 21-23.

Slocum, R. 2008. Thinking Race through Feminist Corporeal Theory: Divisions and Intimacies at the Minneapolis Farmers' Market. *Social and Cultural Geography* 9 (8): 849-69.

Smith, A. 1994. *Canada: An American Nation?* Montreal and Kingston: McGill-Queen's University Press.

–. 2011. Queer Theory and Native Studies: The Heteronormativity of Settler Colonialism. *GLQ: A Journal of Lesbian and Gay Studies* 16 (1-2): 41-68.

–. 2012. Indigeneity, Settler Colonialism, White Supremacy. In *Racial Formation in the Twenty-First Century*, ed. D. Martinez HoSang, O. LaBennett, and L. Pulido, 66-91. Berkeley: University of California Press.

Smith, N., and C. Katz. 1993. Grounding Metaphor: Towards a Spatialized Politics. In *Place and the Politics of Identity*, ed. M. Keith and S. Pile, 67-84. London: Routledge.

Smith, S. 1993. Immigration and Nation-Building in Canada and the United Kingdom. In *Constructions of Race, Place and Nation,* ed. P. Jackson and J. Penrose, 50-81. London: UCL Press.
Smith, W.C. 1939. The Hybrid in Hawaii as Marginal Man. *American Journal of Sociology* 39 (4): 459-68.
Song, M., and D. Parker. 1995. Commonality, Difference and the Dynamics of Disclosure in In-depth Interviewing. *Sociology* 29 (2): 241-56.
Spencer, R. 2004. Beyond Pathology and Cheerleading: Insurgency, Dissolution and Complicity in the Multiracial Idea. In *The Politics of Multiracialism: Challenging Racial Thinking,* ed. Heather Dalmage, 108-16. Albany: State University of New York Press.
–. 2011. *Reproducing Race: The Paradox of Generation Mix.* Boulder, CO: Lynne Rienner.
Spickard, P. 1989. *Mixed Blood: Intermarriage and Ethnic Identity in Twentieth-Century America.* Madison: University of Wisconsin Press.
–. 1992. The Illogic of American Racial Categories. In *Racially Mixed People in America,* ed. M.P.P. Root, 12-24. Newbury Park, CA: Sage.
Squires, C. 2007. *Dispatches from the Color Line: The Press and Multiracial America.* Albany, NY: SUNY Press.
–. 2010. Running through the Trenches, or An Introduction to the Un-dead Culture Wars and Dead Serious Identity Politics. *Journal of Communication Inquiry* 34 (3): 211-14.
Stam, R. 1997. Multiculturalism and the Neoconservatives. In *Dangerous Liaisons: Gender, Nation and Postcolonial Perspectives,* ed. A. McClintock, A. Mufti, and E. Shohat, 188-204. Minneapolis: University of Minnesota Press.
Standen, B. 1996. Without a Template: The Biracial Korean/White Experience. In *The Multiracial Experience: Racial Borders as the New Frontier,* ed. M.P.P. Root, 245-63. London: Sage.
Statistics Canada. 2003. The Ethnic Diversity Survey. http://www23.statcan.gc.ca/imdb/p2SV.pl?Function=getSurvey&SDDS=4508.
Stephan, C.W. 1992. Mixed-Heritage Individuals: Ethnic Identity and Trait Characteristics. In *Racially Mixed People in America,* ed. M.P.P. Root, 50-64. Newbury Park, CA: Sage.
Stolcke, V. 1993. Is Sex to Gender as Race Is to Ethnicity? In *Gendered Anthropology,* ed. T. del Valle, 17-38. London: Routledge.
Stoler, A. 1997. Racial Histories and Their Regimes of Truth. In *Political Power and Social Theory,* vol. 11, ed. D.E. Davis, 183-206. Westport, CT: JAI Press.
–. 2002. Reflections on "Racial Histories and Their Regimes of Truth." In *Race Critical Theories: Text and Context,* ed. P. Essed and D.T. Goldberg, 417-22. London: Blackwell.
Stonequist, E.V. 1937. *The Marginal Man: A Study in Personality and Culture Conflict.* New York: Russell and Russell.
Streeter, C. 1996. Ambiguous Bodies: Locating Black/White Women in Cultural Representations. In *The Multiracial Experience: Racial Borders as the New Frontier,* ed. M.P.P. Root, 305-20. London: Sage.
Swanton, D. 2010. Sorting Bodies: Race, Affect, and Everyday Multiculture in a Mill Town in Northern England. *Environment and Planning A* 42 (10): 2332-50.
Tajima, R. 1996. Site-seeing through Asian America: On the Making of Fortune Cookies. In *Mapping Multiculturalism,* ed. A.F. Gordon and C. Newfield, 263-95. Minneapolis: University of Minnesota Press.
Taylor, C. 1993. *Reconciling the Solitudes: Essays on Canadian Federalism and Nationalism.* Montreal and Kingston: McGill-Queen's University Press.
Taylor, L. 2008. Re-imagining Mixed Race: Explorations of Multiracial Discourse in Canada. PhD diss., Department of Education, York University.
Teillet, J. 2007. Metis Law. LLM thesis, University of Toronto Law School.

–. 2009. *Metis Law Summary*. Toronto: Self-published.

Thobani, S. 2007. *Exalted Subjects: Studies in the Making of Race and Nation in Canada*. Toronto: University of Toronto Press.

Thompson, D. 2010. The Language and the Ethics of Mixed-Race. In *Other Tongues: Mixed-Race Women Speak Out*, ed. A. DeRango-Adem and A. Thompson, 263-99. Toronto: Inanna.

Thornton, M. 1996. Hidden Agendas, Identity Theories and Multiracial People. In *The Multiracial Experience: Racial Borders as the New Frontier*, ed. M.P.P. Root, 101-21. London: Sage.

Thrift, N. 1997. The Still Point: Resistance, Expressive Embodiment and Dance. In *Geographies of Resistance*, ed. S. Pile and M. Keith, 124-52. London: Routledge.

Tizard, B., and A. Phoenix. 1993. *Black, White or Mixed Race? Race and Racism in the Lives of Young People of Mixed Parentage*. London: Routledge.

Twine, F.W. 1996. Brown Skinned White Girls: Class, Culture and the Construction of White Identity in Suburban Communities. *Gender, Place and Culture* 3 (2): 205-24.

–. 2000a. Bearing Blackness in Britain: The Meaning of Racial Difference for White Birth Mothers of African-Descent Children. In *Ideologies and Technologies of Motherhood: Race, Class, Sexuality, Nationalism*, ed. H. Ragone and F.W. Twine, 76-108. New York: Routledge.

–. 2000b. *Racism in a Racial Democracy: The Maintenance of White Supremacy in Brazil*. New Brunswick, NJ: Rutgers University Press.

Ujimoto, V.K. 1991. Multiculturalism, Ethnic Identity, and Inequality. In *Social Issues and Contradictions in Canadian Society*, ed. B.S. Bolaria, 110-34. Toronto: Harcourt Brace Jovanovich.

Vasconcelos, José. 1925. *La Raza Cósmica*. Mexico City: Espasa Calpe, S.A.

Visweswaran, K. 1994. *Fictions of Feminist Ethnography*. Minneapolis: University of Minnesota Press.

Vizenor, G. 1989. *Narrative Chance: Postmodern Discourse on Native American Indian Literatures*. Norman and London: University of Oklahoma Press.

Vonnegut, K., Jr. 1961. *Mother Night*. London: Random House.

Wah, F. 1996. Half-Bred Poetics. *Absinthe* 9 (2): 60-66.

Walcott, R. 2008. The End of George: Civil Rights, Black Power, and Diaspora Consciousness among Black Canadians. Paper presented at the conference Routes of Radicalism: Political and Social Movements in Canada and the U.S. during the "Long Sixties," Princeton University, New Jersey, 22 November.

–. 2011. Disgraceful: Intellectual Dishonesty, White Anxieties, and Multicultural Critique Thirty-Six Years Later. In *Home and Native Land: Unsettling Multiculturalism in Canada*, ed. M. Chazan, L. Helps, A. Stanley, and S. Thakkar, 15-30. Toronto: Between the Lines.

Walker, L. 1995. More Than Just Skin-Deep: Fem(me)ininity and the Subversion of Identity. *Gender, Place and Culture* 2 (1): 71-76.

Wallace, J. 1998. What Does It Mean to Be a Woman? *Times Higher Education Supplement*, 8 May, 16.

Walsh, B. 2012. Dracula at a Desk: Interview with Albert J. Bernstein. *Toronto Metro*, 20 June, 24.

Wardle, F. 1996. Multicultural Education. In *The Multiracial Experience: Racial Borders as the New Frontier*, ed. M.P.P. Root, 380-95. London: Sage.

Ware, V. 1992. *Beyond the Pale: White Women, Racism and History*. London: Verso.

Waters, M. 1990. *Ethnic Options: Choosing Identities in America*. Berkeley: University of California Press.

Weinfeld, M. 1985. Myth and Reality in the Canadian Mosaic: Affective Ethnicity. In *Ethnicity and Ethnic Relations in Canada: A Book of Readings,* ed. R. Bienvenue and J. Goldstein, 23-45. Toronto: Butterworths.

Weir, A. 1996. *Sacrificial Logics: Feminist Theory and the Critique of Identity.* London: Routledge.

Williams, K.M. 2006. *Mark One or More: Civil Rights in Multiracial America.* Ann Arbor: University of Michigan Press.

Williams, P.J. 1997. *Seeing a Colour-Blind Future: The Paradox of Race.* London: Virago.

Williams, T.K. 1992. Prism Lives: Identity of Binational Amerasians. In *Racially Mixed People in America,* ed. M.P.P. Root, 280-304. Newbury Park, CA: Sage.

–. 1996. Race as Process: Reassessing the "What Are You?" Encounters of Biracial Individuals. In *The Multiracial Experience: Racial Borders as the New Frontier,* ed. M.P.P. Root, 191-211. London: Sage.

Winterson, J. 1989. *Sexing the Cherry.* London: Vintage.

Wong, L.M. 1994. Di(s)-secting and Dis(s)-closing Whiteness. In *Shifting Identities, Shifting Racisms: A Feminism and Psychology Reader,* ed. K. Bhavnani and A. Phoenix, 133-55. London: Sage.

Woo, G.L.X. 2011. *Ghost Dancing with Colonialism: Decolonization and Indigenous Rights at the Supreme Court of Canada.* Vancouver: UBC Press.

Young, I.M. 1986. The Ideal of Community and the Politics of Difference. *Social Theory and Practice* 12 (1): 1-26.

Young, R.J.C. 1995. *Colonial Desire: Hybridity in Theory, Culture, and Race.* London: Routledge.

Yu, H. 2003. Tiger Woods Is Not the End of History: Why Sex across the Color Line Won't Save Us All. *American Historical Review* 108 (5): 1406-14.

Yuzyk, P. 1967. *Ukrainian Canadians: Their Place and Role in Canadian Life.* Toronto: Ukrainian Canadian Business and Professional Federation.

Zack, N. 1992. *Race and Mixed Race.* London: Routledge.

–, ed. 1995. *American Mixed Race: The Culture of Microdiversity.* London: Rowman and Littlefield.

–, ed. 1997. *Race/Sex: Their Sameness, Difference, and Interplay.* London: Routledge.

Ziv, A. 2006. *Breeding between the Lines: Why Interracial People Are Healthier and More Attractive.* Fort Lee, NJ: Barricade.

Index

Aboriginal people. *See* Indigeneity; Indigenous Canadians; Metis
Aboriginality. *See* Indigeneity; Indigenous Canadians; Metis
adoption, 74, 76, 78, 128
agency, 7, 26, 37-38, 45, 68, 88, 138, 151, 196, 206, 219, 223-42, 248-50, 256
   See also resistance
Alcoff, L., 4, 33, 129-30, 178, 192
ambiguity. *See* racial ambiguity
anti-black racism. *See* blackness, anti-blackness
antiracist, 27, 42, 45, 72, 74-75, 92, 108, 111, 137-38, 154, 158, 239, 256
   analysis, 53, 135
   legislation, 107
   policy, 107
   stance, 7
   studies, 30
appropriation, 27, 53, 126
assimilation, 8, 55, 98, 166, 213

Bettez, S., 4, 20, 30, 63, 65, 246
bilingualism, 102-5
   See also Royal Commission on Bilingualism and Biculturalism
Bill of Rights, 40-41, 90
   See also Root, Maria
biological determinism. *See* cultural hybridity, vitality; racism, biological

biracial, 6, 35-36, 41, 43, 63-68, 148, 187, 193, 198, 206, 249
bisexual, 73
   See also sexual orientation
blackness, 42-44, 58, 65, 137, 141, 145, 151-56, 161-65
   anti-blackness, 41-44, 225
blood quantum, 55, 124
Boondocks (comic strip), 41-42
"border crossing," 168
   See also Root, Maria
Butler, Judith, 28, 89, 207-16, 224, 229, 238, 241

Camper, Carol, 4, 20, 31, 64-65
Canada Immigration Act, 99
Canadian Consultative Council on Multiculturalism, 104
Canadian Ethnocultural Council, 106
Canadian Heritage Department, 110
Canadian Race Relations Foundation, 107
Chinese Exclusion Act, 99
   See also racism, anti-Chinese
Chinese Immigration Act, 99
   See also racism, anti-Chinese
Chung, Andrew, 50, 53, 56, 255
colonialism, 28, 52
   anti-colonialism, 8, 248, 250-51
   neo-colonialism, 133

settler-colonialism, 5, 56, 130, 139
violence, 53, 56
colour-blind. *See* racism, colour-blind
colourism. *See* shadeism
critical mixed race studies, 7-8, 22, 30-32, 36-37, 45, 54, 92, 153, 183, 243-44, 251
cultural capital, 6, 52, 125, 145, 245, 256
cultural hybridity, 39-42, 197
   degeneracy, 33-35
   Indigenous, 55
   vitality, 34, 68, 152
cultural pluralism, 103

DaCosta, K.M., 4, 7, 20, 62-63, 92, 132, 147, 167, 190, 192, 196, 244
Dalmage, H.M., 4, 166-67, 233
diversity
   racial, 18, 84, 96-113, 120-22, 130-39, 251-52
   social, 168-74, 184
"Diversity: Our Strength" (Toronto motto), 133
double displacement, 40
"double foreigner," 120
Dubois, Jazmine. See *Boondocks* (comic strip)

Elam, M., 4, 6-8, 20, 25-26, 30, 32, 41-43, 51, 131-38, 249
empowerment, 132, 154, 219, 230
Equality Now! (House of Commons report), 106
exoticism, 7, 20, 34, 39, 61, 65, 75, 117-18, 134, 137, 148

"feeling white vs being white," 151
feminism, 26, 38-39, 47, 64, 87-89, 116, 153, 159, 166, 169-74, 185-86, 189, 194, 208, 211
   white, 90-91, 142-43
   See also gender
Feminism and Geography (Rose), 170-73
   See also "paradoxical space"; Rose, Gillian
"feminist kill-joy," 91
fetishization. *See* exoticism
fluidity. *See* identity, fluidity

gay, 211, 233
   See also sexual orientation
gender, 19, 26-28, 31, 34, 38-40, 55, 64-65, 73, 79, 84-86, 94, 109, 145, 153-56, 164, 175, 185-86, 193-95, 204, 218-19, 227, 230, 236-37
social construction, 208-12
genotype, 23-24, 149
Gradual Enfranchisement Act, 55

"half-white," 5, 70, 146-49, 184
heteronormativity, 38-39, 65, 155, 211, 227
   See also sexual orientation
heterosexism. *See* heteronormativity
Hill, Lawrence, 4, 7, 19-20, 30-31, 117, 155, 221
historical amnesia, 3, 17, 92, 122, 136
human geography, 17-18, 87
hybrid. *See* cultural hybridity
hypersexualization. *See* sexualization
hypervisibility, 219
hyphen, 104, 117-19

Ibrahim, Habiba, 4, 9, 20, 30, 32, 39, 43-44, 46, 52, 64-65, 92-97, 129, 137, 139, 145, 244-50, 254-58
identity
   fluidity, 62, 150, 156
   intersections, 8, 62, 114, 144, 155-56, 174, 185, 197, 206, 211, 233, 242, 250
   See also mixed race, identity
Ifekwunigwe, Jayne O., 4, 20, 23, 30-36, 64, 167, 236, 244
immigration, 13, 55
   changes, 105
   compared to US, 118
   policy, 56, 100, 106, 133, 249
   racist history, 98-105
Immigration Act (Canada, 1910), 100
Immigration Act (Canada, 1952), 100
Indigeneity, 31, 49-54, 131, 247-56
Indigenous Canadians, 27, 48-59, 251-54
   erasure, 31, 137, 253
   mixed-race identity, 46, 48, 54-58
institutionalized racism. *See* racism, systemic
interracial relationships, 5-6, 21, 37, 50-51, 78, 91, 121, 136, 247, 254-55
   See also miscegenation
invisibility, 20, 141-43, 147, 156-57, 163
invisible majority. *See* visible minority

Joseph, Ralina, 4, 20, 30, 32, 101, 140, 255

"knapsack of white privilege." *See*
McIntosh, Peggy

lesbian, 211, 233
 white, 143
 See also sexual orientation
light-skin privilege. *See* privilege

Maclear, Kyo, 3, 226
Makalani, Minkah, 4, 6, 9, 43, 46-47, 131, 193, 244-45, 249
McIntosh, Peggy, 142-43, 162
McNeil, Daniel, 4, 6-7, 20, 30-32, 36, 43-44, 51, 62, 95-97, 120, 130-34, 137, 167, 202-3, 245-46, 248, 251
melancholic migrant, 91
Metis, 251-54
metissage, 121, 236
Ministry of Multiculturalism (Canada), 104
miscegenation, 32, 39, 51, 123, 219, 251-53
 anti-miscegenation, 6, 35
 See also interracial relationships
mixed race
 body, 26, 34, 58, 95-97, 130-32, 247, 249
 identity, 3-10, 17, 20-21, 29-39, 44-48, 54-58, 61-65, 68-69, 83, 92, 116, 123-24, 128, 144, 166-68, 179-206, 217-42
mixed-religion, 16
"mobile paradoxical spaces," 167-206
model multiracial, 97-139, 254
Multicultural Act (Canada, 1988), 106
Multicultural Directorate, 104
multicultural policy, 97-120, 136-38
multiculturalism, 5-7, 58, 91, 95-38, 254-55
Multiculturalism Department (Canada), 107, 110
multiracial, 68, 255-56
 association, 80
 citizen, 203
 counselling, 45
 discourse, 44, 56, 65, 97, 183, 256-57
 experience, 37, 45, 49
 feminist, 143
 idea, 32
 identity, 27, 30, 39, 42, 44, 96, 120, 131, 196, 243-44, 254, 258
 ideology, 244
 movement, 65, 95, 132, 244, 247, 249-50
 people, 50, 66, 136, 144

 politics, 44, 64
 status, 253
 studies, 43, 47, 63, 243
 subjects, 46-48, 92, 166, 244, 246, 248
 women, 17, 116
multiracialism, 16, 65-66, 140, 246
 books, 50
 discourses, 97
 liberal, 7, 96
 politics, 43, 64
 representations, 64
 studies, 16, 43
multiraciality, 3-10, 16, 21, 22, 27-65, 84-85, 90-97, 130-32, 138-39, 145, 190-92, 201-3, 227, 244-58

narcissism, 9, 27, 60-94
nationalism, 8, 69, 101, 116, 121-39
neocolonialism, 130
neoliberal, 245, 251-52
 forms of government, 21-22
 identification, 44, 134
 individualism, 245
 multiculturalism, 130-39
 musings, 57
 optimism, 45
 politics, 245-47
 stance, 91, 137
"New Metis," 49-59
new mestiza, 226

Olumide, J., 4, 20, 35, 167
Outside Belongings (Probyn), 169, 174
 See also Probyn, Elspeth

"**p**aradoxical space," 165, 169-74, 179, 197
 See also Feminism and Geography (Rose);
 Rose, Gillian
"parodic proliferations," 212
passing. *See* race, passing and performance
pathology, 32-36, 44-45, 61, 88, 90, 131, 167, 205, 224
phenotypes, 23-24, 34, 42, 64, 84, 108, 116-17, 126, 132, 149-50, 155, 161, 163, 204, 217-42
privilege, 6-8, 33, 44-47, 52, 58, 63, 88, 120, 160, 182-85, 193, 235, 246-49, 255-57
 class, 38-43, 77, 84, 130, 141, 145, 148, 155, 215, 246, 249
 light skin, 84, 155-56, 218

276 INDEX

male, 142, 155
racial, 41, 138, 141, 159, 247
straight, 155
white, 8, 27-28, 38, 140-65, 235
white-skin, 84, 144, 146, 153-54, 160, 164, 235
Probyn, Elspeth, 152, 167-70, 174-77, 188, 193, 205-6, 230, 237, 242
See also Outside Belongings (Probyn)
purity. *See* race, "purity"

Quebec separation, 101

race, 22-27
"bending," 227-28
in Canada, 31, 56, 58, 99, 106, 108-9, 120-4, 248, 251-54
"card," 233
critical theory, 8
discussion of at home, 72-80
geography of, 18-19, 135
passing and performance, 140, 145, 157, 207-9, 212-42, 245
politics, 7, 96
post-race, 17, 29-30, 43, 131-32, 197, 211, 251-45, 258
"purity," 7, 33, 36, 38-40, 78, 148, 182, 220
social construct, 19, 23-27, 36-39, 108, 178, 181-82, 185, 190-91, 211-12, 219, 224, 227, 237, 244-45
"traitor," 159
Race Relations Directorate, 107
racelessness, 29-30, 132
See also racial impotency
racial ambiguity, 7-10, 33, 39-40, 55, 62-63, 90, 119, 132, 135-37, 145, 157, 207-8, 217-36, 240, 245
racial discrimination. *See* racism
racial essentialism, 214
racial neutrality, 19, 27, 95-97, 129, 141-42, 147, 152, 158, 163
racial impotency, 7, 132, 138, 254
See also racelessness
racial trailblazer, 132, 137
racialized, 18, 26, 117, 145-57
bodies, 19, 25, 95, 177, 226
boundaries, 194, 207, 231, 239
categories, 150, 156, 161, 165, 179-80, 189, 193, 206, 224, 228, 257

dualisms, 146
experiences, 6, 10, 65, 183
genders, 39-40, 64-65, 88, 94, 195, 203, 236-37
groups, 4, 16, 53, 56, 143, 246, 254, 256
hierarchies, 31, 139, 150-66, 174, 189
histories, 56, 255, 257
identities, 19-20, 33, 62, 70, 84, 90, 147, 150, 202, 208, 212-29, 241-42
immigrants, 9, 21, 49-57, 100, 253
lenses, 4
matrices, 131
meanings, 211, 222, 229, 232, 237
mixes, 35-36, 46
people, 29-30, 45
performances, 28, 206, 213-16, 226-27
subjects, 154
terrains, 178, 222
vocabulary, 179-80, 206
voices, 122
racism, 7-8, 10, 13-18, 26, 84, 108, 160, 186, 227, 230-33
anti-Chinese, 99
biological, 23-25, 33-36, 112, 123, 182-83, 203, 211-12, 220
colour-blind, 97, 208
internalized, 17, 75, 225
mixed-race as a solution to, 32, 36-45, 91-92, 97, 131-32, 136, 219, 255-56
multicultural policy, 112-18, 121
neoliberal, 92
sexualized, 34
systemic, 107-9, 240, 245, 249
white feminist, 143
resistance, 19, 39-40, 46-47, 87-89, 122, 126, 137, 150, 158-59, 172, 180, 206, 219, 222, 225, 229-42, 249-50
romanticization, 3, 26, 29, 36-59, 121, 127, 177, 198, 219, 243-44, 255-56
See also racism, mixed-race as a solution to
Root, Maria, 21, 37-38, 40, 65-66, 69, 82, 90, 150, 158, 167-68, 196, 208, 219-20, 237
Rose, Gillian, 89, 165, 167-74, 193, 197, 205-6, 220, 222, 238, 241
See also Feminism and Geography (Rose); "paradoxical space"
Royal Commission on Bilingualism and Biculturalism, 101-3

Secretary of State Department (Canada), 104-5
Sexton, J., 4, 8, 19, 20, 23, 30, 32, 36, 41-44, 46, 51, 58, 92, 183, 256
sexual orientation, 28, 39, 43, 73, 84, 154-56, 197, 211, 227, 233, 242
  See also bisexual; gay; lesbian
sexualization, 34, 39, 65, 156, 227
shadeism, 136, 155, 220
Special Committee on Visible Minorities in Canada, 106
Spencer, Rainier, 4, 8, 20, 30, 32, 36, 43, 51, 90, 92, 135, 140, 145, 153, 203, 244, 248
Squires, C., 4, 6, 51, 91, 203
Standing Committee on Multiculturalism, 106-7
Status Indian, 49, 53-56
stereotypes, 4, 6, 41-49, 67, 73, 88, 90, 112-15, 122, 126-27, 130, 138, 181, 196, 223-56
  history, 35-37
  tragic mulatto, 34-37
strategic forgetting, 3, 16-17, 131, 255
Stray Love. See Maclear, Kyo
structural inequality. *See* racism, systemic
symbolic multiculturalism. *See* multiculturalism

"**t**hird force," 100
"third space," 194, 197
Toronto, 3, 13-15, 21, 27, 50, 66, 69-81, 112, 126, 132-35, 138, 180, 185, 190-91, 202, 242
tragic mulatto. *See* stereotypes
transparent reflexivity, 89
"trickster studies," 234-36
Trudeau, Pierre Elliott, 102-4, 115, 127

visible minority, 78, 103, 106, 109-10, 116

"**W**hat are you?" 4, 10, 118
"Where are you from?" 4, 10, 18, 79, 117, 119, 147, 229-30
white beauty ideal, 68
white feminism. *See* feminism, white
white privilege. *See* privilege, white
whiteness, 5, 8, 10, 13, 43, 54-56, 76, 140-65, 211, 224, 233, 235, 246, 248, 254
white-skin privilege. *See* privilege, white-skin
Williams, P.J., 141, 144, 225-26
Williams, T.K., 38, 62, 150, 165